A-Z FOR TOK

TOK

GLOSSARY AND STUDENT COMPANION FOR IB DIPLOMA

Theory of Knowledge

BIANCA PELLET

Elemi
INTERNATIONAL SCHOOLS PUBLISHER

Published by Elemi International Schools Publisher Ltd

Author: Bianca Pellet

Series Editor: Mary James
Specialist Editor: Kay Wright

The author and publisher would like to acknowledge the very valuable input of Jelena Savkovic who reviewed and commented on the manuscript. Jelena is an experienced educator of the IB Diploma and has experience of teaching students in China and elsewhere.

First published 2021

A catalogue record of this title is available from the British Library
British Library Cataloguing in Publication Data

ISBN 978-1-9164131-6-0

Page layout/design by EMC Design Ltd
Cover design by Jayne Martin-Kaye

Contents

Studying TOK as part of your IB Diploma

The core component of the IB Diploma programme named 'Theory of Knowledge' or 'TOK' is a rigorous course which requires you to use some basic vocabulary associated with epistemology – a branch of philosophy dealing with how we think about knowledge (how we get it, how we use it, how we see it, and more). This course seems frightening to many students, as you have not usually come across these ideas before. You are now encountering these challenging ideas not just for the first time but perhaps even in your second, third or fourth language. The TOK course can seem scary, too, because it is compulsory for everyone – you have to do it, regardless of your interests, and must pass it in order to get your IB Diploma. This book aims to help you with the vocabulary and ideas involved, as well as the assessments, so you can achieve your best.

How this resource can help you

Getting through the IB Diploma programme is a time-consuming activity. You may need extra support from your teachers, family members, friends, and other resources. Since your teacher, friends and family are not always available, you may need alternative help to acquire, learn and use the language and ideas of TOK.

This A–Z glossary and companion aims to assist you in this process by 'unpacking' the language and ideas of the TOK course, with a focus on vocabulary, assessment, and some key ideas.

- In this A–Z glossary, you will find key vocabulary, including some philosophical terms, assessment terminology, and other important words and phrases that are used during your course.

- Each word or phrase included in this A–Z glossary has been carefully chosen because we think it will help you in your studies. This resource contains words and phrases from the IB TOK subject guide, as well as subject-specific terms found in many TOK textbooks.

- In each definition, you will also find questions and examples relating to the words in the glossary. Each definition and set of questions includes a tag categorising the entry with possible core and optional themes, as well as areas of knowledge from the TOK course that align well with it. The core and optional themes are Indigenous knowledge, Knowledge and the knower, Language, Politics, Religious knowledge, and Technology. The areas of knowledge that each definition and set of questions could relate to are The Arts, History, Human sciences, Natural sciences, and Mathematics. Please note that when an entry is 'tagged' with themes or areas of knowledge, these are based on what the entry is most likely to relate to. It does not exclude other possible themes or areas of knowledge.

- Do remember that this resource is **not** a dictionary, as it does not contain all possible definitions. It does, however, aim to help you understand the terminology in the context of the TOK course.

- When you see a word in the definition which is written in green text, this means that a glossed definition exists for it somewhere else in the book. This has been done where we thought it would be helpful for you.

- While using this book, you should identify how these terms are useful to you in your own study of epistemology.

- If your teacher gives you some additional words, you might choose to write them into the glossary yourself, so that the book is more like a 'living workbook' for you. Your teacher may also encourage you to extend the current list with extra terms, add to the definitions according to your own ideas and interpretations, or provide alternative examples. Many of the definitions come with questions to help you with this.

- In addition, you will find a section that helps you to prepare for the TOK Essay, and another that helps you to prepare for the Exhibition. These sections walk you through your preparation and planning for these assessments step by step, as well as providing examples.

- These sections also contain grids with phrases that will help you in your essay-writing, as well as sample sections from the TOK essay and exhibition. Where these key phrases are highlighted, you may find them useful in your own work. 'Phrases you can steal' are highlighted in yellow; connectives (also 'phrases you can steal'!) are highlighted in pink. Quotations are highlighted in green.

- Remember when using the sample assessment sections that these are meant to serve as an example of what can be done. They are not 'perfect', 10/10 examples, but are intended to show the level of work that students can produce. They are also not intended to be copied – remember the IB's academic honesty policy at all times.

- This book also comes with a 'frequently asked questions' section for the TOK essay, and a 'frequently asked questions' section for the exhibition. These are based on students' possible questions about the assessments. These sections of the book also provide you with possible planning templates, and checklists to help you make sure you have got everything done.

Note that the nature of epistemology is that it is very far-reaching and requires original thought – so take this book as a starting point to help you achieve your best in TOK, and one that can be at your side whenever you encounter a new idea or assessment. It aims to encourage you to question what you are presented with and to come up with original thoughts of your own.

We wish you the best in your learning journey and, of course, all the best in your assessments!
Bianca and the team at Elemi

a posteriori	Latin for 'knowledge from experience'. This is knowledge that must also come from knowing facts about the world, not just reasoning alone. "Louis XIV reigned from 1643 to 1715." This cannot be worked out via reasoning alone but requires you to know something about the world. History
a priori	Latin for 'knowledge not from experience'. This is knowledge that can come from reasoning alone. "If Lady Jane Grey has reigned for more than four days, then she has reigned for more than three days." This can be worked out by reasoning alone. History
Abductive reasoning	When we infer things logically, we start with observations and try to draw the most likely conclusion from them. If we are trying to diagnose a fault in a machine or in an example of artificial intelligence, this requires abductive reasoning (looking at what is happening with the machine and trying to work out why). Natural sciences, Technology
Ability knowledge	Knowing 'how' to do something, based on a set of procedures and skills. If we need to carry out an operation, we need to know all of the appropriate steps to follow to carry it out safely (eg suturing). Natural sciences
Abnormal	When something is statistically rare, or going away from what is usual or expected. If someone has abnormal liver function, this is a concern as it may mean that their liver is damaged and cannot do its job properly. In TOK, we want to consider how we know something is abnormal. Natural sciences
Absence perception	How we perceive, detect or represent something that is absent. In mathematics, how is zero able to represent nothingness? Cognition of zero can therefore be a type of absence perception. Mathematics
Absent	When something is not present. In TOK, we want to think about why information may be absent. *Has it been left out on purpose? How do we know? How might this absence affect our perceptions?* Language, Politics
Absolute	Something is absolute when we do not look at it relative to other things, but in its own right. For example, £350 million a week might seem like a big number in absolute terms, in terms of funding a national health service, but is relatively little compared, say, to £5 billion currently received weekly by the same country. Mathematics, Human sciences, Politics
Absolute idealism	The idea that only the mind is truly reliable, or the true basis of reality. Physical things are therefore illusory. Absolute idealism implies that there is only one mind; in religious terms, that everything is ultimately God. Religious knowledge
Abstract	Something is abstract when it cannot be seen or touched; it is the opposite of something concrete. It is sometimes also a general idea of something. 'Five', for example, is a very abstract idea, whereas 'five cars' is more concrete: we can see or visualize it in front of us much more easily as well as seeing it in the real world. Mathematics
Absurdism	Absurdism is the conflict between our search for meaning in life, and our inability to find it. We can try to make meaning, but these efforts are transient or temporary. The myth of Sisyphus, as described by the writer and philosopher Albert Camus, is a great example of absurdism. Every time Sisyphus pushes a boulder up a mountain (as punishment for a past deed), it rolls back down again. He is obliged by the punishment to keep pushing it up the hill. From a TOK perspective we can ask: how do we know where the meaning is in Sisyphus' life? Camus concludes that there has to be meaning in the struggle itself. We can also ask ourselves how far we agree with this. The Arts

Academic freedom	This is the freedom to write or publish what we wish as academics. The discussion and publication of controversial views (eg views going against the government or the zeitgeist) are included in this, so that we can all advance academically. *How can we know if there is true academic freedom in a particular country or place? And how far are professors responsible for the work of their PhD students, where does the role of professor stop and censor begin?* Human sciences
Academic honesty	Academic honesty means making sure any sources you have used or quoted from are duly credited. It means not plagiarizing your work. The IBO states that what you submit for your essay and exhibition must be entirely your own work. *How do we know what is academically honest? And how can we know what an original idea looks like?* Knowledge and the knower
Accept	To accept something is to believe in the truth of something, or to reach a state where you tolerate something undesirable. *What impact does the source of knowledge have on our acceptance of it?* Knowledge and the knower
Access	To access something is to be able to see, hear or read it, and to be able to understand it. *Who defines access to resources and what might be some of their possible motivations between providing and denying access? Which groups may lack access to knowledge, and why? What knowledge is it important to have access to, and who decides what 'important' knowledge is? How can access to knowledge be increased? Does there come a point where 'full' access is no longer possible, and why? What difference(s) could this make?* Human sciences
Accomplished	If your work is 'accomplished', it means it is fluent, sophisticated, logically sequenced, and contains your own original ideas. *Who decides what 'accomplished' work looks like? Might this look different from one country or educational system to another? How far can a universal definition of 'accomplished' be reached, particularly given that IB examiners, educators and curriculum designers come from all over the world and have been educated in many different ways?* Human sciences, Language
Account	You can 'hold someone to account', which means making them responsible for their ideas and actions. You can also 'account for' all of your data, which means explaining it and making sure everything you need is there. *What methods may you need to use to ensure that all of your data is accounted for?* *What methods can we use to hold others to account, and how reliable are these methods?* Human sciences, Mathematics, Natural sciences
Accountability	Levels of accountability show us how far someone is accountable or responsible for something. *Do different situations have different levels of accountability? How do we know what these are? Who may need to be held to account, and for what reasons?* Human sciences
Acculturation	The process of fitting in to, or being accepted by a new culture (usually the one that dominates the place we are in). For example, Native Americans have previously adopted Western language, customs, dress or religion on contact with Westerners in order to acculturate. *How far is this acculturation acceptable, desirable or necessary?* Indigenous knowledge, Human sciences
Accumulation	When things build up over time, they accumulate. For instance, intuition is a form of unconscious reasoning whereby we recognize patterns as we accumulate knowledge. You also need to accumulate a minimum of 24 points to gain your IB Diploma! Knowledge and the knower

Accurate	If something is accurate, it can be proved to be correct through repeated testing, where the result of the testing does not change. If something is accurate it is considered a true reflection of a given situation.
	Is there always a trade-off between accuracy and simplicity? Does knowledge become more accurate over time? How do we judge the significance of accuracy in the arts?
	The Arts
Acknowledge	When we recognize the importance of something, we acknowledge it. In your TOK essay, you have to acknowledge, recognize and explore different perspectives.
	What are some of the ways in which you can do this?
	Knowledge and the knower
Acontextual	If information is given to us with no details about who wrote it or where it came from, it could be said to be acontextual (without context). In the study of literature, the theory of New Criticism states that literature (especially poetry) is best appreciated acontextually, with the text being appreciated as an aesthetic object in its own right.
	How far do you agree with this view? How far is acontextual study possible in other fields, such as history?
	The Arts, History
Acquaintance knowledge	Knowledge by acquaintance is when you know it through personal experience. Examples of knowledge by acquaintance are: "I know Bertha", "I know the city of Paris well", and "I know the works of Emily Dickinson".
	Knowledge and the knower
Acquisition	Acquisition refers to how you get or obtain something (in the case of our TOK studies, knowledge).
	Does how we acquire knowledge matter, and why or why not? Can the acquisition of knowledge ever end?
	Knowledge and the knower
Activism	If you fight for or stand up for what you believe in, you are an activist, especially when doing this with a wider group of people (eg going on a protest, signing a petition) and/or if this is your full-time job.
	How do activists know if they are defending appropriate causes? How do we know if our actions, in the name of activism, are morally acceptable? (eg is it OK to set animals free from captivity or break into a public building?)
	Politics
ad hominem	If you argue or react to a person or to their personality or actions, rather than to the argument they are putting forward, this is an ad hominem response. (See also appeal to motive, bulverism, genetic fallacy.)
	"They were wrong then, so they must be wrong now." (This may not be true.) "I look professional; she doesn't." (Judging appearance, rather than ability to govern.)
	Politics
Adduce	To cite as evidence.
	"In support of a 6-month school year, the committee adduced data from other schools."
	How can we assess the reliability of the data that we and others adduce?
	Knowledge and the knower
Adequate	Meets the minimum or average standards expected in order to be acceptable. For example, you might be told by your teacher that your essay shows adequate evidence of independent thinking.
	How do you decide what makes adequate evidence different from analytical or accomplished work?
	Knowledge and the knower

Adherent

If someone is an adherent to a cause, it means they believe in it.

How true is it to say that 'science is progressively more accurate and adherent to reality'?
How do you decide whether to adhere to High Church or Low Church principles, if a Christian?

Natural sciences, Religious knowledge

Aesthetics

Aesthetics is the branch of knowledge dealing with the arts, specifically appearance and beauty, and the appreciation of this.

The principle of 'art for art's sake' prioritizes aesthetic appreciation, rather than the practical function of art in society.

How far do aesthetics matter? Do the arts need to fulfil a practical function? Why or why not?

The Arts

Aetiology

The science and study of causes (rather than end results), especially in relation to diseases. (See also cause and teleology.)

How can we identify the aetiology and sources of illnesses? How can we judge whether causes matter more than effects or results? How do we know if we have accurately established the cause (or aetiology) of something?

Natural sciences

Affect

Affect means 'to influence' or 'to have an effect or impact on'.

Different map projections and types can affect how we see the world (our perception of it) when studying geography.

(See also the Mercator projection, the Hobo-Dyer projection and the Robinson projection.)

Human sciences

Affinity

To have an affinity with something or someone means to feel that you have a strong relationship or connection to, or a lot of things in common with, that person or thing.

Platinum, for instance, has a strong affinity with sulfur.

How can we tell whether a relationship between things exists (as opposed to just putting things together at random)? When we classify and link things in this way, is this the only/best way of linking and classifying them? How do we know? In religion, if someone feels a strong affinity with a particular god or gods, is this based on faith, intuition, reasoning, experience, or something else?

Natural sciences, Religious knowledge

Agenda

The purpose of one's text, or message. For example, a publication might have an agenda to promote a particular set of political ideas. This could be covert or overt.

How can we detect what someone's agenda really is? What evidence would we need to support such a claim?

History, Human sciences, Politics

Agnosis

The lack of knowledge; or, not caring about knowledge, denying knowledge, or rejecting knowledge; or, poor-quality knowledge. If someone says they are agnostic, it usually means they do not know if they believe in God or not.

How can someone decide if they believe in an idea or not?

Religious knowledge

Agree

If you agree with someone, it means you share the same ideas or views that they have.

How can we decide if we agree or disagree with an idea? Are there situations in which it is acceptable to only partially agree? Why might this situation occur?

Knowledge and the knower

Ahistorical

An ahistorical approach ignores history/the past; it lacks historical perspective or context. It can refer to a lack of concern for history or tradition, rather than a lack of knowledge. A film featuring dinosaurs and humans existing side by side might be said to be ahistorical.

Are all concepts governed by what has gone before them? How far is it possible or desirable to study historical events by looking at them out of context? To what extent might some recent examples of activism, such as the toppling of statues, be considered ahistorical?

(See also acontextual.)

The Arts, History

Aim	All tasks usually have a clear aim; what you need to do to achieve something. Aims can also be linked to the idea of agenda (what you want to achieve, and why).
	Who can reasonably decide the aims of an overarching international course like TOK? How are such aims decided on and formulated? Can such aims ever be fully achieved?
	Human sciences
Alternative histories	Alternative histories imagine what our past may have looked like if certain events had been different – and how these changes may have affected the present day. Alternative histories are often explored in speculative fiction.
	If the killing of Franz Ferdinand could have been prevented, how might the present have been altered?
	(This is an example of an alternative history, as this is not what really happened.)
	How can we know? What purpose(s) might alternative histories serve, if any?
	The Arts, History
Ambiguous	If something is ambiguous, it may have more than one meaning, or it could be very difficult to discern the 'true' meaning of the idea. If there is ambiguity in a sentence, this can be due to lots of different things, including homonyms and syntax. Some would argue that the TOK category of 'indigenous knowledge' is ambiguous.
	How far do you agree? Does most knowledge deal with ambiguity? How do we know? How far is this a problem?
	The Arts, Indigenous knowledge
Amoral	If a person is amoral, it means they lack the strong principles of good behaviour. One thing often said to distinguish humans from other animals is morality.
	To what extent do you agree? Is there such a thing as a moral fact, or a single set of morals? Is moral knowledge omnipresent, and how do we acquire it? How far can our sense of humour tell us something about our morals?
	Human sciences, Natural sciences
Analogy	An analogy is an example to help us compare or imagine things, often using a metaphor or simile (comparing a concrete thing to an abstract idea).
	The authors of the Oxford TOK textbook use the analogy of knowledge as a map.
	How far is this a useful analogy?
	Human sciences
Analytical	If you are being analytical, you are not just retelling something in your own words but giving your own ideas and judgments about the topic in question.
	"To achieve at least 7 or 8 out of 10 in your TOK essay, you need to be analytical."
	How can we know if we are being analytical? How far is this a skill we can learn?
	Knowledge and the knower
Analytic-synthetic distinction	This divides propositions into two types: analytic ones, which are true based on meaning alone, and synthetic ones, which are based on both meaning and on knowing how the world is.
	An analytic proposition would be 'bachelors are unmarried'. A synthetic proposition would be 'bachelors are lonely'.
	How do we know whether synthetic propositions are just assumptions?
	Knowledge and the knower
Anecdotal evidence	Anecdotal evidence provides support for an idea through the use of stories of personal experience.
	"I know someone who has smoked cigarettes for decades and never become ill."
	Does this mean that claims about smoking are exaggerated? What are some of the strengths and weaknesses of anecdotal evidence, especially compared to other types of evidence? How far does it help us to gain knowledge?
	Knowledge and the knower

Animism

The belief that all plants, animals, and so on, have a soul. The indigenous Kalash people of Northern Pakistan follow an ancient animist religion, and the Shinto religion of Japan also has many animist aspects.

How can you 'know' if a being or object (human, or non-human) has a soul? How far might animism come from the human desire for a sense of agency in all things?

Indigenous knowledge, Religious knowledge

Annotate

Annotating a text means you make notes around the outside of the text, or inside it (eg by highlighting or underlining). Annotations may help you to label key terms in a text, remind you to look up meanings, add your own thoughts, or ask yourself some questions about what you have read that you can think about later.

Language

Anomaly

Anomalies are results that seem odd because they do not fit into a trend, or observations that do not seem to fit with accepted theories.

IBO officials may investigate schools' marks and methods if there is a big difference between your TOK essay grade and your TOK exhibition grade.

How are such anomalies detected? Are the methods of detection reliable? How do we know? Is it always a problem if anomalies cannot be explained? (See also reproducible anomaly.)

Natural sciences

Anonymous

If something is anonymous, then the creator or speaker's name is unknown to, or deliberately kept secret from, the public.

How far is anonymity necessary, or even desirable, for the true value of artwork to be known or recognized? How do we decide if anonymity is an advantage or disadvantage? Might there be any negative consequences? How does the anonymity of an assertion affect its production by the speaker or writer, and its reception by listeners or readers?

The Arts

Anthropocentric

Anthropocentrism is a theory that regards the human as the most important thing in the universe; it portrays everything through human values and experiences.

An anthropocentric view of climate change would argue that humans are the cause.

How can we know if this is really the case? What might be some problems with an anthropocentric view of the world?

Natural sciences, Politics

Anthropology

Anthropology is the scientific study of humanity, including past and present human behaviour, biology and societies, to understand human origins and evolution.

How does an outsider (anthropologist) understand a world completely different to their own? How far is it possible to remain objective and neutral when studying other cultures? How does our own culture, training or personality influence what we choose to research or learn from respondents?

Human sciences

Anti-vaxxers

'Anti-vaxxers' is popular slang for those who are against vaccination programmes, and/or refuse to be vaccinated. This often relates to conspiracy theories and misinformation regarding vaccines, particularly in terms of fake news perpetuated online. Usually, it relates to parents who do not wish to vaccinate their children.

How big a problem is vaccine hesitancy? How far is it effective, or morally correct, to legislate so that people are obliged to be vaccinated or have their children vaccinated? How do we know whether anti-vaxxers are correct or incorrect? How do we know if vaccines are safe? How do we know whether or not to give anti-vaxxers a platform?

Natural sciences

Appeal to motive

The appeal to motive is a type of ad hominem fallacy which involves questioning someone's motives, rather than the quality of the idea they put forward.

If a football referee is from Manchester, for instance, does it necessarily follow that he is biased when refereeing a match where one of the teams is from Manchester? Is it ever valuable, or ethical, to question a claim-maker's motives? How do we know?

Politics

Appeal to novelty	The appeal to novelty is a type of fallacy when you claim that an idea is superior just because it is new or modern. Companies may claim, for instance, that a new operating system or phone model is automatically superior to the previous one.
	How do we know if this is really the case?
	Human sciences
Appendix	An appendix (plural 'appendices') is a section at the end of an essay where you add extra information which is relevant to your essay, but doesn't really fit into its main body.
	Appendices, end-notes and your bibliography, as well as maps, charts or diagrams, do not count towards the 1600 words of your TOK essay.
	Knowledge and the knower
Applied	Applied knowledge is when we relate our ideas to a specific situation in the real world.
	Is it always important to apply our knowledge to real life, to a practical situation? How far is knowledge valuable for its own sake?
	Knowledge and the knower
Appraisal	When you appraise something, you make an assessment or evaluation of its level or value. This can be in terms of valuing an object before it is sold at auction, or evaluating an employee's performance at work, for example.
	Who decides on the criteria on which appraisals are based? How far do these criteria help us to assess success, importance or value?
	Human sciences
Approach	When you take a particular approach to something, you are looking at it according to your own experiences, aims or values. It can also relate to the methods you use.
	Research can be carried out using lots of different methods, including qualitative, quantitative, and participatory. You can also take different approaches to providing support, reading a text, or even teaching, according to different theories (eg learner-centred, cross-cultural feminist).
	How do we decide which approaches to use? How far can we show or prove which approach(es) might be the most effective?
	Knowledge and the knower
Appropriate	We might decide if our behaviour or language is suitable to the given situation. What we say and do needs to fit with the place and people involved. We also need to choose appropriate methods for the task we are carrying out. 'Appropriate' can be used as a verb too, as an example of taking something, especially something that we are not authorized to take. (See also cultural appropriation.)
	Different measures are appropriate for different moments and contexts; for example, it is more appropriate to measure the weight of a human in kilograms than in grams. It is also inappropriate in most cultures to dress informally for a funeral.
	How do we decide what is appropriate and what is not? Are there ever moments where it is acceptable to be 'inappropriate'?
	Human sciences, Mathematics
Arbiter	An arbiter is a person or group who decides what is acceptable or appropriate, or who passes a judgment.
	Judges serve as arbiters in criminal cases. Magazines can also be arbiters of fashion and taste.
	How far are the opinions of these arbiters valid? When do they become 'fact' (if indeed they do)?
	Human sciences, The Arts
Arbitrary	If something is arbitrary it seems to be decided at random, rather than based on reason. Some argue that the words we use have no real connection to the objects they designate. For example, it could be considered arbitrary that an animal that barks, has four legs, fur and a tail, and is often kept as a house pet, is called a 'dog' rather than, for instance, a 'rog' or a 'yog'.
	Would it matter if you named your cat 'Dog', for instance? How far does our language have meaning, and how far are our names for things arbitrary?
	Language

Areas of knowledge (AOKs)	The IB DP TOK programme consists of five compulsory areas of knowledge: mathematics, human sciences, natural sciences, the arts, and history.
	Prior to the new TOK syllabus issued in 2020, the course also contained three further areas of knowledge: religious knowledge, ethics, and indigenous knowledge. Religion and indigenous societies now feature in the course as optional themes, along with politics, language, and technology, with ethics only featuring in relation to other themes.
	How do creators of IB courses decide what to include and what to exclude? And how do we decide if they are right or wrong to do so?
	Knowledge and the knower
Argument	An argument is when you explain the reasons for your beliefs.
	How far should an argument be balanced? How do we know which reasons and counterarguments to accept and reject when formulating an argument?
	Language, Politics
argumentum ad nauseam	The logical fallacy that something becomes true if you repeat it often enough.
	"What I tell you three times is true."
	This line from the poem 'The Hunting of the Snark', by Lewis Carroll, indirectly asks us how far repetition serves as evidence of truth in itself.
	Can repetition ever be proof of truth?
	The Arts, Human sciences
Armchair theorizing	The notion of the general public disseminating theories from their homes, often online, based mainly on opinion and hearsay, rather than on real expertise. It involves collecting and synergizing existing evidence (frequently anecdotal evidence) rather than the collection of new information.
	Anthropologist Bronislaw Malinowski said it was important to 'go into the field' and live among those you studied, instead of researching from homes and libraries.
	How far is this the case for all disciplines? What might be some possible advantages and disadvantages of studying 'in the field' as opposed to researching from afar?
	Human sciences
Artefact	1. In history, an object from the past that we can study, so that we can learn about how people lived.
	2. In the natural sciences, it is something artificial that does not reflect what we would normally see, especially due to an error or due to a piece of equipment introduced during scientific observation.
	Historically, an artefact might be a Tang dynasty pot or a piece of Roman jewellery. Biologically, an artefact might be a surgical metal clip that appears on an X-ray, obscuring part of the anatomy.
	How can artefacts affect the quality of our knowledge about the world?
	History, natural sciences
Articulate	When you articulate your ideas, you explain them clearly and in detail. If you are articulate, or your essay is, it means you/it do(es) this regularly or throughout.
	Food critics need to be articulate in order to let readers or viewers know their thoughts about the restaurants they visit and the food they eat.
	How far do restaurant critics and oenologists (wine experts) really have superior knowledge to the rest of the population, and how far are they simply more articulate?
	The Arts, Human sciences, Language
Artificial intelligence	Artificial intelligence (also known as AI) is when a machine is created that appears to be 'intelligent' and can carry out some tasks that a human would also be able to do.
	What examples can you think of from your day-to-day life, or from anything you have read in the press, where artificial intelligence has done something that seems really 'clever' or, conversely, rather silly? (For example, a satellite navigation system telling someone to drive into a river.)
	Does anyone really know how to make AI truly smart? How far do you think this is possible or even desirable? How might AI act in ways that are considered unethical?
	Human sciences, Natural sciences, Technology

Artistic licence	If someone uses artistic licence when creating a piece of art, they may change some aspects of real life in order to benefit the artwork.
	Some works originally published as memoirs were later revealed to be more fictional, having made significant use of artistic licence.
	To what extent do artists have a commitment to the truth, as opposed to a commitment to their art?
	The Arts, Language
Arts	The arts is an area of knowledge covering the production of music, artwork, literature, dance, theatre, television, film, and other objects produced for our entertainment.
	How do we judge the importance of the arts in our day-to-day lives? Does art have to be timeless to be classed as art? How far are the arts affected by the political and cultural space in which they are produced?
	The Arts, Politics
Ascribe	When something is ascribed to a particular person, place or time period, it is being associated with it, or thought of as belonging to it.
	Memes often erroneously ascribe quotations to historical figures when they did not in fact say them.
	How can we check the veracity of these claims when something is ascribed to someone?
	The Arts, Technology
Assertion	An idea presented as a fact (though it may or may not be a fact). Usually presented with a degree of confidence which takes it beyond a mere claim.
	How do we know if there is sufficient evidence to back up someone's assertions? How far can we determine if someone's assertions are true? What methods might we use?
	Knowledge and the knower
Assessment instrument	The assessment instruments provided by the IBO are what examiners use to help them mark your work. They usually have a description written next to each mark to show what you would have to do to achieve that mark.
	How subjective or objective are assessment instruments (or mark schemes)? How far can measures be taken to ensure that these are applied reliably, even across thousands of students in a given year?
	Knowledge and the knower
Assimilationism	Assimilationism is the encouragement of minority communities and cultures to fit in (linguistically, culturally, or in terms of appearance) to a given culture or community (usually the dominant one). For example, assimilationist Latin-American families might not want their children to be educated in Spanish in America.
	How far is assimilationism morally correct? How can we identify which social groups are candidates for assimilation?
	Human sciences, Language
Assumption	An opinion based on only partial and/or sometimes inaccurate information; an idea put forward without proof. It can be disproved later by logical argument, rather than necessarily being testable.
	"Science has disproven many common assumptions."
	Might this statement itself be an assumption? How could we prove this? What methods might we use to disprove assumptions? In what situations might assumptions be needed?
	Natural sciences
Astrobiology	The study of life on earth and in space. This considers the early origins, distribution, and future of life in the universe.
	Part of astrobiology is researching the possibility of life on other planets.
	How far can we judge the value of such a quest? And is this a fair representation of the field of astrobiology?
	Natural sciences

Atheist

Atheism is broadly a lack of belief in any god or gods. If someone is atheist, they consider that God does not exist.

Is it truly possible to establish such a belief? How confident can we be in asserting this view?

Religious knowledge

Attainable

If something is attainable, then it is possible to achieve it.

How do we decide what is attainable? Is it appropriate, for instance, to compare the attainability of 'I want to lose 10kg', 'I want to become an astronaut', and 'My goal is to achieve nirvana'? What factors may affect whether something is attainable or not?

Human sciences, Religious knowledge

Audience

The audience of a text, idea or object is whoever will look at or respond to it.

When creating an object, writing a speech, or presenting an idea, I can use demographics to help me reach my audience. If I know that my audience is aged 6, or headteachers, or from South-East Asia, how far will this help me to achieve my goal?

What else might I need to know about my audience in order to succeed? How can I overcome possibly unknowable factors about my audience in order to succeed anyway?

Human sciences, Politics

Authenticity

If something or someone has authenticity, it means they are believable and seem real to us – even if they are fictional or constructed.

Experts certify the authenticity of historical documents or artefacts, which lets us know that they are genuine.

What is the probability of experts being wrong regarding the authenticity of an artefact? How far is it possible for a male author to create a truly authentic female character in a novel? How can politicians make themselves seem authentic, and how far is it important for constituents to relate to them on this basis? What does authenticity on the internet really mean?

The Arts, History, Politics

Authority

If someone or something has authority, it means they have power and are to be believed in or obeyed. If someone is an authority in their field, this can mean they are an expert. Both Hitler and Jesus Christ could be described as authority figures.

How can we judge if somebody has authority or not? Is authority a perceived or actual quality? How far does authority extend? How far is authority a positive quality? And to what extent does authority come from yourself, as opposed to others?

History, Human sciences, Politics

Autobiography

An autobiography is someone's written account of their own life. It explains the most important events of the person's life, from their own point of view. (See also **biography**.)

How reliable are autobiographies as a record of a person's life? Is self-knowledge the most accurate form of knowledge in this situation, or must it be combined with other forms of knowledge?

The Arts, Language

Autoethnography

A type of research which connects your personal experiences to wider social, political and cultural meanings and understanding. Some argue that autoethnography combines the researcher and the researched.

*Might it be possible to argue that autoethnography is a self-absorbed pursuit? How subjective is autoethnography compared to other forms of research? (See also **ethnography**.)*

Human sciences

Axiomatic

If something is axiomatic it is considered to be self-evident or unquestionable. Axioms are mathematical statements which are taken automatically to be true.

Examples of axioms are 'all right angles are equal to one another' or 'the whole is greater than the part'.

How far are axioms 'provable'? Do they cause more problems than they solve?

Mathematics, Natural sciences

Balanced	If something or someone is balanced, it means that equal or even attention is given to different areas.
	The IB learner profile states that by being balanced we become responsible members of our community.
	How do we know whether or not our lives are balanced? To what extent are we, others, and the world, interdependent? How far is it possible to achieve balance in our lives? To what extent is balance necessary for wellbeing?
	Human sciences
Bandwagon effect	The bandwagon effect sees people agreeing with an idea because multiple others are also agreeing with or participating in it. (See also groupthink and herd mentality.)
	People are more likely to vote for the candidate in an election who they believe to be winning. Many people also begin wearing a certain style of clothing when they see others doing so.
	How do we know if people are 'jumping on the bandwagon' or thinking critically? What effects might the bandwagon effect have?
	Human sciences, Politics
Basis	The basis for an idea is the reasons for it or where it comes from originally.
	How do we know on what basis our decisions are made? When might we need to explain on what basis we have made decisions? How do we judge what an idea or assertion is based on?
	Human sciences, Mathematics
Begging the question	This is when you assume the conclusion through the initial premises of your argument. You're not logically wrong, but you're not adding anything to the argument either.
	"I am confident God exists because it says so in the Bible."
	The argument does not support the claim very well as it already assumes it is true.
	How can we tell when someone is 'begging the question'? (See also brain in a vat.)
	Religious knowledge
Behaviourism	The theory that all of our behaviours are acquired through conditioning. That is, all our behaviours are just responses to the environment around us. Behaviourists only study observed or measurable behaviours, rather than emotions or motives. Companies often offer raises to employees who perform well as it reinforces positive behaviour.
	How far can this be said to have nothing to do with motives? What methods could we use in order to judge the effectiveness of a behaviourist approach?
	Human sciences
Belief	An acceptance that something exists or is true. This may be with or without proof.
	What are the differences between a belief that snow is white and a belief in God? How can we revise our beliefs when presented with evidence? Must it be possible for a belief to be expressed in language, or are there non-linguistic beliefs? How far do facts influence our beliefs?
	Natural sciences, Religious knowledge
Belief system	A set of beliefs; these could be religious or non-religious. A belief system helps us to interpret the world and to interact with and within it.
	How far are we free to make decisions, and act, in ways that resonate with our values and belief systems? To what extent should others' belief systems be respected? How do we form or acquire our own belief systems? Does it matter how our beliefs are formed and acquired? For what reasons?
	Human sciences, Politics, Religious knowledge
Bias	If you are biased then you are not fully neutral in your approach to a person, group, object or idea. This prejudice may be for or against the person, group, object or idea, and often results in unfair outcomes. For example, if there is a racial bias in the selection of candidates for a job, the best person for that job may not be selected if candidates are 'filtered out' based on their skin colour.(See also prejudice.)
	Is it possible to be completely unbiased? How can we detect our own biases? How far is it possible to alter our biases? How can we judge the effectiveness of unconscious bias training programmes (which are increasingly popular in schools and workplaces and are designed to eliminate any biases we have that we are unaware of)?
	Human sciences, Politics

Bibliography

A list of sources at the end of your essay, showing in full the names of the texts you have used to support your argument, as well as their authors.

There are lots of different systems for producing a bibliography at the end of your essay (eg MLA, APA, Harvard), as well as lots of online tools to speed up the process (eg Easybib, MyBib, CiteThisForMe).

How do we decide which bibliographical system is the 'best', and which tool(s) – if any – are most reliable in terms of helping you produce one?

Knowledge and the knower

Bilateral

Having, affecting, or relating to both sides. (See also unilateral, multilateral.) For example, a bilateral agreement takes place when you sell a car or a house. Bilateral trade also takes place between two particular countries, and we often talk about countries having a bilateral relationship or alliance.

What might be some advantages and disadvantages of bilateral agreements and approaches?

Human sciences, Natural sciences, Politics

Binary

Related to, made up of, or involving two things. A binary choice indicates that you have two choices.

What might be some problems with a binary view of the world? In what situations might a binary view of the world be desirable?

Knowledge and the knower

Biography

An account of somebody's life written by another person. (See also autobiography.)

How far should a biography be composed of multiple accounts? Is a biography more reliable if based on interviews with the person it is about? How authentic are unauthorized biographies? To what extent is the public persona a reflection of the person's private life?

The Arts, History, Language

Bivalence

The existence of only two truth values: true or false. "There will be a battle tomorrow" implies that the battle will either take place tomorrow, or it will not.

How far is this sort of bivalency transferable to other propositions? What, for instance, might be the problem with a bivalent approach in the case of the proposition 'The apple is red'? or 'Every number is either odd or prime'?

Mathematics

Blackboxing

Blackboxing describes how science and technology are paradoxically made more invisible by their own success. For example, if a device works well, we usually only need to think about input and output (ie I swipe left, and this happens), and not about how it works inside.

How might blackboxing affect our search for knowledge?

Natural sciences

Blatantly

Obviously; clearly; with no attempt to hide an idea or viewpoint. Some people might, for example, accuse politicians of using blatant propaganda to promote their policies.

Is it always, if indeed ever, in our interests to behave blatantly?

Human sciences, Language, Politics

Blind acceptance

Believing an idea to be true without questioning it. (See also face value, gullibility.) If someone is a 'yes man', they always agree with what their boss or other authority figures say, whether they agree or not (or maybe even without thinking about if they agree or not), accepting ideas blindly in the interests of keeping their job and keeping their boss happy.

What might be some problems with blind acceptance? And how far can blind acceptance be equated to faith?

Religious knowledge

Boundary	Where one thing or idea stops and another begins. A boundary can be visible or invisible. Boundary lines on a map can indicate property, or a moment where you pass from one country to another.
	How accurate or useful might boundary lines on a map be? Do boundaries between different subject areas (eg geography and politics, art and science really exist? If so, how do we know where one begins and the other ends? How do we define our own personal boundaries?
	Human sciences
Bounded rationality	The idea that we make decisions rationally, but that this is limited according to the information we have and our own personal abilities. An individual might buy shares based on their earnings and price, but might be unaware of factors making it a high-risk investment (eg default risk, cost of capital).
	How far is it possible to overcome bounded rationality?
	Human sciences
Bowdlerisation	The process of 'sanitizing' or editing a text to make it seem less offensive or indecent. (See also censorship, whitewashing.)
	Recent editions of many works have been bowdlerised to remove the word 'nigger'.
	How can we decide if bowdlerisation is necessary? What might be some implications for authenticity?
	The Arts, Language, Politics
Brain in a vat	A philosophical thought experiment that suggests there is no way for us to know if our experiences are real because we could be just a 'brain in a vat', with a sophisticated computer program manipulating our brains to simulate life-like experiences, and with us not knowing the difference.
	"I know that everything I experience is real. I can see, touch, smell, hear and taste it all myself."
	What would be some ways of proving or disproving this fallacy?
	Knowledge and the knower
Brainwashing	Forcing someone to radically change their beliefs so that they can be manipulated into behaving in a way that advantages the 'brainwasher'. Brainwashing is often linked with cults and viewed as abusive.
	How can we determine whether this is an accurate perception? How far is brainwashing effective, and for how long can it be maintained?
	Knowledge and the knower
Bulverism	A fallacy which assumes your opponent is wrong from the beginning (usually based on their personality, motives, or some other aspect of their identity), and focuses on less important questions to do with the idea, rather than on the main/basic idea itself. One example of bulverism might be "You only think that because you're rich!" (See also ad hominem, genetic fallacy.)
	What might be some flaws in this reasoning?
	Human sciences
Can	A modal verb, meaning 'to be able to', or 'to be permitted to'. 'Can' shows what is possible.
	"I can speak four languages."
	How can we prove that people are really able to do what they say they can? Which methods might be more effective than others in proving this?
	Knowledge and the knower
Cancel culture	When someone is ejected from or rejected by social or professional circles, in real life or online, because of personal beliefs that are thought to be offensive. In this way, they are culturally blocked from having a platform or career. (See also no-platforming.)
	Some researchers claim that they have been victims of cancel culture, with their invitations to speak at universities being rescinded.
	Is cancel culture a mob mentality, or an effective way of speaking the truth to figures in power? How could we decide this?
	Human sciences, Politics

Capability

The ability of a person or thing to do or achieve something.

How can the capabilities of a person or substance be measured most accurately, both in a single moment and over time? What might be some of the most effective methods to use? How do we know this, and therefore how do we choose?

Human sciences, Natural sciences

Caring

If a person is caring, it means that they think about others and consider their needs.

The IB learner profile states that being caring means we show empathy, compassion, and respect towards others.

How do we know whether or not we are doing this? How far is a commitment to service a requirement to lead a morally good life? How do we know whether we have made a positive difference to the lives of those around us, and to the world we live in?

Human sciences

Case study

An example of an individual situation or person which shows more broadly what you are trying to investigate.

If hundreds of case studies exist on a particular subject, how do we know which ones, if any, to cite in our own research? To what extent are case studies reliable? What makes them more reliable, and how can we make them more reliable via their design?

Human sciences, Natural sciences

Categorical imperative

A basis of all rules for life, or a rule that is true in all circumstances; a concern with what people do, rather than the consequences of these actions. It relies on our doing things because we have a duty to do the right thing. (See also hypothetical imperative, moral imperative.)

If truth-telling is a universal duty, should we tell a murderer the location of the person he wants to murder? What might be some problems with always acting according to the categorical imperative (always acting based on a duty to do the right thing)?

Human sciences

Categorization

The act or process of placing items into broad groups. (See also classification, taxonomy.) The signs of many disorders, such as autism, might be said to defy precise categorization.

How do we decide in what broad group something belongs? How far is it problematic for categories to blur, or for something to belong to more than one category?

Human sciences, Natural sciences

Causality

The relationship between cause and effect. (See also causation, determinism.) For example, 'My student opened the window, and the window broke.'

How could we prove a causal link between the two events (ie did my student break the window)? Does the word 'cause' link to anything objective, or do human beings simply interpret what they see as cause and effect?

Human sciences, Natural sciences

Causation

The direct, provable interconnectedness between an event and the reasons for its occurrence. For example, if one event, or variable, increases or decreases due to other events, it can be said that there is causation – 'They threw a brick through my window so the window broke.'

What methods might we use to prove this?

Mathematics

Cause

1. The reason for an event occurring. (Noun)

2. To make something occur. (Verb)

3. A cause can also be a principle or movement that you deeply believe in.

(See also aetiology.)

For example, someone might show great dedication to the cause of citizens' rights. Some materials are also no longer used to make children's toys (such as lead paint) because they are now known to cause poisoning or other harms.

How do we decide what a 'good' cause to believe in might be? How far can we really determine the cause of an event?

Knowledge and the knower

Censorship

When information is deliberately removed, especially from mass media, in order to give a better impression than is really the case.

Letters home from war zones were often censored in the past, with negative information about soldiers' living conditions blacked out, and also any sensitive information about where troops were deployed. Maps are sometimes censored so that politically sensitive areas are not shown.

How far can it be argued that some things should never be censored? How can we determine possible positives of censorship? How far should governments take censorship? How can censorship's impact on free speech be assessed?

Human sciences, Politics

Certainty

When something can be proven beyond all reasonable doubt.

For instance, to what degree of certainty can we know why some diseases spread so quickly? Is certainty objective or subjective? Is there a difference between knowledge and certainty? On what grounds can we say we are certain of something?

Natural sciences

Ceteris paribus

'Default' reasoning; reasoning based on the idea of 'all things being equal'. For example, if the price of bread increases, ceteris paribus, people will buy less bread. Ceteris paribus doesn't consider the price of competing products, how readily the bread is available for purchase, or other factors that would affect customers' decreasing desire to buy bread.

What might be some advantages and disadvantages of a ceteris paribus approach?

Human sciences

Challenge

To present an idea that goes against a person or group's existing beliefs; to stretch and increase our abilities and performance; to question.

How do we know whether to challenge research findings? In what situations might knowledge challenge our pre-existing beliefs? How do we know whether something is 'open to challenge'? How do we know when to challenge a person or idea? Should we challenge every idea with which we are presented?

Human sciences, Natural sciences, Technology

Checks and balances

The sharing of control between different branches of governments or organizations so that one person or group does not have all the power. A system put in place to reduce mistakes and inappropriate behaviour.

What checks and balances might be needed to make institutions more transparent and accountable? To what extent are checks and balances necessary? How can we judge the success of a system that uses checks and balances?

Human sciences, Politics

Cherry-picking

Taking only what is most beneficial to you, especially to help or skew your argument in your favour.

How far does cherry-picking enable exaggeration? How can we evaluate whether someone has cherry-picked to aid their argument? Does the term cherry-picking necessarily imply that one is ignoring significant data?

Human sciences, Mathematics, Natural sciences, Politics

Childhood amnesia

The inability to retain very many memories before the age of 4 (in children) or the age of 10 (in adults).

How can the end of childhood amnesia be determined? To what extent are our memories, and our recollections of them, reliable? What factors might influence the recall of our memories?

Human sciences

Circumstances

The individual situations that people find themselves in; these are affected by multiple factors, including time and place; a condition relevant to an event or action. In some legal cases, for instance, a judge might find that there were mitigating or extenuating circumstances that caused someone to do something, which can ultimately affect the outcome of the case.

How far can the impact of circumstances be assessed? To what degree might circumstances mitigate our behaviour?

Human sciences

Cite	To recognize and acknowledge the sources you have used when writing an essay or forming an argument.
	You should cite a range of types of evidence in your Extended Essay to help increase your marks.
	To what extent might the quality of citation affect our views? What might be some examples of poor citation?
	Knowledge and the knower
Claim	A statement that puts forward an idea as if it were a fact, while acknowledging that it may not be possible to prove it. (See also assertion, false claim.)
	For example, if someone claims that they have been cheated, how can we decide if this is true? What methods can we use to assess the reliability of a claim? How do we decide what the 'best' methods are, and whether or not we ultimately believe a claim?
	Knowledge and the knower
Claims-maker	Someone who makes claims; this person may or may not be in a position of authority.
	How easy is it for claims-makers to persuade us? How can we judge the expertise of any given claims-maker? What sources of knowledge do claims-makers draw on?
	Human sciences, Politics
Classification	A more specific group that can be placed within a broader category. We might also talk about 'the classification process' to show that we are putting things into specific groups (or classifying them). For example, within the broader category of race, we could classify people as African-American, Asian, White, and so on.
	What are the possible benefits and pitfalls of such classifications?
	Human sciences, Natural sciences
Cliché	An idea or phrase which has been repeated so often (usually within a culture or language) that it no longer feels original or exciting.
	"Let's touch base."
	How can we judge the usefulness of such clichés? How far are clichés the same across cultures? Why might such clichés persist? To what extent do clichés reaffirm a confirmation bias, or shut down debates?
	Human sciences, Language, Politics
Clicktivism	A form of activism mainly carried out online (eg by signing petitions or sharing social media posts).
	How do we decide if clicktivism is an effective form of activism? How do we know if 'real' activists (who go out on protests, lobby governments, etc) are 'more effective' activists than those who engage in clicktivism? How can we judge how much effort or commitment clicktivism involves?
	Politics, Technology
Cliodynamics	An area of research which integrates history with sciences and mathematics.
	Cliodynamicists apply mathematical models to explain historical patterns; for example, the rise and fall of empires.
	How far is such an approach useful to the study of history?
	History, Human sciences, Mathematics, Natural sciences
Closed question	A question which invites only a 'yes' or 'no' answer, or only allows for one or two possible answers. (See also leading question, open question.)
	"Would you like the red one, or the blue one?"
	To what extent are closed questions useful in our search for knowledge?
	Knowledge and the knower
Cluster concept	An idea defined by a weighted list of criteria, so that all of the criteria have to be fulfilled for the idea to be legitimized. Some would argue that concepts like 'energy' or 'a species' are cluster concepts.
	How far is it possible to agree with this idea? Where do the criteria for each cluster concept come from, who decides how important they are, and therefore how reliably can we apply them to 'energy' or 'a species'?
	Natural sciences

cogito ergo sum	Literally meaning 'I think, therefore I am' in Latin, it is the idea that the only certainty is the existence of the thinking being.
	Is 'cogito ergo sum' something we know for certain? To what extent is this proposition provable? Could 'cogito ergo sum' possibly be false? Might a 'better' translation be 'I doubt, therefore I am', and for what reason(s)?
	Knowledge and the knower
Cognition	The process of gaining knowledge through thought, experiences, and the senses. (See also **epistemic cognition**, **metacognition**.)
	First-level cognition involves us computing, memorizing, reading, perceiving, and solving problems.
	How far can, or could, humans manage with only this 'first level' of cognition?
	Knowledge and the knower
Cognitive dissonance	The act of holding multiple contradictory beliefs at the same time.
	An example of cognitive dissonance might be telling a lie while believing it is important to tell the truth, or smoking cigarettes despite knowing the damage caused by doing so.
	Under what circumstances might we expect cognitive dissonance to occur? How do we know if we are experiencing cognitive dissonance ourselves?
	Human sciences
Coherence (test)	If something is coherent, it is clear and makes sense. The coherence test involves working out if a belief is consistent with your other beliefs and makes sense in relation to them. (See also **correspondence test**, **pragmatic test**.)
	One criticism of the coherence test is that just because a belief is consistent with your other beliefs, that still does not necessarily make it true.
	How can our beliefs be manipulated so that statements appear to be consistent with each other? What might be some implications of rejecting an idea that does not fit with what we already know?
	Knowledge and the knower
Coincidence	A coincidence takes place at the same time as something else, and may appear to have significance, but turns out to actually have nothing to do with the other thing.
	"I am waiting for my best friend to arrive, but she is late. I hear sirens going past."
	How can I decide whether she is late because she has been involved in an accident, or whether she is late for another reason (and that, therefore, hearing the sirens is a coincidence)? What might be some possible explanations for coincidences occurring? How can we tell coincidences from causation? How can we decide whether or not coincidences are significant? How might coincidence be different from coexistence?
	Human sciences
Collective consciousness	The set of shared beliefs and values that unify a particular society or community.
	How far does a major event, such as a war, affect collective consciousness? How far can collective consciousness be altered? In what situations might this be useful or desirable, or, alternatively, dangerous? How can we detect when or if this might be the case? How can we judge the value of collective consciousness to society?
	History, Human sciences
Collective memory	The shared pool of memories of a particular group or community. This can be shared knowledge, or the continuous process via which memories of events change over time. Collective memory tends to focus on one perspective.
	What are some possible benefits and pitfalls of this? What are some possible differences between history and collective memory?
	History, Human sciences
Commentary	A critical explanation of a text or situation. For your TOK exhibition, you have to produce a commentary about each object.
	How do we know what makes a good commentary?
	Knowledge and the knower

Common knowledge

General knowledge; knowledge known by most people.

It has only become common knowledge relatively recently that bacteria cause disease.

Where does common knowledge come from? How far is common knowledge necessary to our day-to-day lives? How might we determine this? Does common knowledge vary between communities? If so, how and why?

Human sciences, Natural sciences

Common sense

Good practical judgment concerning everyday matters; assumptions about the physical properties, purposes, intentions and behaviour of people and objects, as encountered in ordinary situations.

It could be said that the common sense of modern times was not always 'common' historically.

Is there such a thing as universal 'common sense' that is unchanged by time and place? How might we judge this?

Human sciences

Communication

Exchanging information, whether through speaking, writing, or by other means.

How far is it possible to communicate without words? To what extent are words valuable and valid vehicles to communicate our ideas? How useful is the oral tradition of indigenous and preliterate communities as a form of communication? How far does communication bring people closer to the truth? How might our chosen methods of communicating our knowledge actually distort our knowledge?

Human sciences, Language

Community

A group of people living in the same (small) place, and/or having certain characteristics in common (such as race, religion, or particular attitudes or interests).

In science, what might be the value and weaknesses of community-based trials? What methods might we need to use to study rural and tribal communities accurately?

Human sciences, Indigenous knowledge, Natural sciences

Compare

To discuss and analyse the similarities and differences between two or more entities. Sometimes doctors try to compare scans, for example, to see any differences in the growth of a tumour between the latest scan and the previous one.

Are all comparisons equal? What factors may affect the reliability of a comparison? How can we know whether a comparison is helpful or not?

History, Natural sciences

Compartmentalization

1. In psychology, a psychological defence mechanism used to 'protect' an individual from the effects of trauma, or from having conflicting beliefs and values.

2. In natural sciences, dividing things into groups or parts.

To what extent can psychological disorders be induced or characterized by compartmentalization? How far can, or should, similar disciplines, such as structural geology and stratigraphy, be compartmentalized? How can we detect the possible benefits and pitfalls of compartmentalization?

Human sciences, Natural sciences

Compelling

Especially interesting or intriguing; strong; keeps your attention; persuasive.

To what extent is 'compelling' a subjective concept? What might be some differences between 'adequate evidence' and 'compelling evidence'?

Knowledge and the knower

Competent

If a person or their work is competent, they are considered acceptable and satisfactory as a minimum, and perhaps also efficient and capable.

By what standards do we judge competence? How reliable are those who define competence? How might ideas of competence differ from place to place, or person to person, or even culture to culture?

Human sciences

Competing	Rivalling or attempting to win out over others; opposing, even if both equally valid.
	In an argument or debate, for instance, two opposing or competing views might be very different from each other. However, this does not mean that either view is automatically wrong – just different. Both views might be right or wrong to varying degrees; they are therefore both equally valid.
	How far is it possible for multiple competing ideas to be right at the same time? Why might it be important to scrutinize competing ideas?
	Knowledge and the knower
Complement	Something that contributes extra features to another thing, in a way that enhances it or makes it better. 'To complement' can also be used as a verb. (Not to be confused with 'compliment', which involves saying a nice thing to or about someone else.) Scientific observations can be complemented by interviews, for instance.
	How can we decide what complements knowledge? In what ways can we complement our own knowledge?
	Natural sciences
Complicit	If someone is complicit in an action, they are involved, especially in an activity which is illegal or ethically wrong.
	How far can one be responsible for perpetuating a wrong, or being complicit, if one does not know it's wrong? In what ways might people be complicit in the construction and maintenance of ignorance and the harms that accompany it?
	Human sciences
compos mentis	Having full control of one's mind. If compos mentis you are still thinking clearly and fully responsible for your actions. This might mean that you are not unconscious or intoxicated, or suffering from a condition such as Alzheimer's.
	How can we decide if someone is compos mentis? How far is it possible to suffer from a mental illness and still be compos mentis? How can we know where the boundary is between compos mentis and non compos mentis?
	Natural sciences
Computability theory	Also known as recursion theory, computability theory studies what can be effectively calculated and what can not, putting limitations on what is computable.
	In putting limits on what we understand of scientific and mathematical theory, how far does computability theory also place limits on knowledge?
	Mathematics, Technology
Conceivable	If something is conceivable, we are capable of imagining or understanding it. If something is inconceivable, it is (or seems to be!) just not possible.
	How do we decide on the conceivability of an idea? For instance, is perfection conceivable, even in things that are not completely understood? How many people have to conceive of something for it to be conceivable?
	Knowledge and the knower
Concept	An abstract idea.
	How do concepts change over time, and how do we judge what is the 'right' concept to use?
	Natural sciences
Conception	The forming or devising of a plan or idea; the way in which something is perceived; an abstract idea; an ability to imagine or understand.
	How far can we develop clear conceptions of problems or ideas? What counts as the 'right' conception of the nature of knowledge?
	Knowledge and the knower
Concerns	As a noun, anxieties or worries; as a verb, to involve or relate to.
	How do we decide which concerns are most important to us?
	Human sciences

Conclusion	An end, or finish (eg of a historical event such as a war or interregnum); an overall judgment or decision based on reasoning, often at the end of an essay or argument.
	To what extent can data confirm conclusions? How useful are multiple conclusions to one argument? How can we decide which conclusion is 'more valid', if any? What next steps might be important if your data disagree with previous data or conclusions? How far is any given conclusion definitive?
	Knowledge and the knower
Concrete	Concrete objects and situations exist physically in our real world; typically, they can be seen, touched, or otherwise proven to exist. For example, dense things sink. We can prove this by experiment (eg by dropping a brick into water).
	Are concrete details or examples always helpful? How can we prove the existence of concrete objects (and how far is it possible to fully achieve this?). Is knowledge valuable without concrete examples to go with it?
	Natural sciences
Condition	The circumstances or factors affecting a situation; also, a situation that must exist before something else is possible or permitted.
	There are three necessary conditions for an experiment: at least one experimental and control group; at least one researcher-manipulated variable; some degree of randomization.
	How do we know whether these conditions are met? How far is it important for us to know in what conditions something has been produced, or taken place?
	Human sciences, Natural sciences
Conditioning	Training a human or animal to behave in a certain way based on external stimuli is known as classical conditioning. (See also behaviourism, operant conditioning.)
	"Some would say that conditioning starts as soon as boys are given guns to play with and girls are given dolls."
	To what extent does conditioning allow for free will? How can we decide whether conditioning is problematic? What implications might conditioning have for psychology as a science?
	Human sciences
Confidence	The state of feeling certain, having faith in something or someone, or feeling able to rely on something or someone.
	How far can we have confidence in a given idea? Is confidence sufficient on its own for knowledge? And what knowledge do we require in order to be confident in an idea? To what extent is confidence about odds and percentages? How can confidence be measured? And how far is full confidence in an idea possible?
	Human sciences
Confidence interval	In statistics, confidence intervals are a type of estimate, based on a range of plausible values. They help to show the amount of certainty we have about an idea, in quantifiable terms.
	For example, a researcher measures the heights of 40 randomly chosen men, and gets a mean height of 175cm. The 95% Confidence Interval is 175cm ± 6,2cm. This says the true mean of ALL men (if we could measure all their heights) is likely to be between 168,8cm and 181,2cm. But it might not be: the '95%' says that 95% of experiments of this type will include the true mean, but 5% won't.
	How far can confidence intervals be trusted? Can they lead to unjustified or arbitrary inferences? How far do these methods meet our needs as mathematicians and scientists?
	Mathematics, Natural sciences
Confirmation bias	When you tend to believe, or 'see' more prominently in your day-to-day experiences, evidence that conforms to your existing beliefs.
	Person A is opposed to gun control, and both seeks out and is more likely to believe news sources that support his position.
	How can we tell what our own confirmation biases are? How far do social media in particular reinforce these biases, creating an echo chamber? Is our engagement with confirmation biases overt, or more of an unconscious effort?
	Human sciences

Confirmation holism	Also known as the Duhem-Quine problem, confirmation holism states that it is not possible to prove a hypothesis based on one test or theory alone, as this is always dependent on other theories. (See also meaning holism.)

Confirmation holism

Also known as the Duhem-Quine problem, confirmation holism states that it is not possible to prove a hypothesis based on one test or theory alone, as this is always dependent on other theories. (See also meaning holism.)

For instance, if trying to assess why a planet is not following a predicted path, we have to consider multiple factors, such as whether other scientific 'laws' are erroneous, whether another natural satellite might be in the way, or even if the telescope is set up correctly.

Do experiments only ever confirm or refute entire theories? How can we know if this is the case?

Mathematics, Natural sciences

Conflate

When we conflate two or more ideas, we combine them to make one larger idea, often in a manner which confuses them or mixes them up. For example, it is important not to conflate gossip with real news.

What might be some possible implications of doing so? Why might the conflation of science and technology be a serious problem?

Human sciences, Natural sciences

Conflicting

If two ideas are conflicting, they are incompatible; they do not work well together.

Even large, well-conducted observational studies and randomized controlled trials of drugs can seem to provide conflicting results. How can we distinguish some messages from others when they are conflicting? How far does the 24/7 news cycle result in conflicting messages? How can we decide what to believe? What might be some problems if cognitive dissonance is the result? How do we know what to do if scientific results conflict with each other?

Human sciences, Natural sciences, Mathematics, Politics

Conflict of interest

When someone's professional activities or interests are in conflict with each other, they may benefit personally from their professional actions, which could prevent them from making good decisions.

If an examiner also teaches in a school where that same qualification is taught, they have to declare a conflict of interest so that they do not end up marking their own students' work.

How should employees disclose potential conflicts of interest? How can we tell when we have a conflict of interest ourselves? Are some areas of knowledge immune from conflicts of interest? How do we know if this is really the case?

Human sciences, Natural sciences

Confounding

When something surprises us by going against our expectations, or when something confuses us. (See also confounding variables.)

An example is the study of the effect of smoking tobacco on human health. Smoking, drinking alcohol, and diet are lifestyle activities that are related. A risk assessment that looks at the effects of smoking but does not control for alcohol consumption or diet may overestimate the risk of smoking.

How can we know when confounding is taking place? What can we do to decrease the possibility of confounding?

Natural sciences

Confounding variables

A factor that may influence or confuse our conclusions in a way that is incorrect, by suggesting correlations that are not there, and/or introducing bias. It is related to the supposed cause and supposed effect being studied. (See also extraneous variable.)

If both ice cream sales and murders go up during the summer, weather could be the confounding variable causing both to increase (in cold weather, people tend to stay indoors, as opposed to going out and murdering people, or getting into situations where they might be murdered. In hot weather, people also tend to buy more ice cream).

What might be the 'best' methods to identify confounding variables in an experiment? How do we know if we have identified a confounding variable? How might confounding variables bias our results?

Human sciences, Natural sciences, Mathematics

Conjecture

1. In general, an opinion formed on the basis of incomplete information or guesswork.

2. In mathematics, a statement believed to be true based on observations.

In mathematics, Goldbach's conjecture states that every even whole number greater than 2 is the sum of two prime numbers.

How do we determine the possible differences between conjecture and fact? How useful might 'unsolvable' mathematical conjectures be? More generally, how do we know if decisions or ideas are open to conjecture?

Mathematics

Connection

A link or relationship between people, objects or ideas. For example, there appears to be a strong connection between tight cultures and foreign-language learning.

How can we establish if there is a genuine connection between ideas (such as an experiment and its result), or whether the appearance of a connection is affected by other factors (such as economic ones)?

Knowledge and the knower

Connotation

An idea associated with or triggered by a particular word or image.

"The adjectives 'bloody', 'scarlet' and 'ruby' all mean 'red', but each have very different connotations."

How far can we control how our word choices are perceived by others? And how do we determine whether connotations are positive or negative? To what extent might these be influenced by our cultural context?

The Arts, Language

Conscience

Our 'moral compass' letting us know what is ethically right or wrong.

How far are researchers guided by their academic or scientific conscience? How far is freedom involved in one's religious conscience? What differences, if any, might exist between 'scientific conscience' and 'religious conscience'? How might we decide what such differences are?

Human sciences, Natural sciences, Religious knowledge

Conscious

Being aware of and responding to our surroundings.

*To what extent is it desirable to construct **artificial intelligence** that is, or appears to be, conscious? How far can we know if we, as humans, are fully conscious, or if other objects and forms of life (such as a bat or a toaster) also have consciousness?*

Human sciences, Natural sciences

Conscious competence model

In psychology, the conscious competence model (or 'four stages of competence') shows the process we go through when learning a new skill.

The four stages are as follows: unconscious incompetence (when you don't realise you are bad at something), conscious incompetence (when you do realise you are bad at something), conscious competence (you are aware of your burgeoning skills and improvement, but still have to concentrate to perform well), and unconscious competence (when you are so good at something that you can do it well without thinking too much about it).

How can we judge whether this is an effective model in describing how we learn?

Human sciences

Consensus

An agreement between multiple people on a given topic. For example, there could be a strong consensus between two age groups about which words or images are acceptable in a certain situation and which are offensive.

How do we recognize in what situations a consensus might be valuable? And to what degree does consensus present us with an overly binary view of the world?

Human sciences

Consent

Agreement or permission. (See also Gillick competence.)

"The age of consent varies in different countries, from as young as 9 to as old as 21."

What might be some possible values of having an age of consent in place? How can we tell in what situations it should be applicable? How can we decide whether or not someone is sufficiently informed to give their consent?

Human sciences

Consequentialism	The idea that the morality of an action is determined purely by its consequences. (See also utilitarianism.)
	*If consequentialism requires that we should do whatever results in the best possible outcomes, how do we know what the 'best possible outcomes are'? How far is it possible to apply consequentialism all of the time? What factors may mean a consequentialist approach is not advantageous? How can we measure both the relative and **absolute** 'goodness' of consequences?*
	Human sciences
Conspiracy theory	A belief that a secret organization is responsible for an otherwise unexplained event.
	How far are reliable references possible for any conspiracy theory? For what reasons do conspiracy theories flourish? How far could conspiracy theories be considered truth claims? To what extent are conspiracy theories due to a biased perception of randomness? What else might explain belief in conspiracy theories?
	Human sciences, Politics
Constitute	To compose or make up the content of something.
	"A whole consists of parts; the parts constitute the whole."
	Do all true beliefs constitute knowledge? How do we know by what criteria we should classify knowledge?
	Knowledge and the knower
Constraint	A restriction, which may be natural or artificially imposed/created by humans. Grammar, for example, is a set of constraints particular to an individual language.
	How far does cognitive success involve compliance with constraints? To what degree does knowledge itself have constraints?
	Language
Construct	1. To build or create. (Verb)
	2. An idea or concept. (Noun)
	To what extent is learning achieved through the construction of meaning? How reliable are constructs themselves?
	Knowledge and the knower
Constructionism	The creation of objects to show learning. Theories of constructionism assert that learning can happen most effectively when people actively create tangible objects in the real world.
	How far do digital tools, such as microworlds, and educational tangible tools, such as multilink cubes, enable learners to show their knowledge?
	Mathematics, Technology
Constructivism	The creation of knowledge through the construction of models; the idea that knowledge of the world is always a human and social construction.
	Microworlds like Scratch use constructivist instructional design models that let learners 'play' within an artificial or real environment (eg a Sandbox), and learn by building things.
	To what extent is it possible, through constructivism, to separate the knower and the known?
	Human sciences, Natural sciences
Consumption	The action of using up a resource.
	How can we predict the ways in which human consumption of materials may affect our future? What might be the most appropriate methods to use to calculate this?
	Human sciences, Natural sciences
Contemporary	Taking place at the present time, or at the same time as another historical event.
	How far should we apply contemporary values to historical figures and events? Will there always inevitably be a discord between contemporary and past cultures? Is it possible, or even desirable, to 'update' texts to fit with our contemporary values?
	The Arts, History, Language

C

Contentious

Controversial, or not attracting universal agreement. Contentious deductions might appear acceptable at first sight but may not do so on closer inspection.

What might be some examples of such arguments or deductions? How can we prove the contentiousness of an idea (if indeed we can)?

Knowledge and the knower

Contestable

If something is contestable, then it is possible to disagree with it, or it is debatable.

How can we judge what makes something contestable? Are all ideas ultimately contestable?

Knowledge and the knower

Context

The (historical) time and/or place, society, politics, culture or situation in which something occurs.

How far do events need to be looked at within a larger context? How far are contexts altered by our own perceptions, especially within the field of historiography?

History, Politics

Contextualism

The approach emphasizing the importance of context in the interpretation of actions, events or utterances.

To what extent is a decontextualized approach valuable in the study of the Arts? How far is the word 'know' context-sensitive? Are all knowledge attributions context-sensitive?

The Arts, History

Contingent (on)

Dependent (on); subject to chance.

How can we judge the remoteness of a contingency (how likely it is to take place)? To what extent does contingency depend on time and perspective?

Knowledge and the knower

Contradict

To go against or disagree with an existing idea or norm. In mathematics, proof by contradiction involves starting with the assumption that a proposition is false, and working to prove that falsity until you can, in fact, show that the proposition is true after all.

How far can contradictions be resolved? Are there any situations in which this might be undesirable? To what extent is 'all existence the result of contradiction'?

History, Human sciences, Mathematics

Contrast

A stark or obvious difference between two or more things, people, or ideas. For example, you can compare and contrast two characters in a story, or your beliefs about abortion may contrast with those of your friend – your friend may believe it should be allowed, while you do not. Colours can also contrast, such as black and white.

By what standards are contrasts created? How can we tell whether colour contrasts are creating optical illusions?

Human sciences, Natural sciences

Contrived

Artificial, or artificially set up; not genuine.

Textbook authors often contrive examples that are purportedly by students.

Why might contriving sometimes be necessary? Can all situations be contrived? How can we tell if something is contrived?

Knowledge and the knower

Control

A 'control' in an experiment is a factor that maintains the status quo or behaves in an ordinary way, so that this can be compared to the factor being experimented on. This lets us know if the experiment has an effect or not. For example, we can see what happens with control groups in an experiment, compared with those receiving a treatment.

How do we know what a good example of a control is? What factors could influence a control group in a way that may impact the experiment negatively?

Human sciences, Natural sciences, Mathematics, Technology

Controversy

A public disagreement or argument. (Adjective: controversial)

How far, and/or for what reasons, should we seek to court controversy? What purposes might controversy serve? How far is controversy necessary in order to incite change?

Politics

Convention	Things that appear regularly, or are expected, in a text, culture, or community; a way in which something is usually done.
	Who decides the conventions of a particular text type, such as a poem? How far is the breaking of conventions acceptable (such as an artwork shredding itself after it has been purchased)? How far should we seek to conform to, or subvert, societal conventions?
	The Arts, Human sciences, Language
Convey	To communicate a message, information or idea in an understandable way.
	How do we choose what methods to use in order to convey something most accurately? How far are we able to succeed in this, or indeed control this? What non-linguistic means might there be of conveying ideas, and how do we decide what methods are most effective?
	Language
Convincing	If an argument is convincing, it is believable and backed up by reliable sources.
	Where is the boundary between a convincing and non-convincing explanation? How can we decide this? In what ways might the persuasiveness of explanations alter over time, and for what reasons?
	Language
Core	The fundamental part of something, central to its existence or character.
	The IB core, for example, consists of the Theory of Knowledge course, the Extended Essay, and the Community, Activity, Service component. They are considered 'core' as they are thought to be vital to your academic personal development, and everyone must take them, regardless of academic ability or interests.
	How do we know what the core issues of a topic are? How can the 'core' of something be determined? How might this differ between what is important to individuals and societies, and what methods could be used to measure, identify and record this?
	Human sciences, Religious knowledge
Cornerstone	An important quality on which something is based; a founding principle.
	If importance is subjective, how do we decide what cornerstones are? What might we consider the cornerstones of a free and open society? How far might cornerstones change over time?
	Human sciences
Corollary	A statement, or proposition, following on from one that's already been proved, or something that results from something else. It might be said, for instance, that the corollary of shared profits is shared losses.
	How far can we decide whether something is a genuine corollary that really follows on from previous elements?
	Human sciences
Correlation	A mutual relationship between two or more things; one influences the other.
	How can correlation be determined? How far are variables causally related if there is correlation between them? How can we tell if this is really the case? In what ways might correlation be conflated with prejudice?
	Human sciences, Mathematics, Natural sciences
Correspondence test (theory)	The idea that a statement can only be true or false if it relates/corresponds to what is actually happening in the world around us.
	Correspondence testing means checking for yourself to see if something is true.
	What might be some problems with correspondence testing? Why might other types of evidence be needed?
	Knowledge and the knower
Corroborate	To confirm or give support to an idea or theory.
	"This data is corroborated by research into levels of second-language learning."
	What could be considered the 'best' methods of corroborating a claim? What might be some meaningful differences between 'corroborate' and 'authenticate', 'verify', 'validate', 'substantiate', or 'confirm'?
	Knowledge and the knower

Cosmology

The science of the origin and development of the universe.

Experts in cosmology currently believe that 95 percent of the universe is missing.

To what extent is this claim testable? How can we assess the validity of different approaches to cosmology (eg religious cosmologies, physical cosmology, philosophical cosmology)?

Natural sciences, Religious knowledge

Cosmos

The universe, seen as a well-ordered whole.

How can we know whether the cosmos has an edge, beyond which there is nothing? How might our studies of the cosmos be connected to astronomy? To what extent is the idea of the expansion of the cosmos really testable?

Natural sciences

Cost-benefit analysis

A process to help make decisions. You weigh up how a decision will benefit you, as well as how an alternative decision may disadvantage you, and choose what to do based on what will cause you the least damage or what will help you the most.

To what extent do cost-benefit analyses enable us to make (good) decisions? Are there sometimes too many uncertainties to enable us to carry out a cost-benefit analysis?

Human sciences

Could

The past tense of the verb 'can'. Indicates possibility.

"They could be right."

What might be some advantages of using 'could' in an argument instead of, for example, 'can' or 'are'? What does this modal verb show us about the nature of knowledge?

Language

Counter-argument

An argument or set of claims put forward to oppose an idea developed in an argument, usually before an opponent can come up with these opposing ideas in real life. (See also counterclaim.)

Including and analysing counter-arguments (what others might say about your ideas) can improve the quality of your analysis, and in the case of an assessment like the Extended Essay, your grades.

What might be some benefits and problems of detecting problems within your own argument? How can you be sure that you are developing a reasonable counter-argument, given your own biases? To what extent do counter-arguments enable us to develop a balanced argument?

Language, Politics

Counterclaim

A statement to counteract or rebut a previously made claim (often by an opponent in an argument). (See also counter-argument.)

How can we distinguish between claims and counterclaims? What methods can we use to assess the reliability of counterclaims?

Knowledge and the knower

Counterfactual

Related to or expressing what has not happened/is not the case. In psychology, counterfactual thinking imagines how things could have happened differently.

How can we establish whether or not a claim is counterfactual? What might be some benefits of counterfactual thinking in psychology (eg 'If I hadn't been wearing a seatbelt, I would have been killed')?

Human sciences, Politics

Counterintuitive

Against your intuition or common-sense expectations.

*How do we know if a finding is counterintuitive? Some argue that the **Monty Hall problem** is the most counterintuitive probability problem. How might we prove or disprove this claim?*

Mathematics

Counterproductive

Having the opposite of the effect you originally wanted, or preventing a goal from being achieved.

How far is categorization counterproductive? How can we decide if someone else's, or our own, actions are counterproductive?

Human sciences

Courtier's reply	Claiming someone is mistaken or ignorant without telling them why.
	"You're wrong!"
	How far does the courtier's reply enable people to prevent their arguments from being criticized? How far might a courtier's reply be a valid response?
	Knowledge and the knower
Covert	Hidden or concealed.
	For example, a weekly newspaper may have a covert agenda to promote a particular ideology or political policy.
	How can we detect covert ideas? How far is it deliberate when an idea is covert?
	Knowledge and the knower, Politics
creatio ex materia	Latin for 'creation from materials'. The idea that God created the world from pre-existing materials.
	How can we decide what, if any, creation stories to believe? How could we prove the truth of this particular creation theory?
	Religious knowledge
creatio ex nihilo	Latin for 'creation out of nothing'. The idea that the physical world is not eternal but had to be created by someone (usually a god or gods).
	To what extent do religious texts imply creatio ex nihilo? How far can the idea of creatio ex nihilo be proven?
	Religious knowledge
Credentials	A qualification, achievement, or aspect of a person's background which makes them more credible or suitable for a particular role or situation.
	How can we prove someone's credentials? Who or what determines whether someone's credentials are valuable?
	Knowledge and the knower
Credibility	The quality of being trusted, believed in, or convincing.
	How do we know whether a source is credible? What strategies can researchers adopt to ensure the credibility of their studies' findings? Are understandability, appropriateness, truth and sincerity all equally important in the creation of credibility?
	Human sciences, Natural sciences
Criteria	Principles or standards by which something is decided.
	Is one set of criteria sufficient to make a judgment? Is there any way of alleviating the subjectivity of criteria? How do we know if criteria are specific or accurate enough?
	Knowledge and the knower
Critical	1. Expressing disapproval; analysing merits and faults; important.
	2. In mathematics, showing a point of transition/change.
	3. In natural sciences, maintaining a chain reaction.
	For example, we might say that a project is due to 'go critical' later this year, or that obesity is a critical factor in how seriously one is affected by illness. If seeking critical acclaim, we are looking for approval for our work by famous critics or experts. Critical editions of books usually have introductions and other notes supplied by experts in the field. In our day-to-day lives, we can be critical of a restaurant we visit or a TV programme that we watch. ('Being critical' is often used negatively, but criticism can also be positive; it can just mean analysing or giving our reasoned opinion about something.
	How do we know what thinking critically involves? How can we decide what is of critical importance?
	Knowledge and the knower
Critical realism	An approach distinguishing between the 'real' and 'observable' worlds.
	How far can the 'real' be observed? To what extent are our sense-data reliable?
	Natural sciences

| Criticize | To pass judgment on someone's faults (in a disapproving way); or, a synonym for critique. (Verb) |

How far can value judgments can be rationally defended or criticized? To what extent do we have a duty to criticize? How can we judge whether criticism and problem-solving are equivalent? How can we relativise criticisms and recognize their limitations? Are some criticisms more valuable than others? How do we know?

Human sciences

Critique

1. To evaluate in a detailed way. (Verb)
2. An analytical assessment or review of something. (Noun) Critiques may be positive, negative, or a mixture.

How far are good critiques essential to the continual improvement of everything humans do? Are critics really more well-informed than the rest of us, or just more articulate?

The Arts, Human sciences

Cultural appropriation

The unacknowledged, inappropriate or unwanted adoption of different cultural icons (eg costumes, foods, music) by those from another, unrelated, typically more dominant culture. For example, one celebrity chef was accused of cultural appropriation for calling his rice recipe Jamaican when people from Jamaica did not see traditional Jamaican ingredients in the recipe.

How far is appropriation necessary to human cultural development? How do we know if we are guilty of cultural appropriation? How far does cultural appropriation impinge on freedom of speech? What might be some differences between attribution and appropriation? Can appropriation ever be ethical? To what extent does the intention behind the appropriation matter?

The Arts, Human sciences

Cultural exchange

The sharing of different ideas, traditions, and knowledge with someone who comes from a different background to you.

How far does cultural exchange have to accommodate cultural diversity? Might there be situations in which cultural exchange is not desirable? How might we ascertain this?

Human sciences

Culture

1. In general, the ideas, customs and behaviour of a people or society; pieces of art, and other examples of human achievement, that are collectively well regarded.
2. In biology, the growth of bacteria, tissue cells, etc in an artificial environment providing the necessary conditions (eg nutrients).

To what extent is it morally correct to export a particular culture so that it is the dominant one worldwide? How can we tell whether a biological culture (eg a blood culture) provides the right conditions for growth (eg of bacteria)? How far is it wrong to impose our culture onto others?

The Arts, Human sciences, Natural sciences

cum hoc ergo propter hoc

Latin for 'with this, therefore because of this'. (See also causation, correlation, post hoc.) In other words, A and B are happening at the same time; therefore, one must be causing the other.

What could be some problems with this approach?

Human sciences, Natural sciences

Curiosity

A strong desire to gain information (about someone, or something).

What 'ways of knowing' could curiosity potentially be linked with? To what extent do humans have an innate curiosity? How could we define the differences (if there are any) between curiosity and wonder?

Knowledge and the knower

Curious

Eager to learn or know something.

What are some possible pitfalls of curiosity? How can artificial intelligence be honed to be curious and explore the world? How far is this desirable?

Human sciences, Technology

Data	Sets of numbers, information or statistics that have been collected for research purposes. For example, reports are usually written after analysing data from multiple sources.
	How do we decide what data to collect? What ethical concerns might there be in the data collection process?
	Human sciences, Mathematics, Natural sciences
Data-dredging	Only considering the data that is significant after the experiment, and inventing **post-hoc** conclusions for why that emerged.
	Data dredging is when you choose which data you want to use only after the experiment has taken place, or when you use correlations that have occurred solely by chance rather than representing a true relationship.
	How do we know whether data-dredging has occurred? How can data-dredging be avoided? What implications does data-dredging have for knowledge?
	Human sciences, Mathematics, Natural sciences
de facto	'In reality', regardless of whether the situation or status is legally recognized. For example, someone can serve as a de facto head of department at work without actually holding an official title that indicates this; they essentially do the work that a head of department would do without being rewarded for this in terms of title or salary.
	What might be some advantages or disadvantages of a de facto status/situation – even/ especially if it has no formalized/legalized status? How far can a de facto situation or status be reliably established?
	Human sciences
de jure	Meaning 'by law', this Latin term is used to describe practices that are recognized by the law, even if the practice does not exist in reality. Similarly, something may exist de facto/in reality before it is recognized de jure/in law (such as the existence of a country).
	What value might de jure recognition have? How far might it imply that an idea or situation has no value without legal recognition?
	Human sciences
Debate	To argue about or heatedly discuss a particular subject; to consider a possible course of action in one's mind before making a decision.
	How can we judge the validity of ideas put forward in a debate? What methods can we use to separate ideas from the rhetoric used to describe them? How can rhetoric clarify and obfuscate (obscure/make unclear) ideas within a debate, and affect our judgment?
	Language, Politics
Debunk	To expose the falseness of an idea or belief; to show that something is less important, good or true than it has been made to appear. Something may be believed to be true initially, then debunked later.
	What methods might we use to debunk falsehoods or myths? How can we judge the benefits and pitfalls of doing so? Is there a 'right' way to correct someone when they believe something that is objectively wrong?
	Language
Decanonizing	Diminishing the importance of the canon – or list of works determined to be permanently of the highest quality, over multiple generations – in order to make what we study more ethnically diverse. For example, universities might decanonize their syllabi in order to include voices that had not previously been so widely studied or recognized.
	How far is it possible to demand the abolition of a canon, given that a canon tends to exist more in the minds of people than as a definitive written list? On what basis can we judge whether a canon is problematic? What might be some implications of decanonization?
	The Arts, Language
Deception	The act of deceiving somebody.
	To what extent is magic just clever visual deception? To what extent is deception dependent on context? How do we know if we are being deceived? How far can deception be judged to be always wrong?
	Natural sciences

Decision theory	The study of how choices are made (descriptive decision theory) and how they should be made (normative decision theory). (See also cost-benefit analysis.)
	How far is decision theory based on what is useful, and how far is it based on what is probable? How can we determine the usefulness of decision theories in our everyday lives? How do we know whether groups make decisions that are fundamentally different from, or 'better' than, those of individuals?
	Human sciences, Mathematics
Decolonizing	The process by which a former colony becomes an independent state. More recently, 'decolonizing' is often used to describe the process of making curriculums, organizations, and fields of study more ethnically diverse and being more 'honest' about colonial and Confederate pasts.
	"Architecturally, some buildings from colonial times which survived decolonization have now been restored."
	In terms of art, history, and literature, decolonizing might involve greater understanding of what we know as being based on the story of the 'white victor' and understanding that when we learn history, we are sometimes just learning one version of what happened.
	Many dictionaries do not yet list the latter meaning of decolonization.
	Who decides what decolonization is and whether or when it can be included in dictionaries? How far do we have a moral obligation to decolonize individual states, as well as curriculums and organizations? What might be some implications of this process? Is it architecturally, historically, or aesthetically valuable to maintain colonial buildings as they were in those times?
	History, Human sciences, Politics
Deductive reasoning	Reasoning from one or more general statements (or a theory) to reach a conclusion about a specific situation. An example of deductive reasoning is the series of statements:
	"Philip is a man. All men are mortal. Therefore, Philip is mortal."
	How can we decide whether each statement in a series is true, and therefore if the deductive reasoning is sound?
	Knowledge and the knower
De-emphasize	To make something appear to be less important than it really is. For example, some might de-emphasize grammatical accuracy in favour of communicative fluency.
	Why might somebody want to de-emphasize something? How can we know when something has been de-emphasized?
	Language
Deepfake	A video of a person whose face, voice or body has been altered so that they appear to be somebody else, usually to spread untrue or malicious information. Deepfake software can be easily downloaded and used to create convincing fake videos.
	How far can we trust the format of video, based on phenomena such as deepfakes? How might this improve or deteriorate the spread of misinformation? How can we decide whether deepfakes are amusing or dangerous? How can we detect whether a face is real or computer-generated? Will people be more likely to believe a deepfake, or an information algorithm that flags the video as fabricated? What might be some ethical implications of deepfakes?
	Politics, Technology
Defeasibility theory	The idea that an idea can seem logical on the face of it, but is ultimately not valid. (See also prima facie, defeaters, Gettier problem.)
	Defeasibility theories try to exclude true beliefs that are based on faulty justifications, to create a plausible definition of knowledge. We might believe that someone stole a book from a library if we saw them exiting the library while removing a book concealed under their coat; however, if we later learn that this person has an identical twin who was also at the library that day, the statement becomes defeasible.
	Knowledge and the knower

Defeaters	True statements which undermine available evidence. (See also defeasibility theory, misleading defeater.)

Defeaters
: True statements which undermine available evidence. (See also defeasibility theory, misleading defeater.)

If we believe someone stole a book from a library but are then told they have an identical twin who was also at the library that day, this latter statement counts as a defeater, because it undermines the initial idea.

How do we decide whether defeaters are valid?

Knowledge and the knower

Defence
: The case presented by someone who is accused of a crime; defending your arguments also involves explaining why you think you are correct to those who disagree with you. If you speak or write in defence of something, you are standing up for what you believe in and explaining why you believe in it. For example, you might try to defend murdering a thief by saying that you merely meant to wound them.

On what basis can we decide whether to trust someone's defence, or judge that it is valid? How do we know what constitutes an acceptable defence? To what extent is the justification for a defence culturally dependent?

Human sciences, Language

Deficit model
: 1. In the natural sciences, the deficit model considers that any scepticism or hostility towards scientific belief comes from people having a lack of information, and the divide that is created between experts (who have the information) and everyone else, who does not.
  2. In the human sciences, the deficit model considers how far failure to succeed comes from the individual – as opposed to external factors affecting them, such as socio-economic factors or a lack of education.

How do we know whether simply giving more information to people will change their minds about a topic? How far could we decide what the reasons are for somebody's lack of success? What might be some possible flaws in the deficit model in both cases? To what extent is the deficit model an oversimplification of the issues at hand?

Human sciences, Natural sciences

Define
: To exactly describe the meaning or scope of a word or idea.

Who decides how to define words and ideas? For what reasons might this matter? How far is it possible to 'fully' or 'truly' define something?

Language

Definition
: The statement of the exact meaning of a word or idea; the process of defining something.

To what extent is it possible to develop an exact definition of something? How far is the formation of definitions related to, or important in, forming meaning? For what reasons might we need to create definitions? In what way(s) might definitions cause more problems than they solve? Is there ever such a thing as a universal definition? How do we know?

Language, Human sciences, Natural sciences

Dehumanisation
: Depriving a person or group of positive human qualities; eradicating the unique value of individuals or groups; not treating a person or group with the dignity and respect normally accorded to human beings.

Totalitarian regimes typically dehumanise their populations. Some would argue that "dehumanisation always starts with language".

How far can we determine whether this is really the case? How do we know what criteria describe the process of dehumanization? To what extent does artificial intelligence represent a form of dehumanization? How can we judge the effects of this?

Human sciences, Language, Technology

Demarcation problem
: The question of how to tell the difference between science and non-science.

Why might the demarcation problem be important? To what extent are 'boundaries' like these between different disciplines useful for us as producers of, receivers of, and critical thinkers about, knowledge?

Natural sciences

Democratization	The introduction of a democratic system; the act of making something accessible to everyone.

How far has access to information been democratized through technology? What might be some possible consequences of democratization? How far do we have a duty to export democracy? How can we measure the potential costs of democratization? How can we tell whether a country has truly become democratized, or whether they are just a democracy on paper?

The Arts, Human sciences, Politics

Demographics

The study of a population based on factors such as age, sex, race or class.

How can we decide whether demographic changes cause or are the effect of something else/ other changes? To what extent can demographics explain people's underlying beliefs? How far is demographic analysis helpful to us? What might be some ethical issues behind the obtention of demographic information?

Human sciences, Natural sciences

Denialism

Also known as negationism, this is the act of denying the truth, existence or validity of something in spite of strong evidence.

What drives people to reject scientific truth? To what extent do people have the right to deny scientific truth? How do we know when merely questioning scientific truth crosses over into denialism? How far is denialism based on genuine concerns?

Human sciences, Natural sciences, Politics

Deontology

The study of the nature of duty. (To remember the difference between deontology and ontology, remember that 'duty' begins with d, and so does deontology!)

How do we know what our duties are to others, if any? To what extent is duty an essential component of the ways in which we behave?

Human sciences

Descriptive knowledge

Also known as declarative knowledge, descriptive knowledge describes things, processes and relationships, laying out in factual terms how things are. It refers to information stored in the memory which is considered quite static in nature. It can be described as 'knowing that', as opposed to 'knowing how'. An example of declarative or descriptive knowledge could be "The sun is larger than the earth."

How can we work out whether our descriptive knowledge is accurate? How far is our descriptive knowledge really static?

Natural sciences

Detect

To discover or identify the presence/existence of something.

How can we determine whether what we have detected is accurate?

Natural sciences

Determinism

The idea that everything is caused by some force outside of our own free will.

To what extent are free will and determinism compatible beliefs? If we believe in determinism, does this mean we are no longer morally responsible for our actions? How far do you need to believe in a god or gods to believe in determinism? Is science an ultimately deterministic discipline? Might determinism indicate that only one possible future exists? How do we know if this is really the case?

Human sciences, Natural sciences, Religious knowledge

Devalue

1. Making something seem less valuable or important. We could say, for instance, that some societies devalue old age and older people.

2. In economics, devaluation sees a currency having its official value downgraded. For example, we can say that 'the dinar was devalued by 20%'.

In economics, how can we tell if devaluation might be a useful step to take? How do we know, in the human sciences more generally, what different people and cultures value and devalue?

Human sciences

Devil's advocate	When playing devil's advocate, you deliberately pretend to take the side of the opposing party in order to advance the argument or test the solidity of someone's beliefs.

Devil's advocate

When playing devil's advocate, you deliberately pretend to take the side of the opposing party in order to advance the argument or test the solidity of someone's beliefs.

"I don't really believe all that – I was just playing devil's advocate."

What might be some benefits of this tactic in an argument? How can we tell if someone is playing devil's advocate or genuinely believes in what they are saying?

Human sciences

Dialogue

A conversation or discussion between two or more people or groups. In literature, this refers to any speech taking place; in other situations, it is often used to refer to a conversation that is necessary in order to solve a problem.

How far is a dialogic approach helpful in gaining and interpreting knowledge? What might be some problems with this method?

The Arts, Human sciences, Language

Diametric opposition

When two things, ideas or people are diametrically opposed, they are completely opposite or different from each other.

"I treated her in a manner diametrically opposite to that."

What might be some benefits and pitfalls of diametrically opposed approaches or evidence?

Knowledge and the knower

Dichotomy

1. A division or contrast between two things, approaches, or ideas, showing that they are completely different from each other.
2. In biology, a repeated branching between two parts.

For example, some might say that there is a clear dichotomy between science and mysticism. Others might say that when researching, we should not distinguish between two approaches that some perceive to be different from each other – ie that this represents a false dichotomy.

*How far might dichotomies be said to be an **illusion**? How do we define dichotomies and create a boundary between where one starts and another ends? To what extent is this **possible** or even desirable?*

Knowledge and the knower

Difference

1. A way in which things, people or ideas are not the same; a disagreement or dispute.
2. In mathematics, a quantity by which amounts differ.

For example, an insurance company might refuse to pay the difference between the cost of a repair and the level of cost you are covered for.

What might be some problems inherent in detecting and resolving differences? How can we detect where differences have come from? How can we decide whether differences are statistically significant?

Human sciences, Mathematics, Natural sciences

Differentiate

1. When you differentiate, you enable knowledge to be accessed at multiple levels of understanding. When you differentiate between things, you are showing that you understand the difference(s) between them.
2. In mathematics and sciences, when you differentiate you are finding and showing rates of change.

For example, you can differentiate between species, or differentiate levels of experience, understanding, and reality.

How far can we differentiate between experiences and reality? How do we know if we are differentiating 'correctly'?

Human sciences, Mathematics, Natural sciences

Digital knowledge

Knowledge accessed through digital tools, and also partially processed through digital tools.

*How far can combining datasets help us to build digital knowledge? To what extent do digital technologies facilitate access to knowledge? How far could it be argued that this creates new knowledge ethics? How far is it possible to directly **experience** knowledge digitally? How far does digital knowledge enable a wider range of cognitive processes to be automated, and to what extent is this desirable?*

Technology

Direct realism	Also known as naive realism, the idea that our senses provide us with direct awareness of the external world. (See also critical realism, indirect realism.) For example, if a straw appears bent when seen through a glass of water, am I perceiving the world directly as it is? *How far are there differences between perception and reality? What might be some problems with the theory of direct realism?* Natural sciences
Disagree	To have or express a different opinion from others. *How can we decide whether we agree or disagree with someone or something? How do we know if others have a valid basis for agreeing or disagreeing?* Knowledge and the knower
Discern	To detect; to be able to tell that something is or is not present; to recognize or find out. *By what method(s) might we be able to discern something? How do we decide what method(s) will best allow us to discern what we are trying to find out?* Knowledge and the knower
Discerning	Having or showing good judgment. For example, if you are a discerning investor, you might not want to invest in a business that you do not think will allow you to recoup your investment in the future. *How far is it necessary to be discerning? How do we know if we, or others, are being discerning? Is it possible to know this objectively?* The Arts, Human sciences
Discipline	A branch of knowledge. For example, public administration might be considered a relatively new discipline. *How do we know whether, or when, something qualifies as a whole new discipline or field of knowledge? How far do we benefit from dividing knowledge in this way?* Knowledge and the knower
Discount	To regard an idea or possibility as unworthy because it lacks credibility. "I'd heard rumours, but discounted them." *How do we know when or if to discount an idea?* Knowledge and the knower
Discourse	Written or spoken communication or debate. "Taking a more technical approach would immediately raise the level of discourse." *How far does the language of discourse in a discipline simply reinforce power structures and close off access to knowledge, rather than advancing knowledge? How far is it possible to convey 'truth' (or a form of it) through our discourse?* Language
Discrepancy	When two ideas or facts are incompatible or lack similarity. "There is a discrepancy between your account and his." *How can we detect whether discrepancies exist? What are some possible problems or consequences associated with discrepancies?* Human sciences, Natural sciences
Discussion	Talking about something in order to exchange ideas or make a decision. For example, when trying to draw conclusions from an experiment or assessing the reliability of a report, there might be discussion of issues surrounding the quality of data. *How do we know if there are any topics that it is inappropriate to discuss? How do we know if topics are taboo?* Human sciences, Language, Natural sciences

Disinformation	False information which is intended to mislead. (See also misinformation.) It can, for example, be argued that with the rise of the internet, individual people and even entire systems have been manipulated with disinformation, particularly in relation to elections.
	How do we distinguish between disinformation, misinformation, and fake news?
	Language, Politics, Technology
Disinterested	Unbiased; impartial; not influenced by information or situations that may benefit you. (Not to be confused with 'uninterested', which means not being concerned about something.) (See also uninterested.)
	How far is it possible to be fully disinterested, especially in relation to value judgments (eg deciding whether something is beautiful/ugly, right/wrong, etc)?
	Knowledge and the knower
Disjunctivism	A theory stating that in certain cases, we should reject sense-data as being reliable in our perception of the world.
	Disjunctivists do not think that true sensory experiences and hallucinations have anything in common.
	What is involved in the claims that these experiences differ? Why might one want to be a disjunctivist? What kinds of claims can the disjunctivist make about hallucination and illusion?
	Natural sciences
Dismantle	To destroy the integrity or functioning of an organization or idea; to show that a claim is untrue or incorrect.
	How can we dismantle existing power structures – if indeed we should do so? What methods should we use when attempting to dismantle an argument credibly?
	Human sciences
Dismiss	To treat as unworthy of serious consideration; to deliberately stop thinking about something.
	"He suspected a double meaning in her words, but dismissed the thought." "Rumours that they are about to marry have been dismissed as pure speculation."
	How do we know when, or whether, to dismiss an idea? Is it ever valid to dismiss an idea without discussing it? How would we know when, or if, this is an appropriate course of action?
	Human sciences
Disseminate	To spread information widely. For example, it may be considered good practice to disseminate information to the general public in a transparent way, especially in relation to research that has been carried out.
	How do we judge which are the 'best' methods to disseminate information? What might be some barriers to the dissemination of research? How far can such barriers be broken down? Are there any situations in which information should not be disseminated?
	Human sciences, Natural sciences
Dissenter	A person who dissents, disagrees or rebels.
	How far should dissenters be silenced? What benefits and pitfalls could there be in asking difficult questions? How do we know how to perceive dissenters: as troublemakers, or problem-solvers?
	Knowledge and the knower
Distinction	A difference or contrast between similar things or people. For example, a class distinction might show broader differences between people who work in particular professions (eg welder versus professor) or differences in behaviour.
	What methods might we use to draw distinctions between different groups or ideas? How do we know if such distinctions are useful?
	Human sciences

Distinguish

To recognize or treat something as different.

How do we know whether someone is capable of distinguishing between fantasy and reality? How can we distinguish between cases in which someone knows something and someone else does not?

Some languages distinguish between different types of knowledge: for example, in French you use 'savoir' for knowing a fact and 'connaître' for knowing a person or place.

To what extent are such distinctions useful?

Human sciences, Language

Distort

To give a misleading or false account or impression of something; to warp or twist out of shape.

For example, many factors can distort scientific results. We can also ask ourselves in what ways our thinking can be distorted. How can we judge if an idea has become distorted? How can we separate a distorted image from its reality?

Natural sciences

Documentary evidence

Evidence in the form of anything on paper or existing digitally (such as text messages, letters or photographs), as opposed to oral testimony. For example, new documentary evidence can cause us to see an historical event differently.

How far can documentary evidence support or undermine oral testimony? How can we assess the reliability of documentary evidence in general? What might be some ethical considerations relating to the use of certain types of documentary evidence?

History, Human sciences

Dogma

1. A principle or set of principles presented as being incontrovertibly true. For example, some churches may phrase or formulate a particular dogma in the same way, or they may not.

2. In biology, the 'Central Dogma' is the process by which the instructions in DNA are converted into a functional product. The Central Dogma can be described as the process by which information 'gets into' a protein and is transformed into something else.

For what reasons might we wish to challenge a particular dogma? How can we judge whether or not a particular dogma is effective?

Natural sciences, Religious knowledge

Dogmatism

The tendency to present ideas as being undeniably true, without considering others' evidence or opinions. It can be argued that if dogmatism is absent, then there is an openness to alternative readings of a text or situation, without the proponent becoming too 'preachy'.

What might be some problems with dogmatism? How can we better understand what drives dogmatism from a cognitive perspective? For what reasons might dogmatic people not choose to seek out further information, even when unsure?

Human sciences, Religious knowledge

Dominate

To have power or influence over others. For instance, arguments can be dominated by one particular viewpoint.

To what extent should we strive to eradicate dominance? Are there some situations in which it is necessary or desirable to dominate? How do we judge what those situations are? How do we know when it is necessary or important to challenge a dominant narrative or viewpoint?

Knowledge and the knower

Doublespeak

When you deliberately use euphemisms, or vague/obscure language, in order to prevent others from understanding, or to deceive them. Some would describe doublespeak as 'public lying'.

How can we judge the validity of this claim? How do we know when doublespeak is occurring? What are some of its possible ethical implications?

Language, Politics

Double standard

A rule or principle that is unfairly applied in different ways to different people or groups. Some would say that in society there are double standards between men and women, whereby some behaviours are accepted in men but criticized in women.

How can we judge whether this is really the case? Are there any situations in which it could be beneficial to judge or treat men and women differently? How far might this be culturally dependent?

Human sciences, Politics

Doubt	A feeling of uncertainty.
	How can we tell whether to doubt or believe? In what situations might we doubt the authenticity of an account? For what reasons might doubt be a vital human instinct? How far is doubt based on reason?
	Knowledge and the knower
Downplay	Making something seem less important than it really is. (See also de-emphasize.) For example, some politicians downplay the seriousness of global warming.
	For what reasons might people choose to downplay an idea? How can we judge whether downplaying an idea is wise?
	Knowledge and the knower
Doxastic	Relating to someone's beliefs. Doxastic logic allows for reasoning about belief, rather than knowledge.
	How can we differentiate between belief and knowledge? To what extent is it justified to do so?
	Religious knowledge
Draft	A draft of your essay is like the first version of it, before any edits have been made or feedback has been given. Note that this is different to an essay plan.
	How do we know when an essay is finished? How do we judge the quality of an essay (especially in its draft stages)?
	Knowledge and the knower
Dream argument	The idea that dreams show our senses to be unreliable, and that therefore everything we experience through our senses should be tested in order to determine whether what we have experienced is a dream or reality. The dream argument states that dreams and waking life can have the same content.
	How far are dreams and reality similar? What methods can we use to distinguish between the two?
	Human sciences, Natural sciences
Dualism	1. A theory that separates something into two distinctly different and separate ideas, such as mind and matter, or body and soul.
	2. In religion, dualism is the idea that the world is divided into good and evil.
	Dualism in some places, for example, might value the mind over the body.
	How far is dualism an effective way of seeing the world? What are some possible pitfalls of this worldview?
	Natural sciences, Religious knowledge
Dunning-Kruger effect	When people with low ability in a task overestimate their ability, as they lack the cognitive ability to see their own incompetence. (See also imposter syndrome.) The Dunning-Kruger effect might prevent people from stepping back and looking at their own behaviour and abilities from another's/outside view.
	How can we avoid falling prey to the Dunning-Kruger effect? To what extent is the Dunning-Kruger effect influenced by cultural norms?
	Human sciences
Duty	A moral or legal obligation; a responsibility. (See also categorical imperative.)
	"It's my duty to uphold the law."
	How do we know what our duties are? How far is it possible to live a life that is free of obligation? To what extent do we have duties to ourselves?
	Human sciences
Dysphemism	A derogatory or unpleasant term that is used in the place of a pleasant or neutral one. (See also euphemism.) For example, some people might refer to cigarettes as 'cancer sticks'.
	How do we know when someone is using a dysphemistic phrase? How can we assess the reasons for which people might use them?
	Language, Politics

Echo chamber

An environment in which you only encounter beliefs that you already agree with, and in which opposing beliefs are actively excluded and discredited. (See also confirmation bias, epistemic bubble, filter bubble.)

What might be some problems caused by echo chambers? How can we work out the differences between echo chambers and epistemic bubbles?

Human sciences, Technology

Ecofeminism

The theory that both ecological and feminist concerns come from the male domination of society.

*How far can 'oppression' mean the same thing when it's applied to women and when it's applied to nature? What kind of evidence, and what volume of evidence could possibly be **adduced** to support the idea of a link between the oppression of women and nature?*

Human sciences, Natural sciences, Politics

Economics

A human science concerned with the production, distribution, and consumption of goods and services. For example, it's perhaps necessary to look at the economics behind political policies, rather than just taking the ideas at face value/as being fine on principle.

To what extent should governments intervene in markets? How do we know what goods and services to produce, and how much of each to produce? How far does it matter who owns and controls particular companies?

Human sciences

Econophysics

A field that uses theories and methods originally developed by physicists in order to solve problems in economics, usually those involving uncertainty.

Econophysicists might argue that the economic world behaves like a collection of electrons that interact with each other, and use new tools of statistical physics to help us understand chaotic economic systems, and make links between markets and other natural phenomena. For example, after a large economic crash, markets show 'aftershocks' similar to what is seen after earthquakes.

How far do the principles of physics apply to economics? To what extent are physicists just coming up with analogies that merely rephrase established economic phenomena (or existing knowledge), as opposed to creating new knowledge?

Human sciences, Mathematics, Natural sciences

Effect

1. The observable consequence or change resulting from an event. (Noun)

2. To cause something to happen. (Verb)

(See also aetiology, affect.)

Prime ministers may, for instance, have effected changes during their tenure, or radiation leaks might have an effect on the environment.

How can we tell if one thing has caused another? How do we measure the magnitude or consequences of a particular effect? How far is it possible to decide or prove whether something has had an effect or not?

Knowledge and the knower

Effect size

The size of the difference between two groups after an experiment; the measurement of the relationship between two variables. For example, 0.2 might be considered a small effect size, while 0.8 could be considered a large one.

What might be some problems of using effect size to measure the effectiveness of interventions? To what extent is effect size useful in the interpretation of results? How can knowledge about effect sizes be most effectively combined? How can corrections for bias be made?

Human sciences, Natural sciences

Eliminativism

Also called eliminative materialism, this is the theory that certain types of mental states that most people believe in do not exist, and will be proved non-existent by future science.

Eliminativists believe that widely-accepted ideas, such as the soul, beliefs, desires or the subjective sensation of pain, will be proved to be non-existent by the science of the future.

How far can we judge if this is really the case? What might be some problems with eliminative materialism? To what extent could it be described as a circular argument?

Human sciences, Natural sciences

Embed	To place firmly within a surrounding mass or into a larger text or context. For instance, fossils might be embedded in stones, or cultural values can be embedded in poetry.
	How can professionals embed awareness of cognitive and social knowledge processes into their practice? How far are cultural expectations embedded within us?
	The Arts, Human sciences, Natural sciences
Emotion	A strong feeling derived from our mood, circumstances, and relationships with others. For example, it is sometimes appropriate to respond with emotion, whereas at other times, it is more appropriate to respond differently (eg based on hindsight).
	To what extent is emotion a valuable way of knowing? In what ways could emotions be accused of skewing the epistemic landscape? How far do emotions enable us to reach rational conclusions? Can we establish whether emotions are diametrically opposed to reason?
	Human sciences, Natural sciences
Empathy	The ability to understand and share the feelings of others, by imagining or knowing what it is like to be in that person's situation. Some societies show a lot of empathy and understanding of the condition of the elderly, for instance, while in others this is less true.
	How far is empathy the primary epistemic means of knowing other minds? How can we establish the epistemic and moral values of empathy? What limits does empathy have? What might be some differences between empathy and compassion?
	Human sciences, Natural sciences
Emphasize	To give special importance or value to something in speaking or writing. For example, schools might emphasize their former students' success.
	How can we judge in what ways, and for what reasons, people or organizations emphasize particular ideas over others?
	Knowledge and the knower, Politics
Empirical evidence	Information received through our senses, especially through experiments. Also, evidence of how things 'really are', instead of how they should be. (See also external validity, internal validity, is-ought problem, normative.)
	How far can theoretical developments be linked to empirical evidence? How can we make sense of data we have gathered via experimentation? What problems might exist with empirical evidence?
	Human sciences, Natural sciences
Enable	To make something possible; to give someone the authority or means to do something.
	How far does evidence enable us to arrive at firm conclusions? What are the criteria of truth that enable us to identify it and distinguish it from falsity?
	Knowledge and the knower
Enculturation	Gradually acquiring the characteristics and norms of a culture or group by another person or culture. (See also acculturation.)
	It can be said that we all go through a process of enculturation, regardless of where we grow up.
	How might enculturation and individuation (the process by which one achieves a sense of individual self) be related in early learning? How can we assess whether challenges to norms alter the process of enculturation? How far is it important to enculturate? How can we gauge this importance?
	Human sciences
Endnote	An endnote is a piece of extra information that can enhance a piece of written work – for example, an extended explanation of an idea, or a relevant digression – that would get in the way of the essay's 'flow' if included in the main body, so it is numbered and included at the end of the entire piece of work. (See also footnote.)
	What are some possible consequences of using endnotes rather than footnotes in a piece of work? What might be some possible implications for the development of our knowledge?
	Knowledge and the knower

Endorse

To publicly support or approve of something.

How do we know whether to endorse someone's views or not? To what extent can endorsements – especially celebrity ones – be trusted? How do we know whether or not to trust someone's endorsement of a person, product, or idea?

Language, Politics

Engage

To participate or become involved in; to occupy or attract attention in a positive way.

How do we know what qualities make something or someone engaging? What methods can be used to engage others?

Human sciences

Epistemic bubble

Not to be confused with an echo chamber, an epistemic bubble is when you lack knowledge because other relevant voices have been left out accidentally. Epistemic bubbles can therefore be 'popped' by being exposed to evidence. However, being exposed to evidence can reinforce echo chambers.

How far does social media constitute an epistemic bubble? How can we assess the potential damage caused by epistemic bubbles? How can we tell if epistemic bubbles are inherently bad, or if they are only bad if they generate false beliefs?

Human sciences, Technology

Epistemic cognition

The process of thinking about your knowledge and ways of knowing. Those studying epistemic cognition are interested in how people decide that they 'know' versus 'think' or 'believe' or 'doubt' the truth of something.

On what basis can we make these decisions? How far can people be helped to make 'better' decisions about what they 'know'? What counts as evidence, and how else do we create knowledge from data, experience, and logic?

Knowledge and the knower

Epistemic injustice

A kind of injustice in which someone is specifically wronged in their capacity as a knower.

"Some would say that epistemic injustice occurs when people are not allowed to speak for themselves about their own interests, because others claim to know what those interests are."

How might epistemic injustice contribute to what is included in, or excluded from, shared knowledge? What might be some possible consequences of this?

Human sciences, Indigenous knowledge

Epistemic modal logic

Logical reasoning about knowledge. Epistemic modal logic often uses the possible worlds model (analysing ways the world is or could have been) in order to assess what we do and don't know.

What limitations might the 'possible worlds' model have? How far is epistemic modal logic an idealised account of knowledge? To what extent does it explain objective, rather than subjective, knowledge?

Mathematics

Epistemic pluralism

The idea that you need multiple different ways of knowing things in order to achieve full understanding of a subject or field. (See also dualism, monism.)

How far can we judge if this is really the case? How can we judge the importance of this for the research that we carry out? Might there be some fields where a more monistic approach is generally accepted and valued, and if so, for what reasons?

Knowledge and the knower

Epistemological idealism

The idea that what you know about an object exists only in your mind. Epistemological idealism might argue that consciousness is the only thing that we can truly 'know'.

What are some possible consequences of epistemological idealism?

Knowledge and the knower

Epistemological realism

The idea that what you know about an object exists independently of your mind. For example, some would say that the existence of the moon, and the fact that it is spherical, does not change depending on what anyone says or thinks about this – and that this is epistemological realism in action.

How far can epistemological realism be applied to all ideas?

Natural sciences

Epistemological subjectivism	The idea that the standards of rational belief are those of the individual believer or those of the believer's community. Epistemological subjectivism suggests that our beliefs are rational if they meet our community's standards – or the standards of experts within that community.
	How do we know that adhering to such standards will reliably produce true beliefs?
	Human sciences
Epistemology	The branch of philosophy concerned with knowledge. Some might say that epistemology is more theoretical, and that while TOK is based on this, that TOK is a more practical version of epistemology.
	"Epistemology mainly aims to explain how perception can give us justified beliefs – or knowledge – about the world around us."
	On this basis, how can we be really sure if we know anything at all?
	Knowledge and the knower
Eradicate	To completely remove or destroy something.
	"The disease smallpox was eradicated in the 1980s."
	What are some possible challenges inherent in the eradication of infectious diseases? How far can scientific modelling be used to address these challenges?
	Natural sciences
Erasure	1. The removal of writing, recorded material, or data; the complete removal of something.
	2. The practice of collective indifference that renders certain people and groups invisible.
	How do we know if erasures exist in a text? What are some implications of the Right of Erasure (also known as the Right to be Forgotten), in terms of what data is held about us? To what extent is full digital erasure possible? What are some ethical implications of erasing bad memories? If few people follow a case until those from a minority who are affected by it call attention to it, how far can this be described as 'erasure'? How far can erasure be considered a form of violence?
	History, Human sciences, Language, Politics
Error	A mistake, or a failure in logical reasoning.
	How do we decide on the severity of an error? To what extent can errors be avoided and corrected? How do we detect whether or not an error has been made?
	Knowledge and the knower
Essay	An essay is a detailed, structured explanation of your ideas about a particular topic.
	Your TOK essay is a 1600-word exploration of a prompt that you choose from a list provided by the IBO.
	How do we know what makes a 'good' essay?
	Knowledge and the knower
Essay plan	An overview of your ideas, in note form, as to what your essay will contain, and in what order. This usually takes the form of bullet points or a spider diagram and is not the same as a draft of your essay.
	An essay plan helps you to decide what's going to be in your essay before you write it.
	How do you know what to include in an essay, and in what order?
	Knowledge and the knower
Ethical naturalism	A form of ethical realism, this is the idea that moral terms can be defined in terms of facts about the natural world (including facts about human beings, human nature, and human societies) and is based on empirical scientific methods of observation.
	How far is it possible to accumulate evidence about what is morally right or wrong, as ethical naturalists believe you can? To what extent are ethics based on facts? How can we determine whether empirical evidence (and thereby morals) change according to context?
	Natural sciences

Ethical realism

The idea that there are objective moral facts that cannot be disputed. Ethical realists might say that in ethics there is such a thing as a 'right' answer.

Is there too much disagreement in ethics for there to be facts about it? How far do we require ethical facts to create civilised societies?

Human sciences

Ethical relativism

The idea that whether an action is right or wrong depends on the moral norms of the society in which it is practised.

*How often are crimes and denials of freedom justified by ethical relativism? How far can we establish differences between different cultures' moral codes? To what extent does ethical disagreement have a rational bearing on the truth? Are moral matters in any way factual? How can we judge whether morality is just a cultural **artefact**? How far can we argue that moral relativism destroys morality altogether? How can we tell if our culture's ethics are 'better' than those of another?*

Human sciences

Ethical subjectivism

The idea that the 'truth' of morals is dependent on the attitudes of individuals. Ethical subjectivists suggest no objective moral truths exist.

How far does ethical subjectivism have a coherent form? How can we judge whether morals are more than just statements about individuals' feelings? If moral statements have no objective truth, then how can we blame people for behaving in a way that 'is wrong'?

Human sciences

Ethics

Your moral values or moral code which govern how you behave. This is considered part of the knowledge framework in your TOK course of study.

How far does extra education in ethics have an impact on the jobs that we do (for example, in terms of protecting patients' autonomy in nursing)? Is there such a thing as global ethics? How far can we argue that ethical decisions should be left to 'ethics experts'?

Human sciences

Ethics committee

An organization within an institution (such as a university) which is responsible for ensuring that medical experimentation and human subject research are carried out in a legally and morally correct manner.

How far should the advice of ethics committees be advisory, as opposed to being mandatory? How do we know under what circumstances it might be required to seek approval from an ethics committee?

Human sciences

Ethnobiology

The study of past and present interrelationships between human cultures and the plants, animals, and other organisms in their environment.

Some countries have a long history of applying ethnobiology to what they do; this can include the use of sustainable agriculture based on apiculture and interactions between plants and their pollinators.

How might a society's view of the natural world inform their perspective? Different societies divide the living world up in different ways: how far is it possible for an outsider to understand these?

Human sciences, Indigenous knowledge, Natural sciences

Ethnobotany

A branch of ethnobiology, this is the scientific study of the traditional knowledge and customs of a people concerning plants and their medical, religious, and other uses.

Ethnobotany might be described as the relationship between people and plants.

How is indigenous and local knowledge in ethnobotanical research best represented? What methods can 'best' capture the dynamic nature of local/traditional botanical knowledge? What overlaps may exist between other disciplines, such as economics, and how far are these overlaps useful? Some compare the loss of knowledge of indigenous healers to the burning down of a library containing books that are irreplaceable. How can we judge whether this is a valid observation?

Human sciences, Indigenous knowledge, Natural sciences, Religious knowledge

Ethnography	Part of the field of anthropology, this is the scientific study of single cultures, or specific structures within a culture, by someone who has lived in it. (See also ethnology.)

Ethnography

Part of the field of anthropology, this is the scientific study of single cultures, or specific structures within a culture, by someone who has lived in it. (See also ethnology.)

How far does ethnography contribute to an understanding of the human race? To what extent is it useful to distinguish between ethnography and ethnology? How far can we consider ethnography a strong or valid discipline? Is it possible to remain an objective researcher when living among the community you are researching?

Human sciences

Ethnology

Part of the field of anthropology, this is the study of the members and structures of cultures, and the relationship of members to their culture. (See also ethnography.)

How far might it be possible to construct a 'perfect ethnology' which shows us all the differences among a society's social groups? What might be some problems in attempting to do this?

Human sciences

Ethos

The rhetorical use of your own moral credibility in an argument, to convince others to believe in what you are saying. A company's or person's ethos also sets out what they believe in morally. For example, how far can we trust an organization that is sponsored by PETA or the NRA?

What might this tell us about their ethos, or moral credibility? How can we judge a person or organization's overall ethos?

Human sciences, Politics

Etymological fallacy

The belief that an earlier, or the earliest, meaning of a word is necessarily the right one. (See also descriptive knowledge, prescriptive knowledge.) If words' meanings change over time, etymological fallacy can become possible.

How far is it possible to determine the 'true meaning' of a word? To what extent should a word's meaning be based on its origins, as opposed to how it is commonly used? What problems could etymological fallacies cause in our day-to-day lives?

Language

Etymology

The study of the origin of words and the ways in which their meanings have changed throughout history.

How far can etymology be judged to be more important than the popular sense of the word? How can we judge the significance of the way words' meanings have evolved over time? How far does it matter if a word's current meaning has strayed a significant distance from its etymology? To what extent can we be certain of words' etymology?

Language

Euphemism

A mild or indirect word or expression used instead of a harsh, embarrassing or rude one, in order to minimize the emotional impact on others. (See also dysphemism.) A house for sale might be euphemistically described as 'rustic' when it in fact requires a lot of repair work, or companies may say they want to 'downsize' when they really mean that lots of people will lose their jobs.

To what extent do euphemisms obscure the truth, as opposed to illuminating it? How do we know when it is advisable to use a euphemistic expression?

Language, Politics

Evaluate

1. To assess; to form an idea of the amount, number, value or impact of.

2. In mathematics, 'to evaluate' means to find a numerical expression or equivalent for an equation, formula, or function.

For example, studies can evaluate the impact of recent changes. A mathematical example might be 'Evaluate the expression 2x for x=3.'

How do we know if we have effectively or correctly evaluated a situation or (in maths) a formulaic expression, or not? What methods can we use to ensure that we do so as far as possible?

Mathematics, Knowledge and the knower

Evidence

Available information to let us know whether something is true or not.

How do we know whether credible evidence has been provided? How might the collection of the 'best available' information present ethical constraints when carrying out experiments in the human sciences, or caring for patients? How far does evidence go beyond what works on average, as opposed to in specific/obscure situations, or for pertinent subgroups? How do we decide what counts as useful evidence? How do we know what the 'best' course of action is when evidence is inconclusive? How can we tell if evidence is flawed?

Human sciences, Natural sciences

Evil demon problem

A thought experiment invoking the possibility of a being who could make you doubt all of your beliefs. (See also dream argument, scepticism.) According to this problem, everything can be a deception of an Evil Demon, but the very fact that we are being deceived means that we would first have to exist.

How far can we be sure of our existence and all that we perceive within it?

Knowledge and the knower

Evolve

To change gradually over time.

How far must things constantly evolve in order to survive. How might we measure rates of evolution? How can we tell whether something is really evolving?

Language, Natural sciences

ex nihilo nihil fit

Latin for 'nothing comes from nothing'; the view that all things were formed from things that existed before them. The theory of the zero-energy universe puts forward that matter can be created from nothing due to a vacuum fluctuation.

How would we assess whether or not this is true? Is ex nihilo nihil fit incompatible with non-religious belief?

Natural sciences, Religious knowledge

Exacerbate

To make something worse. For example, the high cost of houses might be exacerbated by the fact that wages have not risen in line with inflation.

How far is our own quest for knowledge exacerbated by the internet? How do we know when a situation has been exacerbated, and judge how/why it has been exacerbated?

Human sciences, Technology

Exaggerate

To represent something as being larger, better, or worse than it really is. For example, hypochondriacs might exaggerate any aches and pains.

How can we tell if someone is exaggerating? What might be some possible implications of exaggeration in the formation of our own knowledge?

Language

Examine

To inspect thoroughly; to test someone's knowledge; to formally question in a court of law.

For instance, witnesses can be cross-examined during trials. After a medical examination, doctors may also decide to carry out a particular procedure, such as a Caesarean section. Colleges and schools also assess the suitability of candidates by examining them.

How do we identify possible problems that can arise during the process of examination? To what extent can such problems be prevented?

Human sciences, Natural sciences

Example

A concrete thing that is illustrative of a general idea; a person or thing in terms of whether they/their behaviour should be imitated or not.

How far do we have a duty to set a good example to others? How do we decide whether or not something is a 'good' example?

Knowledge and the knower

Exception

A person or thing which is excluded from a general statement or does not follow a general rule.

"There are exceptions to every rule."

How can we establish whether or not this is truly the case? What are some possible implications of exceptions in our search for knowledge?

Knowledge and the knower

Exceptionalism	The belief that something is exceptional (unusual or atypical in a positive way).
	"The people from this country suffer from a strange sort of exceptionalism, believing that they are better than other countries for no real reason."
	To what extent is exceptionalism problematic? What implications might it have for historiography? How can we judge whether or not exceptionalism is justified?
	History, Human sciences, Politics
Exchange	1. Giving one thing and receiving another, similar thing in return.
	2. A short conversation or argument.
	How far is it the case that we discover other minds, and our own, mainly through conversational exchange? How could we test this?
	Human sciences, Language
Exclude	1. To deliberately leave out (information or people).
	2. To deny access to a place, group, or privilege; to remove from consideration.
	How far is it the case that modern society excludes women and ethnic minorities from inquiry? What are some possible implications of excluding particular people or pieces of information? How do we judge when or whether it is necessary to exclude information? How might excluding information advance our knowledge?
	Knowledge and the knower
Exhibition	A public display of items of interest.
	Your TOK exhibition will showcase (whether in person or digitally) three items of interest.
	How do you know what to choose to include in your exhibition?
	The Arts, Knowledge and the knower
Existence	1. The fact or state of living, or having objective reality; a way of living; all that exists.
	2. In religion, your past lives.
	(See also materialism.)
	Can we logically prove that anything really exists? How far is it possible to differentiate between non-existent entities? How far is existence a valid philosophical concept?
	Religious knowledge
Existentialism	The belief that the world has no meaning, and so people have to make that meaning through being free agents, with total control over their actions and choices; the exploration of human existence, centring on individuals' lived experiences. (See also absurdism, nihilism).
	If you are struggling to define yourself and understand the purpose of your existence, it can be said that you are facing an existential crisis.
	How far is 'being' the source of knowing? How far do the arts help us to resolve our own individual existential crises?
	The Arts
Exoticize	To portray something or someone unfamiliar as exotic or unusual.
	Some artworks are accused of exoticizing particular areas of the world.
	What are some possible implications of exoticizing the cultures of others? What might this mean for the development of our own knowledge?
	The Arts, Human sciences
Expectation	1. A strong belief that something will happen or be the case, or that someone will or should achieve something.
	2. In mathematics, another term for 'expected value'.
	For example, your family might have high expectations for your future. In mathematics, an expectation can be, for instance, a generalization of a weighted average.
	How can we judge whether or not expectations are accurate reflections of the reality of a situation?
	Human sciences, Mathematics

Experience	Practical contact with, and observation of, facts and real-life events; to go through an event or occurrence; to feel an emotion or sensation.
	How can we judge the value of experience in developing our own knowledge?
	Knowledge and the knower
Experiential	Based on experience and observation. (See also a posteriori, empirical evidence.) For instance, it can be considered that lessons for young children need to give them a chance to be creative and to be based on experiential methods of teaching.
	How can we judge the necessity of experiential knowledge? Can experiential knowledge be used as an argument against God's omniscience? What might be some ethical considerations to bear in mind when using experiential learning or experiments?
	Human sciences, Natural sciences, Religious knowledge
Experimental	New and innovative; based on trials and experiments; not fully established or finalised. For example, medicines go through an experimental stage before being prescribed to a wider public.
	How do we know what the goals of experimental research are? How far can our hypotheses be proven via experimental means?
	Human sciences, Natural sciences
Expert	1. A person who is particularly knowledgeable or skilled in a certain area. (Noun)
	2. Having or involving a great deal of knowledge or skill. (Adjective)
	To what extent can someone become an expert empirically, as opposed to through specialised training? How far do experts close off knowledge to ordinary people? How far do they open up knowledge to ordinary people?
	Knowledge and the knower
Expertise	Expert skill or knowledge in a particular field.
	What proportion of expertise is about how others perceive you? How do we decide what expertise is or where it comes from?
	Knowledge and the knower
experto crede	Latin for 'trust the expert', or 'believe one who has experience in the matter'. Usually used as an aside in academic writing to further indicate the writer's (or someone else's) expertise and that they should be believed. Sometimes 'crede' can be followed by the name of the expert.
	Is experience sufficient to define expertise? How do we know whether someone is an expert? When is it more rational to think for oneself or to defer to the relevant expert? How far is it wise to act according to our own good reasons rather than expert authority?
	Knowledge and the knower
Explain	Explaining is when you give details about and reasons for your ideas, along with examples to support them. You may be asked to explain to a person orally, or in writing (eg in an essay).
	What distinction is being made in the statement "I don't argue; I explain"? How do we know what differences there are, if any, between 'argue' and 'explain'?
	Language
Explicit	Stated clearly and in detail; leaving no room for confusion or doubt.
	Ideas can be expressed more explicitly or clearly in some languages than others; for example, the Amazonian tribe of the Amondawa people have no word for 'time' in their language, or indeed for time periods such as 'month' or 'year'.
	How far can ideas truly be expressed explicitly, especially when collaborating cross-culturally? How can we judge whether explicit knowledge is, in fact, a spectrum of expression of belief?
	Indigenous knowledge, Language
Explore	To examine, inquire into, or discuss an idea in detail.
	The TOK course sets out to explore fundamental questions about how we know what we know.
	How far can we define the process of exploration? To what extent is it possible to complete a process of exploration?
	Knowledge and the knower

Extent	The particular degree, or how far, something is (or believed to be) the case. For example, to what extent is compromise necessary?
	How can we decide how far we agree or disagree with an idea? How useful is a spectrum of agreement or disagreement when formulating our ideas?
	Knowledge and the knower
External assessment	An external assessment is marked solely by IB officials – not by your teacher. Your TOK essay will be externally assessed.
	How can we detect or measure the advantages and disadvantages of this method of assessment?
	Knowledge and the knower
Externalism	1. The idea that mental acts are dependent on the world outside the mind.
	2. In religion, the idea that belief requires physical external proof.
	(See also internalism.)
	What might be some implications of, or problems with, an externalist viewpoint? To what extent are our thoughts dependent on our environment? How can we judge the reliability of an externalist worldview? How far can externalism 'prove' God's existence?
	Natural sciences, Religious knowledge
External validity	How far the results of a study can be generalized to other settings. For instance, your results may apply to men, but not to women; or your results may apply to the elderly, but not to those in their teens and early 20s. External validity ultimately asks whether research can be applied to the 'real world'?
	How might we go about answering such a question? To what extent is it fully answerable?
	Human sciences, Natural sciences
Extraneous variable	In a scientific experiment, variables which are not the independent variable, but which could still affect the result of the experiment. For example, if a participant who has performed a memory test was tired, dyslexic or had poor eyesight, this could affect their performance and the results of the experiment.
	How do we determine what the extraneous variables could be in the case of each experiment? What methods might we use to try to control extraneous variables? How far is it possible to control these?
	Human sciences, Natural sciences
Extrapolate	To apply a method or conclusion to an unknown situation, by assuming existing trends will continue or that the same methods will be relevant. For instance, mathematicians and scientists want to know if their results can be extrapolated to other groups or situations.
	How far can we extrapolate knowledge from one area to another? How do we know if this is possible or not?
	Mathematics, Natural sciences
Extrinsic	Coming or operating from outside an entity; environmental; not integral to a thing itself.
	"Extrinsic ageing – or how old you appear to be – can be worsened by external factors, such as sun exposure and smoking."
	How do we recognize or determine whether something is caused by an extrinsic or intrinsic factor?
	Knowledge and the knower

E

Face value

What something appears to be worth. If a statement is convincing enough, people might choose to take it at face value, without investigating it further.

What might be some problems with interpreting a statement at face value? Are there some moments where it may, conversely, be useful to accept things at face value? How do we know when such moments are? How do we know whether we can take something – or, indeed, in mathematics, a number – at face value?

Language, Mathematics

Fact

A thing that is known or has been proven to be true.

How do we know whether something is a fact? How far can we ignore facts when assessing a situation? How far can we advance our knowledge of the world via facts alone? How important is it for our cultures to be fact-based? To what extent are facts independent of our awareness of them? How do we know whether facts are finite?

Knowledge and the knower

Fact checker

A person or organization that seeks to verify whether information is correct, and whose job it is to explain to others why it is true or false. Can also be used as a verb ('to fact check').

Credible news outlets often have their own fact-checking departments to verify if what their journalists have said is true before their work is published.

How do fact-checkers verify the information they hold? How can we judge the effectiveness of fully automated fact-checkers (such as online machines)? What moral responsibilities might fact-checkers have? How far is it possible for fact-checkers to remain fully neutral?

Language, Politics, Technology

Fairness

Just and impartial treatment, without discrimination or favouritism.

How do you know when something is unfair? To what extent does 'being fair' always mean treating people equally? How can we judge whether it is fair to have different rules for different people?

Human sciences

Faith

A feeling of strong trust or conviction; a strongly held belief based on spiritual conviction rather than proof. Some might describe it as a combination of emotional factors (such as a deep commitment) and ethical factors (such as the feeling that things will work out for the best).

If a cancer patient is facing a treatment with a low probability of success, they may nonetheless have faith that the treatment will work.

Is scientific faith different to religious faith? How far might we describe scientific 'faith' in a different way? How far are faith and religion different? And how far is faith compatible with other forms of knowledge?

Religious knowledge

Fake news

False or misleading information presented as news.

How can we assess the possible impact of fake news? In the internet age, how far is it possible that fake news will or can be eradicated?

Language, Politics

Fallacy

A mistaken belief, especially one based on unsound arguments; a failure of reasoning which means an argument is no longer valid.

Common fallacies might be that only men are good at maths, or that women are bad drivers.

How far can fallacies in everyday discourse be eradicated? How can we decide what purpose a fallacy serves, whether used deliberately/rhetorically or accidentally?

Knowledge and the knower

Fallacy of amphiboly

Amphiboly is a fallacy of relevance that relies on an ambiguous phrase and/or grammatical structure to confuse or mislead an audience. (See also fallacy of equivocation.)

If an advertisement for an apartment says '3 rooms, river view, private phone, bath, kitchen, utilities included', you might reasonably expect to find a bathroom and kitchen included in the apartment, when in fact when you get there, you find that these facilities are shared with other residents. (The ad didn't say anything about a private bath or a private kitchen. All the ad said was 'private phone'.) As such, the advertisement could be said to be amphibolous.

For what reasons might the fallacy of amphiboly occur? How can we judge the motives behind this?

Language, Politics

Fallacy of equivocation	When single words are vague or have more than one meaning, enabling them to be used in one way in one part of an argument, and in another way in a later part of an argument, or according to the speaker's own definition, as opposed to the definition that is generally understood. (See also doublespeak.)
	"I have the right to say whatever I want, so it's right for me to do so."
	Another example of the fallacy of equivocation would be if a politician said they had voted in favour of overseas citizens' rights every time since they'd been elected to office. However, what if there were simply no overseas citizens' rights bills voted on during their term? While the candidate's statement wouldn't be entirely false, it would say something different about his voting record.
	How can we tell the difference between equivocation and lying? What are some potential moral implications of equivocation?
	Language, Politics
Fallibilism	The idea that statements based on empirical knowledge can be accepted even though they can't be proven with certainty. (See also scepticism.) Some fallibilists, however, consider axioms to be an exception.
	How far is absolute certainty about knowledge possible? How far can humans still err even when working with allegedly infallible systems, such as axioms? If our knowledge has to be constantly revised, because we and the systems we use are fallible, how far can knowledge be said to exist?
	Mathematics
Fallibility	The tendency to make mistakes or be wrong.
	Are our senses always fallible? How far does fallibility affect our capability?
	Human sciences
False balance	A media bias in which journalists present an issue with more balance than the evidence suggests is justified, potentially by omitting information that would discredit the other side.
	For instance, in the debate on global warming, most scientists believe global warming to be caused by the industrial revolution; however, a very small number of scientists dispute this. If both sides are given an equal voice, it can seem like there is a serious disagreement within the scientific community, when in reality there is an overwhelming consensus.
	What might be some differences between presenting opposing ideas fairly and presenting them equally? How far does false balance avoid bias, and how far does it accentuate it? To what extent is it possible for broadcasters to be completely impartial? What are the possible impacts of false balance on credibility?
	Language, Politics
False claim	When somebody presents an idea as if it were true, when it is not; this can be distinct from lying, as the person making the false claim may still believe it to be true. Some people may judge, for example, that some refugees make false claims about their age, as they have more rights if they are under the age of 18.
	How can we judge what leads people to make false claims? What are some possible implications of false claims?
	Human sciences
False dilemma	Sometimes called a 'false dichotomy', this is a situation where an 'either/or' situation is assumed when in reality there are more than two possible choices or outcomes.
	"You are for us, or you are against us."
	What are some possible advantages, and pitfalls, of this binary view of the world? How might false dilemmas obscure our search for knowledge?
	Knowledge and the knower
False memories	When people remember events differently from the way they happened or even remember events that never happened at all.
	False memory can be caused by misinformation or by misattribution of the original source of the information.
	How can we identify whether our memories are true or false? Are false memories as important as 'true' memories? How could we establish this? How far can the wording of questions we are asked about a past event affect our memory of it?
	Human sciences, Language

False positive

When a test result wrongly indicates a particular condition or attribute. For instance, false positive (or false negative) results can occur in the sciences if cases and controls are not matched in their background. It is also possible, in very rare cases, to have a false-positive pregnancy test result. This means you're not pregnant but the test says you are.

How do we know whether a 'positive' is in fact a false positive? How far can we assess the reliability of a diagnostic test?

Human sciences, Natural sciences

Falsehood

The state of being untrue; a lie.

How can we understand the difference between truth and falsehoods? How can we tell when someone is lying to us? To what extent is lying an unavoidable part of human nature? How can we decide whether there is a good intention behind a lie, or what would count as a 'good' intention? How far do people always have a right to know the truth of a matter?

Human sciences

Falsifiability

Also known as falsificationism, this is the idea that theories cannot be proved but that theories or hypotheses can be disproved, or falsified. For example, the statement 'All swans are white' is falsifiable because one can observe that black swans exist.

How far does something need to be falsifiable in order to be scientific? Is refutation only acceptable when a new theory is empirically better than an old one?

Natural sciences

Falsity

The fact of being untrue, incorrect, or insincere.

Professional analysts can, for instance, demonstrate the truth or the falsity of claims that are made. How can we show whether a claim is true or false? How far does falsity exist in the perceiver, and how far in the object being perceived?

Knowledge and the knower

Fate

1. The development of events outside our control, as determined by a supernatural power (eg God, the universe).

2. An unavoidable, often unpleasant outcome; more broadly, the future.

*To what extent is it possible to decide our own fate? How far can we distinguish between fate and destiny? To what degree is a belief in fate compatible with **agnosis**?*

Religious knowledge

Feasibility study

The process of working out how far a proposed plan is practical/how well it can be carried out in the real world.

Feasibility studies usually cover a range of matters, including location, ethics, time scale, and so on.

How can we establish whether a plan or idea is feasible? Via what methods can the probability of success be calculated? How far can this be done accurately? How do we know what constitutes appropriate data to be gathered as part of a feasibility study?

Human sciences, Natural sciences

Fictionalism

1. The idea that statements appearing to be descriptions of the world should be understood as cases of 'make believe', or pretending to treat something as literally true.

2. In mathematics, the theory that any talk of numbers is just a convenience for doing science.

(See also Platonism.)

Fictionalism holds that our mathematical sentences and theories are mainly about abstract mathematical objects, but if there are no such things as abstract objects, our mathematical theories are not true. For instance, sentences like "3 is prime" might be useful, but ultimately false.

How far does fictionalism advance our quest for knowledge? To what extent is fictionalism plausible compared to other views of how we know what we know?

Mathematics, Natural sciences

Fideism	Also known as sola fide, the idea that religious knowledge depends on faith or revelation (something being revealed to you, particularly by a divine entity, such as God). (See also Pascal's wager, sola scriptura.)
	To what extent is fideism only blind belief and uncritical obedience of tradition? What methods could we use to establish whether this is really the case? How far does fideism imply that faith is superior at arriving at particular truths? To what extent must we 'deny knowledge in order to make room for faith'? How far does fideism reject the correspondence theory, and what implications might this have? How do we know whether God's existence can be demonstrated via reason? To what extent can 'blind faith' be considered 'true faith'?
	Religious knowledge
Figurative	Something that is representative, symbolic, or non-literal. Examples of figurative language include metaphors, similes, idioms, and proverbs (eg "it's raining cats and dogs" or "a rolling stone gathers no moss").
	In what ways can figurative language clarify an idea? In what ways can it obscure the transmission of knowledge? To what extent does figurative language reflect the cultural and intellectual environment of its users?
	Language
Filter	1. To process items or ideas to decide what is unwanted and can be rejected.
	2. In technology and the natural sciences, to pass through a device to remove unwanted material; a light-absorbing substance.
	For instance, our eyes filter out ultraviolet radiation, and filters can reduce haze in photography. "To have no filter" means to say exactly what is on your mind without considering the consequences.
	How far should we see art through the filter of present-day concerns? If you have no filter, what could be some possible consequences of this? How far should parents' ideas filter down to their children? To what extent are emotions a reasonable shortcut to help us filter large amounts of information? How far is it important to filter what we say and do? To what extent are the use of photographic filters significant in how we process information? How far does it matter whether or not we know that they have been used? How do we know what the 'best' filters are to use in an experiment? How do we decide, when filtering information or ideas, what to accept or reject?
	Language, Natural sciences, Technology
Filter bubble	A situation in which an internet user encounters only information and opinions that conform to and reinforce their own beliefs, caused by algorithms that personalize an individual's online experience. (See also confirmation bias, echo chamber, epistemic bubble, information bias.)
	How transparent are the choices made by algorithms – and thus the methods of creation of filter bubbles? Algorithms are designed to show us online material of the same type we have accessed before and liked – how can we counteract the possible problems created by this? How can we ascertain whether such algorithms have sinister intentions behind them? How can we determine the implications of filter bubbles for our discourse, and the construction of our own identities?
	Technology
First-order knowledge	Knowledge relating to objects or concepts in the world. For instance, "There are an infinite number of prime numbers" is a first-order knowledge claim.
	How do we determine the validity of first-order knowledge claims?
	Knowledge and the knower
Fixation	1. An obsessive interest in a thing or person; setting something at a particular level.
	2. In the natural sciences, the process by which plants assimilate nitrogen and CO_2; the process of preserving or stabilizing a medical specimen in a chemical substance before examination; keeping your sight fixed on something; or the connection of molecules of fixed tissue compounds.
	For example, some businesses might consider that they are innovating through the fixation of employment quotas.
	Why might the fixation of quotas be problematic? How do we know whether someone is fixated on something? In the natural sciences, how do we know what 'good' histochemical fixation looks like? To what extent might fixation affect our common sense?
	Human sciences, Natural sciences

Fixation error

When you get stuck on a small thing when trying to work on a big thing and can't move on until you have remembered what the small thing was. For instance, you might find yourself working to a tight deadline, or trying to solve an important problem quickly, and becoming stuck; in this case, you can't progress until you remember a piece of information that is on the tip of your tongue.

How might fixation errors prevent us from moving on in our pursuit of knowledge? How far might different fields (eg aviation vs medicine) assess the risk of fixation error differently?

Knowledge and the knower

Flawed

Having a significant weakness or imperfection. For example, software can be flawed by poor programming, or our own strategies can be fatally flawed, meaning that they will not work.

How can we determine whether or not someone or something is flawed? To what extent are we able to recognize flaws in ourselves? How far might this be important in the advancement of knowledge?

Human sciences, Technology

Folk knowledge

The set of knowledge possessed by a particular (small) society or group of people; this can include songs, memories, recipes and medicines.

How far is it important if folk knowledge counteracts related scientific knowledge? What relationships might exist between folk knowledge and scientific knowledge? What might be some of the benefits and limitations of folk knowledge? In what ways could folk knowledge relate to academic skills? How do we decide which is more 'valuable'?

Human sciences, Indigenous knowledge

Folklore

The knowledge and traditions of a particular society or group of people, passed along via word of mouth, often (but not always) in story form.

To what extent does the reliability of folklore matter? How can we establish the possible value of folklore? Does folklore lose something of value if recorded for posterity? How far is it possible to compare the folklores of different communities?

The Arts, Human sciences, Indigenous knowledge, Language

Folk psychology

The ability of ordinary, untrained people to explain and predict the behaviours and mental states of others. For instance, there is evidence to suggest that those with autism spectrum conditions can find it difficult to 'read' others' emotions or motivations – in short, to engage in folk psychology.

To what extent is folk psychology useful in our everyday lives? How far is folk psychology also useful for academic purposes? What could be some problems associated with folk psychology?

Human sciences

Foolproof

Incapable of going wrong or being misused.

How far is it possible for anything to be foolproof? To what extent is it worth sacrificing imagination in order to make something foolproof?

Knowledge and the knower

Footnote

An additional piece of information printed at the bottom of a page, usually in non-fiction books or essays, but occasionally also in fiction. (See also endnote.)

The IB recommends that you should not have too many footnotes in your TOK essay – most of your words should be in the main body of the essay itself.

What could be some disadvantages of extended footnotes? How might we decide whether footnotes or endnotes are 'better' when writing? What could this choice imply about how we display and process knowledge?

Language

Foreseeability

In law, reasonable anticipation of whether or not the consequences of an action could have been predicted. For instance, foreseeability might involve aspects such as subject, time, standard, extent, and the content to foresee.

How can we judge whether or not somebody could or should have foreseen/been able to predict the consequences of their actions? How do we know what foreseeability does, or should, mean?

Human sciences

Forgery	The act of illegally copying or faking paperwork, art, literature, signatures, or, in one famous case, musical recordings.

How can we tell whether or not something is a forgery? How might a forger's skill alter our understanding of the history of ideas? What are some possible ethical implications of forgery? How can a forgery be proven? How are scientific forgeries possible? To what extent is a lack of artistic or scientific integrity the main problem of forgery?

The Arts, Human sciences, Natural sciences

Formation	1. The action or process of being formed or created; a structure. Some rock formations might generate sand bars on which grass grows, for example.
	2. In philosophy, empiricism focuses on the role of experience in the formation of ideas. Certain social and psychological formations from different historical periods can also be seen in artworks.

How can we tell what has led to particular formations (whether of rocks or social structures)? How far do emotions contribute reliably to the formation of ideas?

The Arts, Human sciences, Natural sciences

Foundational beliefs	Also known as basic beliefs, these are beliefs that do not depend on any others in order to be justified. If you question all of your beliefs until you find something that is indisputably true, this might be called a foundational belief.

How far can our senses be counted on to provide us with foundational beliefs? In what ways might foundational beliefs change over time? How do we know what makes something a foundational belief?

Knowledge and the knower

Foundationalism	The idea that our ideas can be justified based on other ideas that we have direct proof of. For instance, you can know that you have cancer only if you know some other things to be true – for example, that your doctors have reported this and that your doctor is reliable. Your first belief being dependent on these other two beliefs is an example of foundationalism.

For what reasons might foundational beliefs be needed? What might be some problems with foundationalism?

Knowledge and the knower

Fragment	1. A small piece broken off or left over from a bigger item. (Noun)
	2. To break, or cause to break, into small or separate parts, away from a main area, idea, or thing. (Verb)

If political systems become fragmented, for instance, such a system may fail to account for the population's broader interests. Archaeologically, sometimes all that remains of an item are fragments.

How far can we make inferences about historical events, places or people based on fragments? How reliable are the impressions that we form based on fragments? How can we judge the value of something that has become fragmented?

The Arts, History, Natural sciences, Politics

Free will	The ability to behave as you wish, unconstrained by ideas of fate.

To what extent is free will a form of personal power? How far do we really have the ability to do what we want to do? Is the free will we seem to experience just an illusion? For what reasons might some people object to the idea of free will? To what extent is the idea of free will compatible with religious belief? What might be the necessary conditions for an action to be regarded as a free choice?

Religious knowledge

Freedom of speech	The idea that an individual, outlet, or community should be able to express their views without fear of retaliation.

Many would argue, for example, that freedom of speech is intrinsic to democracy along with other fundamental rights, such as the right to vote.

To what extent does freedom of speech improve a society? How can we judge what limits, if any, should exist on what people are allowed to say? How far might this vary between cultures? How can we decide whether freedom of speech is desirable?

Human sciences, Language, Politics

Freedom of the press

The principle that journalists should have the freedom to report news and circulate opinions without government interference. (See also **freedom of speech**.)

What may restrict the freedom of the press? When might freedom of the press become an invasion of privacy? What are some possible consequences of freedom of the press? To what extent might freedom of the press be considered a negative thing? What might be some limitations of freedom of the press, and how can we judge whether these should be in place?

Human sciences, Language, Politics

Freethought

The idea that beliefs should be reached based on logic, reason, and experience, as opposed to authority and tradition.

How far does freethought liberate us from societal expectations? To what extent must we reject traditional social or religious belief systems in order to be 'true' freethinkers?

Religious knowledge

Frequency illusion

Also known as the Baader-Meinhof phenomenon, frequency illusion is a type of bias that makes you think something is happening more often than it really is, often based on your own personal circumstances. In reality, you are just noticing it more – it is not really appearing any more frequently than before.

A woman who desperately wants to have a baby may suddenly find she is 'always' seeing babies (in advertisements, in the street, etc). Another example would be if you have recently read about a particular thing online, but suddenly seem to hear it a lot in conversation or find it cropping up regularly in other things you are reading.

How might the frequency illusion affect our everyday lives? How significant are these illusions? How are they different to coincidences? How might they become conflated with religious 'signs' from a God or gods?

Human sciences, Religious knowledge

Function

The use or purpose of a person or thing; to work in a normal way.

What is the role (or function) of scepticism in our studies of epistemology? To what extent must something have a function in order to be valuable?

Function-first epistemology focuses on the role of epistemic evaluation in human life.

How far is this a useful way of seeing TOK?

Knowledge and the knower

Fundamental

Forming a necessary base; of essential importance. For example, revolutions might be said to cause fundamental changes in countries.

How can we tell if something is fundamental? To what extent is it something we can know at the time of the event (as opposed to only with hindsight)?

Knowledge and the knower

Fuzzy logic

1. In mathematics, a form of many-valued logic in which the truth values of variables may be any real number between 0 and 1 inclusive.
2. More generally, it is the observation that people make decisions based on imprecise and non-numerical information.

How far does fuzzy logic help us to identify those 'in-between' states of feelings or situations? One example of fuzzy logic might be air conditioning. Some units are set to minimum and maximum room temperatures, with the unit switching itself off when the lower number is reached, and switching itself back on when the temperature hits the higher point. In more modern systems, though, fuzzy logic doesn't rely on these two 'extremes', instead managing the temperature so that it remains steady, by sensing slight changes and making adjustments. How can we judge the reliability of fuzzy logic?

Mathematics, Technology

Gambler's fallacy	Also known as the Monte Carlo fallacy, this is the mistake in thinking that a certain event is more likely or less likely than it was before, given previous events, when each event should be considered independently, as the others going before it have no effect on it.

For example, if you repeatedly toss a coin, it will come up heads or tails equally after a certain number of tosses, as per the law of large numbers, even after a run of heads or tails may lead you to believe that one is more likely than the other. It is also a common belief after many male or female children in a family, that the parents must be due a baby of the opposite sex the next time, when there is no way of predicting or influencing this outcome and previous births of boys or girls do not affect the sex of any subsequent children.

What gaps might the gambler's fallacy show us between our perceptions and reality? What might be some possible relationships between our beliefs and probability?

Mathematics |
| Gaslighting | Manipulating someone into doubting their own abilities and/or questioning their sanity. (See also illusory truth effect.)

If one party gaslights another in a relationship, through the use of phrases such as "I only did it because I love you" or "I'm not cheating, you're just paranoid", it can affect the self-esteem of the person being gaslighted.

How do you know if gaslighting is happening to you? How far can we judge whether gaslighters are aware of what they do? How might gaslighting affect someone's cognitive processes? In what ways might we distinguish gaslighting from silencing? What is the role of fabricated evidence in gaslighting?

Human sciences |
| General knowledge | Knowledge of a broad range of facts about a variety of different subjects, which you do not need specialised training to know. Not to be confused with common knowledge. For instance, if you think someone only has general or basic knowledge of something, you might choose to provide some background or overview of an issue.

How can we judge the usefulness, and possible limitations, of general knowledge? To what extent is general knowledge 'fixed' or static?

Knowledge and the knower |
| Generalization | A general statement or concept, arrived at based on ideas from a few specific cases. An example of generalization could be the idea that headdresses are worn by all indigenous peoples.

Where do generalizations come from? Why are they used? How do we know whether generalization is useful or damaging?

Knowledge and the knower |
| Generic | 1. Relating to a whole group of things; not specific.

2. In medicine, it refers to a consumer drug that is not sold under a brand name; in biology, it relates to a genus (an overall class of plants or animals that is larger than a single species, such as Rosa, which contains more than 100 species of roses).

For instance, some doctors might be encouraged by the healthcare systems in which they work to prescribe generic drugs because they are cheaper than brand-named versions.

How can we assess whether or not a generic term is useful? Are there any reasons why using a generic term might be a disadvantage? How do we weigh up the benefits of using a generic term, compared to any potential pitfalls? How far is epistemology itself a generic discipline?

Natural sciences |
| Genetic fallacy | Assessing the quality of an argument based only on its source, history or origin (or that of the person making the argument). Some examples of genetic fallacies are "My parents told me God exists, so God exists", and "He is a teacher in a public school, so any claims he makes about that system are bound to be biased and untrue."

Is genetic reasoning always fallacious? How do we know? In what situations might causal or historical factors be relevant in evaluating a belief?

History, Human sciences, Religious knowledge |

Geocentrism

The now discredited/disproved idea that the sun and other planets revolve around the earth. Geocentric theories prevailed for over 1700 years.

How far is the development of technology (eg telescopes), important in helping us prove and disprove ideas?

History, Natural sciences, Technology

Geography

The study of the earth's physical features and atmosphere, the nature and relative arrangement of people and places, and how human activity affects these things. (See also **Hobo-Dyer projection**, **Mercator projection**, **Robinson projection**.) For instance, living well in old age involves a variety of factors, including geography, chance, and available wealth.

How can we assess the consequences of the physical state of where people live on other aspects of their lives? What might be some possible consequences of geographical ignorance? How might geographical concerns affect our problem-solving strategies in different areas of the world? What particular values, if any, should be conveyed through good geography teaching? How can we decide? On what basis have countries' borders and map projections been delineated, and how do we know whether these were 'correct'?

Human sciences, Natural sciences

Gettier problem

The idea that true knowledge and justified true belief are not the same – we can believe something sincerely based on all the facts we have and still be wrong. (See also **no false lemmas**.)

For instance, if you look at a clock and it says 2:15, you are likely to decide that that's really what the time is. On this occasion it is actually 2:15, but the clock is broken, so it always says 2:15 – meaning that on this occasion, you were just lucky to be correct – meaning that your justified true belief did not equate to true knowledge.

How can we tell whether the information we have is 'true' knowledge, or just a belief? What might Gettier problems tell us about information and how we process it?

Knowledge and the knower

Gillick competence

A term used in medical law in England and Wales to decide whether a child (under age 16) is informed enough to be able to consent to their own medical treatment (as opposed to an adult needing to give permission for them). Courts may sometimes make decisions about vulnerable people, however, based on the state's power to intervene, without taking Gillick competence into account.

What must be understood by minors in order for them to be deemed competent? What might be some possible problems with the concept of Gillick competence? How far does competence confer on minors the authority to refuse as well as to accept medical treatment? In what situations might Gillick competence be irrelevant?

Human sciences, Natural sciences

Global impression

1. In medicine, the Clinical Global Impression scales assess the seriousness of symptoms and the effectiveness of treatments.

2. In assessment, 'global impression marking' means your essay or exhibition is given the mark that overall is the 'best fit' for your work (so one mark for the whole piece of work, as opposed to lots of individual aspects of the work being marked and then added together to create the total).

Global impression marking means that, for example, if organization-wise your essay scores 10 but your critical thinking is more like a 6, the examiner might give a 'best fit' mark of 8 overall.

How far does this 'meet in the middle' approach show a student's abilities? In medicine, how can we assess the validity of the Clinical Global Impression scale? How can its effectiveness at predicting treatment outcomes be established? How can we decide whether such 'global impression' approaches are specific enough, and whether 'good enough' (as opposed to 'perfect') is good enough?

Human sciences, Natural sciences

gnaritas nullius

In Latin, 'no one's knowledge'. For example, indigenous knowledge has often been treated as gnaritas nullius in terms of intellectual property rights, and has therefore become part of the public domain.

Who decides what type of knowledge is valuable, and why? What are some possible ethical implications of gnaritas nullius? To what extent could it be considered the erasure of indigenous intellectual property rights? How far does knowledge (of any kind) require legal protection?

Indigenous knowledge

Gnosis	Personal knowledge of spiritual or religious matters; divine knowledge; knowledge of the self and God. We might, for example, distinguish between the 'knowledge' (gnosis) and 'wisdom' (sophia) of God.

To what extent can we distinguish between knowledge and wisdom, if indeed we can? How can we differentiate (if at all) between shared and personal knowledge in this regard?

Religious knowledge

Gnosticism	In religion, the emphasis on personal spiritual knowledge over traditional church teachings and authority.

If you are gnostic, you might consider being religiously 'saved' to be direct knowledge of God. If you are religious, to what extent is gnosticism important to salvation (being 'saved')? How do we know? How far does gnosticism's emphasis on direct experience allow for a wide variety of religious teachings? How far is it possible or desirable to 'standardize' gnosticism into one system?

Religious knowledge

God paradox	Also known as the omnipotence paradox, this is the idea that if God is all-powerful, they are able to make anything – including a stone they cannot lift. If this is not possible (because God is, in theory, strong enough to lift anything) then they cannot make such a stone. This means that either way, they are not all-powerful. However, some would say that what we mere humans would consider to be contradictions and impossibilities do not apply to God, as God is all-powerful.

How far do you agree with this? How can we decide whether the omnipotence paradox is a sufficient argument for or against God's existence? How far do thought experiments of this kind – what we might call exercises in imagination – contribute to religious knowledge?

Religious knowledge

Good faith	An important idea within law and business, this means accepting an idea within common standards of honesty and decency. (See also face value.) If a company acts in good faith, it trusts the ideas presented to it and makes decisions based on these.

To what extent can we judge 'acting in good faith' to mean simply acting without due care and attention? How far can we judge somebody's reliability in order to act in good faith?

Human sciences

Greenwashing	Greenwashing is when a company or organization spends more time and money on marketing themselves as environmentally friendly than on minimizing their environmental impact. (See also whitewashing.) Some people might describe greenwashing as deceitful, or as an advertising gimmick designed to mislead those who prefer to buy from environmentally conscious brands.

How can we judge whether or not this is the case? How do we know whether greenwashing has taken place? What are some possible ethical implications of greenwashing? What repercussions might greenwashing have for knowledge?

Human sciences, Politics

Grounds	Reasons; factors that help us decide whether to take action or to believe something. For example, we might judge that there are grounds for optimism (= reasons to think that something will turn out well).

How can we decide if there is enough evidence, or sufficient reasons, for us to believe in something or not?

Knowledge and the knower

| Groupthink | When a group of individuals reach a consensus without critical reasoning, or analysis of possible consequences or alternatives; blindly following and participating in the views of a group you are part of, possibly out of a desire to fit in. Also known as herd mentality. |

For example, if a political leader decides to invade, groupthink can be seen when others allow them to proceed despite their own concerns. Similarly, if a group of people believes in their own hype, that they can do no wrong, and that they always make the right decisions, this, too, is groupthink.

How can we define some necessary conditions for groupthink? How far is it possible to design institutions that avoid (aspects of) groupthink? How do we know whether groupthink has been successfully avoided? What are some possible implications of groupthink on our quest for knowledge? How can we decide if groupthink has any positive aspects?

Human sciences

Gullibility

The ability to be easily tricked or manipulated; believing anything you are told (adjective: gullible).

How can we detect what – if anything – causes gullibility? How do we know if we or others are gullible? What are some possible implications of gullibility on our search for knowledge?

Human sciences

Habits of mind

Routines of the affective system (the system of our emotions), which help us to link our feelings with experiences; they can also be mental qualities that help us with critical and creative thinking, such as self-discipline and orderly thinking. Other definitions describe 'habits of mind' as ways of behaving and reacting intelligently even when you don't know how to solve a problem.

It can be said that each discipline requires its own set of 'habits of mind'. For example, in mathematics, appropriate habits of mind might involve making connections, developing new ways to describe situations and make predictions, and conjecturing.

How far do habits of mind help us to advance our knowledge? To what extent are 'habits of mind' innate, and how far do they have to be learned?

Human sciences, Mathematics

Hallucination

Perceiving the presence of something which is not actually there.

How can we assess if we are hallucinating, or if someone else is? How far is it possible to distinguish hallucinations from other phenomena, such as divine revelation?

Human sciences, Natural sciences

Hawthorne effect

When people change their behaviour because they know they are being watched.

One example of the Hawthorne effect can be that people perform better in a study when they know they are taking part in one. What are some possible implications of the Hawthorne effect for experiments carried out in the human sciences? How far should we take this effect into account when drawing conclusions?

Human sciences

Hearsay

Rumours; information heard from others which cannot be backed up with evidence.

How can we identify if a statement is hearsay or not? How can the validity of hearsay be established?

Human sciences, Language

Heliocentrism

The idea of the earth and other planets revolving around the sun, as opposed to geocentrism.

In medieval times, heliocentrism was not taken seriously. However, in the 16th century, a mathematical model of a heliocentric system was presented.

To what extent is a heliocentric model useful? What are some of its possible limitations? How do we know?

Natural sciences

Herd mentality	Acting collectively as part of a group, often causing you to make decisions that you wouldn't make by yourself. (See also bandwagon effect, groupthink.) Examples of herd mentality (also known as herd behaviour) in human populations include riots and panic-buying.
	To what extent might herding exaggerate economic and social problems? What are some possible advantages of herding? What fallacies and other cognitive errors can be caused by herding?
	Human sciences
Hermeneutics	The study of interpretation, especially of literary texts. For example, if you recompose a piece of music, there might be both musical consequences and hermeneutic consequences (= consequences for how we interpret the piece). Some would argue that hermeneutics involves both understanding, and making ourselves understood.
	How do we differentiate between communication and hermeneutics? What are the conditions for us understanding something? How does the digital revolution change our understanding of texts? How far can we meaningfully interpret and integrate words, signs and events into a meaningful whole? To what extent can we interpret and understand something we have not personally experienced? How far is understanding based on a self-contained consciousness (as opposed to, for example, interactions with others)?
	The Arts, Language, Technology
Herstory	History viewed or told from a feminist perspective. (See also historiography.) Herstory came about during the 1970s and 1980s, when some started to see the study of history as male-dominated intellectually.
	How far can 'herstory' be seen as a means of adequate compensation for this? To what extent is herstory an infusion of education with ideology, at the expense of knowledge? How far does the concept of 'herstory' enable progress?
	History, Language, Politics
Heuristics	An approach to problem-solving based on experience which encourages the use of the best solution we have, even if it is not perfect or optimal. Some might describe heuristics as mental shortcuts which make it easier for us to make decisions; these could also be classed as educated guesses.
	In what ways could heuristics lead to bias?
	Knowledge and the knower
Hierarchy	A formal or informal system ranking individual members or organizations according to status/ power or authority/expertise.
	How do we know what causes some beings/entities to have higher status than others? How do we know if a hierarchy is justified?
	Human sciences
Hierarchy of evidence	A structure that shows or suggests how some evidence may be more useful or important than others. The hierarchy of evidence consists of (from least to most important/useful): opinions or background information; individual case studies; cohort studies; randomized controlled trials; metastudies and systematic reviews.
	Who decides what evidence is most important or useful, and how? To what extent can the hierarchy of evidence change?
	Human sciences, Natural sciences
Hinder	To get in the way of something else; to make it difficult for someone to do something, or for something to happen.
	How far do language barriers hinder communication? How do we know what aids and hinders communication? How might this affect the development of our knowledge?
	Language

Hindsight bias

People's tendency to see past events as having been more predictable than they actually were.

"I always knew it was a bad idea!"

How might hindsight bias affect our decision-making? To what extent might the hindsight bias be dangerous? How do we know whether we are experiencing it? How far can the hindsight bias be avoided?

Human sciences

Historiography

The study of how history is written.

"Civil War historiography used to focus mainly on military aspects, which is less the case today."

How can we assess the reliability of various histories of the world?

History, Language, Politics

History

The past, or the study of it. (See also alternative histories, herstory, historiography.)

How can we distinguish, if at all, between history and historiography? How can we make sure all histories are told with equal exposure? To what extent might we consider this a desirable outcome? What role(s) might 'official' histories play? What are some possible benefits and pitfalls of these?

History, Politics

Hobo-Dyer projection

A way of presenting a map of the world which preserves area rather than scale, which means the landmasses appear the size that they actually are. (See also Mercator projection, Robinson projection.) The Hobo Dyer projection initially came printed on two sides – one side had north at the 'top', while the other had south at the top. This was meant to challenge perceptions of which side should be 'up' and 'down'.

How can we decide what an 'accurate' view of the world looks like? Why might different groups of people favour different map projections?

Human sciences

Holistic

1. Taking the view that all of the parts of something are interconnected and that you cannot discuss just one part of it without referring to the whole.
2. In medicine, this involves treating the whole person, including mental and social factors, rather than just symptoms of a disease.

For instance, holistic ecology treats humans and the environment as a single system.

To what extent is a holistic approach useful? How far can we distinguish individual factors from a whole entity?

Natural sciences

Holophrastic indeterminacy

The idea that the process of translation is indeterminate – that it is not possible to construct a unique translation that is 'better' than any other.

How far is it possible to reduce or eliminate holophrastic indeterminacy by living among and observing the people whose language you are trying to translate? How do we know what makes a 'good' translation?

Human sciences, Language

Human sciences

Also known as social sciences, human sciences are fields of academic study that base their research on how people interact. Human sciences include, but are not limited to, law, psychology, sociology, anthropology, and economics.

How do we decide what counts as a human science (some would argue, for instance, that economics is a branch of mathematics, or that psychology is a natural science)? To what extent are such categorizations of fields of study useful? In addition, many of the examples and definitions in this book are tied to human sciences as a category (even if alongside others). How far can we say that the construction of personal knowledge is dependent on our interactions with others?

Human sciences

| Humanism | The belief that human matters are more important than divine or supernatural matters. Humanists might see the advancement of the human race as being dependent on aspects such as criticism, discussion, open communication, and unforced consensus, rather than on divine elements. |

To what extent do we require a belief in a God or gods to satisfy our spiritual needs? How do we decide what we believe about life's purpose? How far is humanism incompatible with other belief systems?

Religious knowledge

| Humanity | The human race; also, the qualities that make us human, such as the ability to love, or to show understanding towards others. |

How do we decide what humanity is? How far might some qualities of humanity be transferable to other species (especially those considered highly intelligent, such as primates)? To what extent does our use of technology affect our humanity?

Human sciences, Natural sciences, Technology

| Humility | Having a modest view of your own importance. |

Not all people have the humility to admit when they are wrong.

Why might humility be important to our study of epistemology? What dangers might exist in being too humble?

Human sciences

| Hunch | A feeling or a guess, based on intuition. Scientists might begin with a hunch and then begin gathering data to prove or disprove it. |

How can we know what a hunch is based on, and whether or not it is reliable? What might be some differences between a hunch and a guess? To what extent can hunches be considered evidence?

Knowledge and the knower

| Hypothesis | A proposed explanation, made based on some limited evidence, as a basis for further investigation; a statement that can be proved or disproved. An example of a hypothesis might be that watching too much TV decreases your ability to concentrate. |

What methods can you use to prove a hypothesis? How do we know whether the results of our experiment support our hypothesis? And how do we know whether or not our hypothesis is valid in the first place?

Human sciences, Natural sciences

| Hypothetical imperative | When our motivation comes not from duty but from our desire to achieve a certain goal. (See also categorical imperative.) |

Hypothetical imperatives tell us how to act so that we can achieve a specific goal, with reason applying only on certain conditions (eg "I must study hard in order to get a degree.") To what extent do hypothetical imperatives have moral worth? In what situations might hypothetical imperatives prove problematic?

Knowledge and the knower

IA prompt	The 36 IA prompts are published by the IB in the TOK guide, and you need to choose one of them to base your TOK exhibition on. *Who decides on what the IA prompts are, and how? What makes a 'good' IA prompt? How do you know which IA prompt to choose?* Knowledge and the knower
Idealised	1. Something or someone regarded or represented as perfect, or as better than what it/they really is/are. This is common in the arts but can also happen in real life. 2. In the sciences, idealisation might take place when scientific models assume facts about the phenomenon being modelled; these are technically false, but make models easier to solve or understand. *For what reasons might we idealise something? What biases might these reasons reveal? How do we know when we are idealising something or someone? What might be some benefits, and/or some pitfalls, of scientific idealisation?* The Arts, Human sciences, Natural sciences
Identify	To establish or indicate who or what something or someone is. For instance, you might identify as a feminist, or choose to identify closely with a particular event or cause (such as a protest). In a court of law, witnesses may not always be identified, being referred to using epithets such as Boy A; this is to protect them. *How do we know whether we have reliably identified something or someone? What may be some ethical implications of revealing what we have identified? To what extent can what we have identified change over time?* Human sciences, Politics
Identity	The qualities, beliefs, personality, looks and/or expressions that make a person or group what they are. *What gives us a sense of identity? What might cause us to lose our identities? To what extent is our identity fully discoverable? How do we truly know who we 'really' are?* Human sciences
Identity-prejudicial credibility deficit	When what someone says is taken less seriously than it should be because of a factor key to someone's identity, such as their race, gender, class, or age. When identity-prejudicial credibility deficit happens, individuals are given less credibility due to stereotypes. *What are some possible ethical implications of identity-prejudicial credibility deficit? What might the opposite – a credibility excess – involve? How might this affect the information we receive?* Human sciences, Politics
Ideology	A system of ideas, ideals and principles; a set of beliefs, especially held by an organization. For instance, someone's ideology may be very influential to a large group. *How can we judge what an ideology is based on, as well as whether it is beneficial or dangerous?* Human sciences
If	On the condition that; in the event that; despite; regardless of. "Even if it takes me seven years, I will do it." Conditional words like 'if' imagine what might happen. *How far is this imaginative or hypothetical exploration of ideas useful to the development of our personal and shared knowledge?* Language
If-by-whiskey fallacy	This fallacy means the opinion of the speaker is dependent on the opinion of those listening to them. Both sides are presented so that multiple opinions can be covered, without the speaker committing to one view over the other. (See also doublespeak.) "If by whiskey you mean the devil's brew that destroys the home, then certainly I am against it. If by whiskey you mean the oil of conversation and warm glow of contentment, then I am certainly for it." *How far can knowledge be created by 'sitting on the fence' (ie not committing to an opinion) in this way? To what extent can politicians be accused of deception through hedging their bets (supporting both sides) in this way?* Language, Politics

Ignorance	A lack of knowledge, education or information.
	How can we decide whether ignorance is accidental or wilful? To what extent can ignorance be considered bliss? How far can ignorance be remedied?
	Human sciences
Ignore	To refuse to take notice of or acknowledge; to intentionally disregard; to fail to consider something significant.
	How do we know whether we can legitimately ignore or leave out information?
	Knowledge and the knower
Illusion	A vision of something that is not really there; when your senses (especially sight) deceive you. For example, one famous optical illusion looks like a duck when viewed one way, but like a rabbit when viewed in another way.
	Who are some famous examples of creators of optical illusions? For what reasons might artists and magicians create optical illusions? For what reasons do we believe in them, and want to believe in them? To what extent do optical illusions counteract our search for knowledge?
	Human sciences, Natural sciences
Illusory	Not real; based on illusion. An illusory inference is when you jump to the wrong conclusion because you have not thought through all the possibilities; in psychology, illusory superiority is when you think you are better than others.
	What might be some possible implications of making illusory inferences, or of illusory superiority? How do we know when or if they are illusory, especially in ourselves?
	Human sciences
Illusory truth effect	Also known as the illusion-of-truth effect, this is the tendency to believe that false information is correct after being exposed to it multiple times. The illusory truth effect can also take effect even if we have only encountered part of a statement before.
	How do we come to believe information that might be misleading or unknown? What role might the illusory truth effect play in our cognitive processes? To what extent can familiarity overpower rationality?
	Human sciences
Imagination	The ability to create ideas or images in one's head when these are not physically present or happening.
	How far can evidence of imagination be reliably produced? To what extent is our imagination to be trusted? What is the role of imagination in the creation of artwork? What are some possible intersections between imagination and memory as ways of knowing?
	Knowledge and the knower
Imbalance	Being out of proportion or equilibrium; lacking stability or equality. For instance, there can be significant economic imbalances between countries.
	How can we detect an imbalance between people or places? To what extent can imbalances be resolved? What methods might we use in order to try to achieve this?
	Human sciences, Politics
Impact	The effect or influence on something or someone. For example, high interest rates usually have an impact on retail spending.
	How do we know whether something has really had an impact on something else, or just appears to have done so? How do we judge whether an impact is positive or negative? How do we know if something has had an impact on us personally? How might this link to different ways of knowing?
	Knowledge and the knower
Impartiality	Fairness; equal treatment; neutrality. Entries to competitions are sometimes submitted anonymously to help ensure impartiality in the judging process.
	To what extent is it possible to be fully impartial in our approach?
	Human sciences

Impede	To delay, prevent, obstruct or hinder someone (from carrying out what they wish to do) or something (from happening).
	What factors may impede the transmission of knowledge?
	Knowledge and the knower
Impinge	'To impinge on' something means to have a negative effect on it. For example, things may happen in our houses that we do not notice – for example, on the roof – until they impinge on areas that we can experience. Courts can also decide if a bill impinges on fundamental human rights, such as the right to free speech.
	How far does the right to free speech impinge on other rights? How can we tell if one right is impinging on another? How does the use of our senses impinge on what we know and don't know? To what extent do non-epistemic issues impinge on knowing, and knowledge?
	Knowledge and the knower
Implication	Consequence; something that may happen as a result; conclusions that can be drawn from an idea even if they are not explicitly stated.
	How far are implications objective and factual? What are some possible implications of epistemology/TOK itself?
	Knowledge and the knower
Implicit	Suggested, but not directly expressed. For example, our comments might be seen as implicit criticisms of something, even if we do not say outright what we do not like about it.
	How can we tell what somebody might be implying through their words or actions? How far does implicit information advance our search for knowledge?
	Human sciences, Language
Imposter syndrome	Believing you are not as competent as others think you are. (See also **Dunning-Kruger effect**.)
	Many high-achieving people suffer from imposter syndrome. What does imposter syndrome show us about possible gaps between appearance and reality, or the perception of them? How can we ascertain where imposter syndrome might come from?
	Human sciences
in dubio pro reo	Latin for '[when] in doubt for the accused', meaning that you cannot convict someone of a crime if there are still doubts about their guilt.
	In dubio pro reo might be more commonly phrased as 'innocent until proven guilty'; when assessing evidence in criminal cases, judges must interpret doubts in the accused's favour, so that either a less serious offence is presumed or the accused is acquitted (deemed not guilty/ free to go).
	What are some possible moral implications of being innocent until proven guilty?
	Human sciences
Include	To contain as part of a whole (text, object, group, etc).
	For example, we might decide to include both infants and older children in a scientific study. How do we decide what information to include, and what to leave out? What are some possible consequences of this? How does the deliberate inclusion or exclusion of people or groups affect the development of knowledge? How far is it possible, or desirable, to include everything and/or everybody?
	Knowledge and the knower
Incomplete	Not having all of the necessary or appropriate parts or information.
	How far is it possible to have complete understanding? How do we know if information is incomplete? What might be some possible implications of incomplete knowledge?
	Knowledge and the knower
Inconclusive	Not leading to a firm result; not ending doubt or dispute. For example, an experiment's inconclusive results might mean that scientists cannot tell whether an artefact is genuine or not.
	How can we tell whether results are inconclusive? How can, or should, we interpret inconclusive results? What might be some possible implications of these? To what extent is human interaction inconclusive? Why is it still important to report inconclusive results?
	Human sciences, Natural sciences

Incongruous	Does not fit in with its surroundings; unexpected. For instance, it might seem incongruous to have a woman editing a men's fashion magazine. In comedy, the theory of incongruity explains why we find unexpected phrases, answers, or events funny.
	How can we tell whether or not something is incongruous? To what extent is congruity ('fitting in') important? How do we know what causes some incongruities to be funny, and not others?
	The Arts, Human sciences, Politics
Incremental	Relating to gradual changes, especially increases. For example, incremental changes in an experiment's independent variables, and their immediate effects on the dependent variable, can be used as the basis for projections over time.
	How might we detect incremental changes? How far is this possible? How can we determine the causes of incremental changes?
	Natural sciences
Indefeasibility condition	When a claim has no evidence to defeat or challenge it, it can be said to satisfy the condition of indefeasibility. If something is indefeasible, we are sure that all doubts and objections have been attended to.
	How far is true indefeasibility possible?
	Knowledge and the knower
Independent	Free from outside control; uninvolved; not subject to authority; self-governing; thinking or acting for oneself. For instance, independent advisers can be brought in to resolve conflicts between people or groups. If you are an independent thinker, you filter information in your own way, to help inform your thoughts.
	How far is it possible to be a truly independent thinker or party? To what extent are questions the key to independence? How can independent thinking skills be developed? How far is this cultural?
	Human sciences
Indeterminacy of reference	The idea that when translating single words, we try to determine what exactly a certain word is referring to, and that our answer will always be relative to our own background language. This means that a translation will always be naturally flawed.
	Some would argue that many terms are referentially indeterminate – meaning there is no factual basis for what they mean.
	How far can the indeterminacy of reference be avoided? To what extent can we establish the existence of this indeterminacy altogether?
	Language
Indigenous	Originating or occurring naturally in a particular place; native.
	How can we decide who the indigenous people of a population are? Given that many indigenous populations rely on oral histories, how might determining such a thing become problematic? How can we successfully and respectfully define indigenous values? How far can indigenous peoples be described as subaltern?
	Human sciences, Indigenous knowledge
Indirect realism	Also known as representationalism, this is the idea that we do not and cannot perceive the world as it really is – that is, we only experience perceptions or representations of the world, which vary from person to person and cannot be objective.
	For example, some people might see colour differently to others. The viral 'The dress' phenomenon is one example of this: https://en.wikipedia.org/wiki/The_dress
	How far does the theory of indirect realism lead to scepticism about the nature and existence of the external world? How can we decide whether this is a good or bad thing? What are some possible differences between sensing and knowing? How can we assess the reliability of sense data? To what extent do direct realism and indirect realism represent a false dichotomy?
	Natural sciences
Individual	Single or separate; striking, unusual, or original. For instance, depending on their species, animals might live as individuals or in groups.
	How far does, and should, epistemology focus on individual knowers? What implications do individual differences in reasoning have for rationality? To what extent can individuals be reliably compared? How far is experience independent from individual thought?
	Human sciences, Natural sciences

Individuation

The achievement of a sense of individuality, and the process of achieving this, especially in terms of what makes us distinct from other members of the group we belong to. Also, the general idea of how a thing is identified as an individual thing that 'is not something else'. (See also self-actualization.)

How far is individuation achievable? What methods could we use to help work this out?

Human sciences

Indoctrination

The process of teaching a person or group to accept a set of beliefs uncritically.

"Some people believe that children should not be subjected to religious indoctrination."

How can we distinguish beliefs and practices we have been brought up with (eg meat-eating) from indoctrination?

To what extent do our parents indoctrinate us? How can we know if we are being, or have been, indoctrinated? What are some possible ethical implications of indoctrination?

Knowledge and the knower

Inductive reasoning

A process of reasoning whereby we can use specific examples and experiences to come up with a general truth. (See also deductive reasoning.)

An example of inductive reasoning would be if a teacher notices that his students learn more when hands-on activities are incorporated into lessons. He therefore decides to include a hands-on component in his future lessons regularly.

What might be some problems with inductive reasoning? To what extent can we achieve a more reliable and successful result by relying on a combination of inductive and deductive reasoning?

Knowledge and the knower

Inevitable

Certain to happen; unavoidable. If a study is particularly complex, some might say it is inevitable that some information will be left out.

How can we tell if something is inevitable? To what extent is life itself an inevitable, deterministic series of events? How can we know whether or not this is the case (if indeed we can)?

Human sciences, Religious knowledge

Infallibilism

The idea that a proposition is supported by such strong evidence that it cannot possibly be wrong. Infallibilists might say that you can rationally justify fallible beliefs, but that these do not count as knowledge unless evidence proves them to be absolutely true.

Must all of our justifications be infallible in order to achieve knowledge? To what extent can infallibilism be arrived at via faith or intuition, instead of reason? How far is it possible for us, as imperfect humans, to believe infallibly?

Knowledge and the knower

Inference

1. The process of working out what someone is suggesting when they have not said so directly; reaching conclusions based on evidence and reasoning.
2. In mathematics, Bayesian inference is when you update the probability for a hypothesis as more information or data becomes available.

For instance, we draw inferences from data in the sciences and in mathematics.

How do we know if what we have inferred is correct? What might be some methods of checking this? In mathematics, how do we know that our processes of inferences are not subjective? What are some possible risks of Bayesian inference? How might these affect our search for knowledge?

Language, Mathematics, Natural sciences

Inferior

Lower in status, quality or rank than other similar things.

"I would never lend my name to an inferior product."

How can we judge what causes feelings of inferiority in a person? How do we know if one product or performance is inferior to another? Are some forms of knowledge inferior to others? How do we know?

Human sciences

Infinitism	The idea that knowledge can be justified with an infinite chain of reasons. (See also foundationalism.) Infinitism is similar to when toddlers ask 'why?' in response to every answer you give to questions they have asked.
	How far does reasoning improve the justification of a belief? What are some possible problems with an infinitist approach? To what extent might infinitism be considered humans' natural or default state?
	Knowledge and the knower
Influence	The ability to affect someone's behaviour or development, or the effect itself. For example, we might consider that we are greatly influenced by our parents, or our parents might consider that a friend of ours is a bad influence on us.
	How do we know whether influence is a positive or negative thing?
	Human sciences
Inform	To let someone know something; to give somebody facts about something. (See also disinformation, misinformation.)
	How can we 'best' inform, or communicate knowledge to, others? How do we know whether we have been fully informed?
	Language
Information	Facts provided or learned about something or someone. (See also information bias.)
	How do we know whether we can trust information we have been given? How can we judge whether the information we have is useful or not? What is the relationship between information and knowledge? How do we know what to do with imperfect information?
	Human sciences, Language
Information bias	Also called observation bias or measurement bias, this is any difference from the truth that occurs in the collection, recording, and handling of data in a study, including how missing data is dealt with.
	Examples of information bias in medicine could be incomplete medical records, recording errors in a patient's medical history, misinterpreting symptoms, or patients completing questionnaires incorrectly (because they don't understand the question or don't accurately remember the correct response).
	To what extent can information bias be avoided? What might be some methods of doing so? What are some possible consequences of information bias? How do self-selection and self-reporting affect information bias?
	Mathematics, Natural sciences
Inherent	Permanent, essential, inbuilt, or characteristic.
	Extreme sports have inherent dangers.
	How do we know if an idea, design, product or person has an inherent flaw or contradiction embedded in it? What ethical questions might be inherent in our study of epistemology?
	Knowledge and the knower
Innate	Indicating something you are born with; deriving from the mind or intellect rather than experience.
	How do we know whether something is innate or learned? What are some possible advantages and pitfalls of innate qualities? To what extent might our innate qualities be changeable? How far are we 'blank slates', as opposed to being born with certain knowledge or abilities already?
	Natural sciences
Inquirer	If you are an inquirer, you are naturally curious and want to find things out. According to the IB learner profile, inquirers learn enthusiastically, are lifelong learners, and know how to learn both independently and with others.
	How do we know if we are good inquirers? To what extent is lifelong learning important? How do we know if we are independent learners? How far is it possible, necessary or important to always learn enthusiastically?
	Knowledge and the knower

I

Inquiry

Also spelled 'enquiry', this refers to a question or questions you are trying to answer. Often used in the phrase 'line of inquiry' to mean a whole argument. An inquiry is also an official attempt to establish the facts about something. For example, citizens might demand a legal inquiry into how governments have handled a major crime or event.

How can we decide on the 'best' methods to use when carrying out an inquiry? How do we know whether a legal inquiry is necessary? What does it mean to have a sense of inquiry? If the goal of inquiry is truth, or something resembling it, how far is this achievable?

Human sciences

Insightful

Having accurate and deep understanding; showing original ideas that make people think.

In order to gain high marks in the TOK essay and exhibition, you need to be insightful.

How far can insight be developed, as opposed to being a natural ability that you either have or don't have? How do we know whether somebody is being insightful or not? To what extent can we, as imperfect humans, gain 'true' insight into the nature of knowledge itself?

Knowledge and the knower

Insurmountable

Describing something that is too big to be overcome, especially a problem.

If you are determined enough, can it be said that "nothing is insurmountable"?

How can we decide whether or not this is true? How do we know what, if anything, counts as an insurmountable obstacle?

Human sciences

Intangible

Unable to be seen or touched; not present physically. For instance, charisma might be considered an intangible quality.

How do we know whether something is really intangible, or whether our senses are just not subtle enough to detect its presence? If something is intangible, how far can we know what it really is?

Human sciences, Natural sciences

Integral

Necessary in order to complete something else/make it whole. For instance, microchips are an integral part of modern cars.

How do we know whether something is an integral part of something else?

Technology

Integrity

Honesty; relating to strong moral principles.

How do we preserve the cultural integrity of communities? How far is this possible or desirable? How can we tell whether something, or someone, has integrity? Are there situations in which we might suffer for our integrity, and if so, how might we know what these are? How can we judge whether it is best to uphold integrity at all costs?

Human sciences

Intellectual

1. Relating to the brain and our cognitive skills. (Adjective)

2. A person of high intelligence who engages in critical thinking and reasoning. (Noun)

"She is a real intellectual who can study anything that she wants to when she goes to university." "He needs intellectual stimulation in order to do well."

To what extent can 'intellect' be deemed a scientific term, and to what extent a cultural one? How do we decide what is intellectual and what is not? How far is intellect active, and how far is it passive? How do we know?

Human sciences, Natural sciences

Intellectual property

Intangible property that is the result of creativity, such as copyrights or patents. For instance, remakes of older films can be said to be based on existing intellectual property.

How far does intellectual property enable creativity, and how far does it stifle it? How far is it possible to legally protect our ideas?

The Arts, Human sciences

Intelligence

The ability to acquire and apply knowledge and skills.

How can we measure individual intelligence? How can we decide whether one person is more intelligent than another? To what extent can we judge whether intelligence is something we are born with, or something we can develop, or both? How far is intelligence static? How might different cultures view intelligence differently?

Human sciences, Natural sciences

Intelligible

Detectable; able to be understood. It could be said that good writers make complex ideas intelligible to the average reader.

How can we judge whether something is intelligible? What might be the importance of emotional intelligibility in our quest for knowledge? How can we ensure mutual intelligibility among speakers from different cultures?

Language, Human sciences

Intention

Something that is intended; an aim or a plan.

"It wasn't my intention to exclude her from the list – I just forgot her."

How far can an author's intentions determine the meaning of a text? What role do readers' assumptions about writers' intentions play in our understanding of a text? How can we truly judge what somebody's intentions are?

The Arts, Language, Human sciences

Interact

To work or communicate with others; for multiple elements in a process to affect others. For example, children typically enjoy interacting with each other. In the natural sciences, we can observe how different chemicals interact.

How do we know if an interaction is positive or negative? How do we know what effects different elements in a process are having on others? How do we decide what type of interactions are beneficial? To what extent do interactions with others assist us in our search for knowledge?

Human sciences, Natural sciences

Interchangeable

Can be swapped or exchanged easily without consequence; appearing to be identical or very similar.

How do we know whether certain ideas, words or objects are interchangeable? To what extent might this be culturally dependent? What might be some benefits or limitations of interchangeable words, objects or ideas? How do we know what these are?

Language

Intercultural

Taking place between cultures, or coming from multiple cultures.

What aspects of a culture do you think it is essential to know about? How might this vary between different people? What is the relationship between culture and perception? How might the differing worldviews of diverse cultures present challenges for intercultural communication? Do you feel you know enough about your own culture to enable intercultural understanding? How do we decide what 'our own' culture is?

Human sciences, Indigenous knowledge

Interdependence

Two or more organizations or people relying equally on one another. For example, the interdependence of aspects such as age, time period and cohort might make it mathematically very difficult to separate out the effects of each one.

How can we tell whether interdependence is truly present? How far can interdependence be judged to be a positive quality? How might interdependent factors affect the quality of our research?

Knowledge and the knower

Interdisciplinary

Relating to more than one branch or field of knowledge.

"She favours an interdisciplinary approach in her teaching of English."

How far is it possible to put boundaries between different disciplines? What might be some advantages or problems of an interdisciplinary approach in the search for knowledge? What might be some methodological and cognitive barriers? To what extent are certain practices firmly domain-specific?

Knowledge and the knower

Intergenerational

Relating to, involving, or affecting multiple generations of a group or family. If a piece of technology is described as intergenerational, for instance, it has the ability to improve the situation and quality of life for all people.

How do we know whether the youth can learn from the elderly, and vice versa? How far does language learning rely on intergenerational transmission? What challenges and opportunities might pervade the process of intergenerational learning?

Human sciences, Language, Technology

Internal assessment

An assessment in the IB programme that is marked by your teacher, with the marks then being checked/moderated by IB officials to ensure that they are accurate.

Your TOK exhibition is an example of an internal assessment.

How can we establish the possible advantages and disadvantages of this method of assessment?

Knowledge and the knower

Internalism

The idea that our own desires and beliefs, and other qualities internal to ourselves (whether physical or mental), are sufficient reasons for action, and that facts and the environment alone cannot provide this. (See also externalism.)

Internalism means that knowledge is grounded by your own experience and by your own ability to reason: internalists might say that if you can't see for yourself why you should believe something, you don't actually know it.

To what extent is internalism completely separate from external realities? What might be some possible advantages and disadvantages of this perspective?

Human sciences

Internal validity

Internal validity refers to how well a study is conducted – it gives us confidence that the effects we observe can be attributed to the intervention or program, not other factors. For instance, for an experiment to have accurate internal validity, participants might need to have no other health problems apart from the one being observed.

How do we know whether a study has internal validity?

Human sciences, Mathematics, Natural sciences

Interpretation

Explaining the meaning of something; someone's individual understanding of an idea or situation; an artist's representation of an existing artwork. For example, we can say that an action is open to a number of interpretations, or that our interpretation of data adds meaning to the information we have and helps us to draw conclusions.

How far is it possible to eliminate bias when interpreting data? How do we choose what methods to use to help us interpret data? To what extent can interpretation be objective? How far does this matter? To what extent do individual interpretations help us to advance our collective knowledge? How do we know if our interpretation of a given situation is correct?

The Arts, Language, Mathematics, Natural sciences

Intrinsic

Belonging naturally to something; essential to something; in and of itself.

How far should we judge objects and people by their artistic, emotional, intellectual and spiritual (what might be called intrinsic) value, as opposed to their extrinsic value (what those qualities are worth in material terms, or outward usefulness, such as advancing your career or what you can sell something for)? How do we know if there is a correlation between intrinsic and extrinsic value? To what extent is knowledge intrinsically valuable, regardless of what we can/do use it for?

The Arts, Human sciences

Introspection

Thinking about your own emotional and mental processes in depth. (adjective: introspective)

How do you know whether your assessment of yourself, or situations you have found yourself in, are accurate? How far does this matter? To what extent can introspection be judged the most valuable way of knowing yourself? What might be some possible limits of introspection? What is the role of bias in introspection? How far does introspection help us to develop self-knowledge?

Human sciences

| Intuition | Understanding something by instinct, in a way that does not need conscious reasoning; knowing something 'naturally', without having been taught it. |

"I can't explain how I knew – I just had an intuition that you'd been involved in an accident."

If you have no clear evidence one way or the other, do you have to base your judgment on intuition? How do we know whether our intuitions are correct? What might be some situations in which our intuition is the most valuable source of knowledge? What might be some risks based on 'knowing' by intuition? How far does intuition further our knowledge overall? Intuition is not measurable and demonstrable; how far does this diminish its value as a way of knowing?

Human sciences

| Invaluable | Extremely useful; essential. For example, a person or place can be described as an invaluable source of information. |

How do we judge the value of something or someone? How do we know whether our valuations are accurate? To what extent does this matter?

Human sciences

| Invisible | Cannot be seen. For example, carbon monoxide is an invisible gas. |

How can we prove the presence or existence of something if it is invisible (such as a gas, love, or God)? How do you make an invisible problem visible?

Mathematics, Natural sciences, Religious knowledge

| ipso facto | By that very fact, or by that very act; as such; by default; by definition; therefore. |

"The enemy of your enemy may be ipso facto a friend."

What are some possible advantages of something being ipso facto true, or being able to say that it is? How far might the ipso facto principle be deemed a form of jumping to conclusions without sufficient evidence? How do we decide or know if something is ipso facto true?

Knowledge and the knower

| Is-ought problem | A fallacy when we believe that when things are a certain way, it is because they should be that way; or, conversely, that if something is not happening now, this means it should not occur. |

One example of the is-ought problem could be:

"We do not currently regulate the amount of nicotine in an individual cigarette; therefore we need not do this."

If someone has knowledge of how the world is, how far does this mean they also have knowledge of how the world should be? How far is it possible to say how things should be based on how things are now?

Knowledge and the knower

| Issue | 1. A problem; an important topic that should be debated. (Noun) |

2. To give out; or, to result/come from. (Verb)

Charities exist to tackle various issues, including racism. You can also issue things to others, such as driver's licences.

When and how does an issue become philosophical in nature? How do we decide when something is actually an issue/problem, and when it is merely perceived as one? How do we decide who to issue information to, and when, and why?

Human sciences

| Iteration | Repeating a process or utterance; or, a previous version of something. |

For example, a friend of mine designed the current iteration of my logo for my private tuition business.

In TOK, epistemic iteration is when scientists revisit their knowledge claims to try to improve them.

How far does repeating a task enable us to improve our knowledge? How can we judge whether a new version of something is truly an improvement of the old version? At what point can we judge whether something has been through so many iterations that nothing of the original concept remains?

Knowledge and the knower

Jargon

Words specific to a particular profession that others from outside that profession find difficult to understand. When a writer's work is free of jargon, for example, they are not using a lot of technical terms that could prevent a wider readership from understanding it.

To what extent does jargon exclude people outside a group? How far is jargon used deliberately? How could we judge whether jargon has any particular advantages? To what extent does jargon make you look like, or make you into, an expert?

Language

Judgment

A decision; an opinion; an ability to come to a sensible conclusion. A mistake might be deemed 'an error of judgment'.

How far can our judgments be neutral? To what extent is this desirable? How could we judge whether human judgments, or judgments made by machines/artificial intelligence, are more effective? How do we know whether a judgment is morally correct?

Human sciences

Justice

Fairness; the legal authority, such as a court, responsible for maintaining fairness in our society. For example, if the winner of a race has been disqualified for cheating, it could be said that justice has been done.

How do we know what justice is, and/or whether or not it has been carried out? To what extent do ideas of justice vary? How far is the idea of justice compatible with religious belief?

Human sciences, Religious knowledge

Justification

The action of showing something to be right or reasonable; a good reason for something being right or wrong.

"There is no justification for an increase in charges."

How do we know if something is justified or not? Is it possible to ensure that a certain rule is 'right' without having to resort to justifications in an infinite spiral? What might be some differences between justification and evidence?

Knowledge and the knower

Justified true belief

A belief that you think you have solid justification/reasons for; to an outsider, these reasons would also seem valid and acceptable. However, a justified true belief can still turn out to be wrong. (See also Gettier problem.)

The idea of justified true beliefs allegedly give us the necessary and sufficient conditions for someone having knowledge.

Do we have to believe what we (think we) know? How do we know whether we can know something for sure? What differences might exist between belief and mere opinion?

Knowledge and the knower

Keyboard warrior

Someone who makes abusive or aggressive posts online, typically a person who hides their true identity.

How valuable is the anonymity of the internet? To what extent is it ethical or possible to identify users of the internet by their true names and identities?

Technology

KK thesis

The idea that if you know something, you know that you know it.

"The KK thesis suggests that knowers have self-knowledge, meaning that those who have no concept of the self – such as dogs or very small children – have no knowledge at all."

How do we know if this is plausible? How far is it possible to have knowledge that we are unaware of? What reasons might there be to accept, or reject, the KK principle? To what extent does the KK principle prove that knowledge is infallible?

Knowledge and the knower

Knock-on effects	Indirect effects following an initial action. For example, it could be said that the decline of bees could have multiple knock-on effects, including food shortages and higher food prices, as bees pollinate many plants that provide food for people.

How can we know what knock-on effects will occur as a result of a particular action? How can we assess the severity of possible knock-on effects? Is it possible or desirable to entirely eliminate knock-on effects?

Knowledge and the knower, Natural sciences

Knower

A person who knows, understands, or perceives ideas and information.

How far is it important to be a 'doer' and how does this compare with the importance of being a knower? To what extent is the relationship between the knower and the known a reciprocal one? How far are our knowledge claims consistent with our best psychological account of ourselves as knowers?

Knowledge and the knower

Knowledge

Facts, information and skills acquired through education and experience; the understanding of the theory and/or practices of a subject.

In what ways might our knowledge, and our acquisition of it, be limited? How do we decide how to use our knowledge?

Knowledge and the knower

Knowledgeable

If you are knowledgeable, you are able to retain lots of facts and ideas and apply them to different situations. According to the IB learner profile, learners are knowledgeable if they are developing and using their understanding, explore knowledge across a range of disciplines, and engage with ideas that are globally important.

How far is it necessary to engage across multiple areas of knowledge in order to be knowledgeable?

Knowledge and the knower

Knowledge claim

A statement that the knower – the person producing or saying the statement – believes to be true, even if that statement is wrong, cannot be checked, or has not been verified yet.

An example of a first-order knowledge claim might be "mammals cannot fly"; an example of a second-order knowledge claim might be "mathematical knowledge is always certain".

How could we assess whether or not these knowledge claims are true? How can we rationally criticize a knowledge claim? What makes a knowledge claim valuable?

Knowledge and the knower

Knowledge framework

Within TOK, a knowledge framework is a list of concepts that should be explored within each area of knowledge. The knowledge framework consists of four elements: ethics, methods and tools, perspective, and scope.

How do we decide if all of the elements of this knowledge framework are of equal importance? How might each of them improve or limit our search for knowledge? How far might such knowledge frameworks be considered too prescriptive?

Knowledge and the knower

Knowledge gaps

The pieces of information you do not have. The knowledge gap hypothesis puts forward that gaps in our knowledge are spread throughout society based on socio-economic status, meaning wealthier, more highly-educated people acquire information faster, making knowledge gaps even wider.

To what extent are knowledge, education and interest interdependent? How far is it possible to close a wide knowledge gap present in a society? To what extent can the internet close or widen knowledge gaps (in individuals and/or larger groups)?

Human sciences, Technology

Knowledge neglect

Knowledge neglect is when people fail to retrieve and apply previously stored knowledge appropriately into a current situation. (See also semantic illusion.)

If you have knowledge neglect, you have relevant information, but don't use it. A famous example of knowledge neglect is the question "How many of each animal did Moses bring onto his ark?". Many people will automatically answer 'Two', even though it was Noah, not Moses, who brought the animals onto the ark in the famous Bible story.

What might the role of knowledge neglect be in the context of misinformation, disinformation, and echo chambers? How can we detect how knowledge neglect occurs? To what extent does knowledge neglect have a cultural basis? Is knowledge neglect just 'not reading the question properly', or is there more to it?

Human sciences

Knowledge question (KQ)

A question about the nature of knowledge itself, rather than a question about specific content or situations. (See also first-order knowledge, second-order knowledge.)

Knowledge questions are characterized by being open – they do not have just 'yes' or 'no' answers. An example of a knowledge question might be "At what point does a belief become knowledge?"

The vast majority of the results on the first five pages of Google results when "knowledge question" is searched for are to do with TOK/this specific IB course.

What might this tell us about the phrase and its origins? To what extent can it be argued to 'exist' outside of the TOK context?

Knowledge and the knower, Technology

Knowledge system

1. An organization or structure of knowledge.

2. In computer science, an expert system.

A knowledge system could be within a society, culture, company, or even a machine.

"By 2040, digitalization will have transformed science, technology, research and education into a new integrated knowledge system, with abundant real-time and historic data accessible through AI devices, and education making extensive use of digital tools."

To what extent is defining knowledge systems dependent on the area of knowledge we are working in? How far does information about, and research into, cultural knowledge systems provide us with tools for translating cultural knowledge? What possible roles do knowledge systems play? What might be some of their limitations? How far do knowledge systems enable us to access knowledge?

Indigenous knowledge, Technology

Knowledge transfer

Sharing and disseminating information; providing input to problem-solving.

How do we judge whether knowledge transfers are useful? How do we know if knowledge transfers actually change our day-to-day practices? How far can the perspectives of the knowledge producer and knowledge user be balanced in the process of knowledge transfer? How can the usefulness of knowledge transfers be assessed?

Knowledge and the knower

Kuhn cycle

A cycle model describing how we progress our scientific knowledge, starting with 'normal science' (the foundation for scientific practice), followed by 'model drift' (the appearance of a problem or phenomenon that the existing system can't handle, which can be restored by a solution 'returning' the system to 'normal science'), 'model crisis' (when the problem cannot be solved), 'model revolution' (when new models or systems are created from trying to solve the crisis), and finally, a 'paradigm change' (also called a paradigm shift), where the new model of understanding (or paradigm) is taught to newcomers to the field. When accepted, this returns the field to a state of 'normal science', and the Kuhn cycle is thus completed.

"It is sometimes said that the Kuhn cycle challenged the world's previous conception of science, which worked on the basis that science was a steady progression of the accumulation of new ideas."

How do we know if one day the concept of the Kuhn cycle itself might not be challenged? What might be some possible problems with the Kuhn cycle?

Natural sciences

Language	Human communication through words, structured in a particular way, and conveyed through speech (including elements such as tone of voice), writing, or gesture (body language).
	Who decides when or whether a new word enters our language? How can we establish the possible goals of language? What are some possible intersections between language and other areas of knowledge? To what extent could language be considered the 'main' or 'ultimate' way of knowing? How far does linguistic competence require knowledge of language?
	Language, Politics
Law of excluded middle	The idea that any proposition in the form P vs non-P (ie a pair of statements) is true in one way or another. Any 'middle' possibility has been excluded. Unlike bivalence, it is mainly to do with how the idea of truth or 'not-truth' is structured, as opposed to the actual 'meaning' of truth. (See also bivalence, law of identity, law of non-contradiction.)
	For example, "Nigel is bald" implies the opposite proposition, "Nigel is not bald". Another example of the law of excluded middle is that a number is either even or not even; according to the law of excluded middle, one of these has to be true.
	What could be some problems with this way of thinking?
	Mathematics
Law of identity	The idea that everything in existence has a specific nature. Each entity exists as something in particular and it has characteristics that are a part of what it is. This can be formally expressed as $A = A$.
	We usually use adjectives to show an object's specific nature; for example, "This leaf is red, solid, dry, rough, and flammable." "This book is white, and has 312 pages." "This coin is round, dense, smooth, and has a picture on it."
	How far does the law of identity mean that we have only one identity? To what extent is one object different to others of the same type (eg a particular species of hamster)? To what extent does reality have a definite nature?
	Human sciences, Mathematics, Natural sciences
Law of non-contradiction	The idea that two statements with opposite meanings cannot both be true at the same time.
	For instance, in the Fargo episode 'The Law of Non-Contradiction', the episode's main character is still the acting chief of police, even though she has already been demoted from the position, and tries to investigate a man that both is and isn't her stepfather. In Roald Dahl's *Charlie and the Chocolate Factory*, we are also told that 'the square sweets looked round'.
	How can we determine whether or not the law of non-contradiction has been broken? How can we decide whether this law of thought is valid in general?
	Knowledge and the knower
Leading question	A question phrased in such a way that it suggests what the answer should be, or encourages the answer that the questioner wants to hear; the phrasing of a leading question can also make the interviewee look guilty of something, even if they have not done it.
	A question such as "You were there last night, weren't you?" is a leading question, whereas "Were you there last night?" is not.
	How do we know if leading questions have been used? What are some possible ethical implications of using leading questions, particularly from a legal or scientific perspective?
	Human sciences
Legend	A traditional story, often regarded as historical, but usually not authenticated/verified as true.
	How do we differentiate between legend and truth? Why do legends arise? Is it possible or desirable to authenticate them, and for what reasons? How do we judge their value? To what extent is our society based on myth and legend? How far does it matter whether we believe in a particular legend as being true or not?
	The Arts, History, Language

Legitimate

Conforming to the law or rules; logically valid. For example, you can have a legitimate excuse for being late. If a document is legitimate, it is genuine/has been proved to be real.

Historically, births were recorded as illegitimate if the parents of the child were not married. In some countries and cultures this is still the case.

Who defines the idea of legitimacy, and how? In what ways might legal and societal legitimacy differ? How do we decide if something is legitimate or not? How might ideas of what is legitimate change over time?

History, Human sciences

Lens

A critical viewpoint through which an argument is analysed, influencing the ways in which we perceive, understand and evaluate the ideas involved. We might, for example, read a novel through different lenses, including feminist, psychoanalytical, or post-colonial.

What are some possible benefits, and pitfalls, to viewing a text through a particular critical lens? How may this approach refine or limit our search for knowledge?

The Arts, Language, History, Politics

Liar's paradox

When a liar states that he/she is lying. If a known liar says "I am lying", then we take this to be the truth; however, if they lie about everything, then they are lying about lying.

Are there any possible resolutions to the liar's paradox? How do we know? How far is it possible for the liar's paradox to exist in some languages but not others?

Human sciences, Language

Limitations

A restriction; a defect or failing; a limiting rule or circumstance.

How do we know what our own limitations are? How do we assess the limitations that exist in some of the research methods that we use – such as case studies, questionnaires, and interviews? In our search for knowledge, how do we know whether the limitations are present in the areas of knowledge, or in our ways of knowing, or both?

Knowledge and the knower

Linear

Progressing in a logical sequence; arranged or extending along a straight (or nearly straight) line. For example, we might conclude that a linear relationship exists between jet fuel cost and flight cost.

What methods can we use to help establish whether or not a linear relationship exists between two factors? To what extent is progress linear? If progress is not linear, how can we judge whether or not someone or something is improving?

Mathematics, Natural sciences

Link

A relationship or connection between two things, people or ideas. (See also causation, correlation.) For example, researchers might try to establish if there is a link between pollution and forest decline.

How can we establish whether a link between two things or ideas really exists? How do we know if it is in someone's interest to emphasize or downplay a real link that exists between two things or ideas?

Knowledge and the knower

Lip service

When you 'pay lip service' to something/to an idea, it means that what you say does not match up with what you actually do.

Why might people pay lip service to religion, or to other fundamental aspects of life, such as human rights? How do we know if somebody is genuinely involved/sincere, or just paying lip service to an idea? What are some possible ethical implications of only paying lip service to an idea?

Human sciences

Literacy	Basic reading and writing skills; competence or knowledge in a certain area.
	For example, we might nowadays say that computer literacy is essential, whereas in the 1980s or 1990s it might have just been considered a nice extra skill to have. Literacy rates more generally – showing the percentage of adults who are able to read and write to a reasonable level – can be one thing that lets us know how developed a country is.
	How do we know whether somebody is literate? To what extent can literacy be judged merely through the correct use of spelling and grammar? How can we work out what causes literacy problems? How far are literacy and epistemology separate? Why might digital or media literacy, in particular, be important to our study of TOK?
	Language, Technology
Literal	Basic or usual; without metaphor, exaggeration, or hidden meaning. In translation, the exact words of the original text, rather than just the general sense of them.
	For example, we might say when studying *The Great Gatsby* that the green light has a symbolic meaning throughout the text, going beyond its literal function. When translating a text, we might also say that an idiom, such as 'it's brass monkeys out there', cannot be translated literally. Someone might be described as taking instructions too literally if, when told to 'pull their socks up', they actually pulled their socks up; as opposed to following the non-literal meaning of the phrase, meaning 'to work harder'.
	How do we know if we have taken something too literally? How can we detect whether a writer has only used a literal meaning, or whether they have gone beyond this to add other layers of meaning? What are some possible advantages and disadvantages of literal, or word-for-word, translation?
	The Arts, Language
Locus	A place where something occurs or is situated. For example, we might say that the locus of power within a community lies with the church, or with the local council.
	How can we determine the locus of something? To what extent is TOK itself the locus of competence?
	Knowledge and the knower
Logic	The use of sound reasoning to reach a conclusion; the rules and processes used to achieve this. For instance, we might find it logical that someone should help us, since they helped us before. Some toys are also designed to teach children logical and problem-solving skills (for example, if they can work out how cogs in the toy help it to move).
	What are some possible strengths and weaknesses of logic as a way of knowing? To what extent can knowledge be accessed through a 'step-by-step', logical approach? How far is the human mind set up for rational thought? How does logic interact with other ways of knowing? Might there be situations in which information logically follows from a premise, but is still wrong?
	Mathematics
Logical positivism	The idea that scientific knowledge is the only type of factual knowledge; or, a viewpoint committed to verification (the ability to check facts).
	How far does logical positivism help us to advance our knowledge? How far is it possible to 'prove' something? To what extent can the idea of logical positivism itself be proved? How far does logical positivism allow for some forms of proof to be stronger than others? How can we establish what makes a form or area of knowledge 'unobservable' or 'unverifiable'? To what extent does every area of knowledge contain 'unobservables'?
	Natural sciences
Logos	Arguments based on reason, facts, and statistics, as opposed to emotions or the speaker's moral credibility. (See also ethos, pathos.)
	Logos (pronounced log-oss) is the Ancient Greek word for the use of logic in an argument to help persuade the listener. It often depends on the use of inductive or deductive reasoning; for example, the idea that fair trade agreements worked for one farmer, so might also work for others.
	How can we judge the effectiveness of logos as a tool of persuasion, especially relative to the impact of pathos or ethos? How do we know whether a speaker has provided complete and accurate information about an issue? To what extent can data fully support our claims?
	Human sciences, Language, Mathematics, Natural sciences, Politics

Loophole	When a small mistake in the law or a set of rules allows people to misbehave or act illegally/ wrongly. For example, it may not be allowed to send a certain foodstuff by post into another country. However, if someone is then able to bring that foodstuff to you in a box by car, this might be considered a loophole.

How far can technology and legal mechanisms close all existing loopholes in sets of rules and laws? What are some possible ethical implications of loopholes?

Human sciences, Technology |
| **Lucid** | Clear; easy to understand.

In order to gain full marks for your TOK essay and exhibition, one of the things they have to be is lucid.

How do we know whether we are expressing our arguments lucidly or not? What methods could we use to check if this is the case or not? In lucid dreams, the dreamer becomes aware that they are dreaming; how far are their perceptions of the dream reliable?

Human sciences, Language |
| **Ludic fallacy** | Mistaking the kind of uncertainty found in games for the same type of uncertainty experienced in real life.

An example of a ludic fallacy would be treating gambling on the stock market like a game with clearly defined rules and algorithms (like in a casino), whereas the real risk exists outside our spreadsheets and gamification of the process – in the real world where nobody knows the rules and you don't know which variables contribute to which result.

How far can we calculate odds in relation to real-life situations? For what reasons might the ludic fallacy be damaging? How can we judge the usefulness of simplified versions of real-world phenomena?

Human sciences, Mathematics |
| **Magical thinking** | The belief that unconnected events are in fact connected when there is no plausible evidence for this.

"If I use this mug, I'll have a good day!" "If I want it badly enough, it'll happen!" "If I restart my phone, that text I'm waiting for might arrive!"

For what reasons might people cling to what could be considered 'odd' rituals (such as having a 'lucky' hat)? How far can 'false confidence' caused by magical thinking help people to do well? To what extent might our own thoughts be genuinely connected to outside events? How far is prayer a form of magical thinking? Does it matter if we really believe magical thinking will affect outcomes? What are some possible downsides of magical thinking? What connections might exist between magical thinking and mental health disorders?

Human sciences |
| **Maladaptive** | Not adjusting appropriately to the environment or situation.

For instance, excessive alcohol consumption may be considered a maladaptive coping strategy. In evolution, it can be said that all organisms have maladaptive traits. Post-traumatic stress disorder may also be due to what can be called 'maladaptive' memories; how far can this knowledge be used to improve treatment outcomes for patients with PTSD?

How can we judge the possible causes of maladaptive behaviour? How do we know whether a trait of an organism is adaptive or maladaptive? To what extent is it possible or desirable to 'rewrite' maladaptive memories? How do we know whether a memory has been disrupted or altered (ie maladapted)?

Human sciences, Natural sciences |
| **Manifest** | 1. 'To make manifest' or 'to manifest itself' means 'to make clear or easy to notice'.

2. 'Manifest' can also be used as an adjective meaning 'clear' or 'obvious'.

For example, workers can manifest their dissatisfaction by striking. Illnesses can also manifest themselves through initially innocuous symptoms, such as stomach pains.

How do you decide on the best way(s) to make your ideas or feelings manifest? How far is our own knowledge manifest? How can medical personnel know if they are interpreting what appear to be manifest signs or symptoms correctly?

Human sciences, Natural sciences |

Manifesto	A document whereby a person or organization sets out their political beliefs, aims, or policies. Political parties, especially, send out manifestos before an election so that voters know what the party believes in.
	How do we know whether a manifesto truly reflects the motives and intentions of the person or group who has produced it? What are some possible implications of this for politics? What might be some possible limitations of manifestos?
	Language, Politics
Manipulation	1. Changing or influencing something, sometimes in such a way that a person does not know that they are being changed or influenced.
	2. Controlling or moving using the hands.
	People may argue, for instance, that the media manipulates the facts. On a more day-to-day basis, some medical treatments or specialities, such as osteopathy, involve massage and manipulation of the bones and joints.
	How do we know whether manipulation is beneficial, or damaging? What are some possible implications of manipulation from an ethical perspective (including medical ethics)?
	Language, Natural sciences, Politics
Many-valued logic	A form of logic in which there are more than two truth values. (See also bivalence.)
	Many-valued propositions have both a modal outcome ('yes', 'no', 'maybe'), and statements to do with probability.
	How do we decide which form(s) of many-valued logic might be most useful to us: three-valued logic (true/false/unknown), finite-valued logic (more than three values), or infinite-valued logic (in which 'truth' is a continuous range)?
	Mathematics
Marginalization	Treating a person, group or idea as unimportant. For instance, some might say that women are marginalized in the workplace.
	How do we know when/if people or communities are being marginalized? How can we overcome our own biases and prejudices so as to reduce marginalization? To what extent is the elimination or reduction of marginalization possible or desirable? How do we know whether our intervention in marginalized people's lives or communities is having a positive impact? How much power might we be taking away from marginalized people by collecting and holding data about them? What methods can be used to protect marginalized communities without disempowering them? If an individual does not recognize their life as marginalized, by what legitimacy can they be considered by others to be marginalized?
	Human sciences, Indigenous knowledge, Politics
Marxism	The idea that we live in a class-based world (eg of workers, of capitalists, of aristocrats), that this model exploits the workers (creating constant struggle between the classes), and that this needs to change to a more equal model.
	Marxism might be described as an idea of a world, and how people should live, where everyone shares everything equally, but some people argue that this is too complicated to actually put into place.
	To what extent has history been pushed forward by class struggles? How far does society develop based on people's material needs being met first? How can we decide whether a classless society is a desirable goal? How far can Marxism be described as a failed ideology?
	History, Politics
Material world	Anything to do with matter (a substance that has mass, and takes up space and volume); nature; the physical world. The material world can be quite a bleak place at times, making immaterial things (such as dreams) very appealing.
	What might the material world be able to offer us in our search for meaning? What are some of its possible limitations in helping us form meaning? How do human relationships with the material world help us create meaning? How can we judge whether the material world is eternal or ephemeral?
	Natural sciences

Materialism	1. The idea that all things, including mental states and consciousness, are based on matter and material interactions.
	2. The idea of putting material comfort and possessions above spiritual values.
	How do we judge the value of materialism? To what extent is materialism incompatible with religious belief? How far can physics and materialism account for life and consciousness? To what extent are we "a self-centred society, preoccupied by materialism"?
	Natural sciences, Religious knowledge
Mathematics	The science of number, quantity, and space, using reasoning and a system of symbols or rules in order to make calculations, either for its own sake (pure mathematics) or in relation to other subjects, like physics or engineering (applied mathematics).
	Some people would say that mathematics is the main tool through which we can understand the truth of the world.
	How far can it be argued that this is the case? What might be some weaknesses of mathematics as a tool for understanding the world around us? To what extent can mathematical proof be truly achieved? How far can mathematics be considered an empirical science (based on experience and observation)? How far is the theory that "everything is mathematics" (the theory of mathematicism) a valid one?
	Mathematics
Mathiness	The misuse of mathematics when analysing economics, mostly by making the maths seem more complicated than it needs to be by adding lots of extra elements, or because the language used to discuss the maths involved becomes disconnected from the maths itself. In short, adding or using maths in ways that are scientifically unsound.
	Some might say that mathiness hides unrealistic assumptions – or even just hypotheses – behind math, and therefore the use of math is more about politics than science in this situation.
	How far does mathiness cause the field of mathematics, or the field of economics, to lose credibility? To what extent does mathiness equal lying? What are some possible intersections between maths and politics? How far is it possible to 'match' maths with the words we use to express mathematical ideas? To what extent is it 'fair' to ask for 'better' writing from mathematicians?
	Language, Mathematics, Politics
May	A modal verb showing possibility; a wish or a hope; or that you are permitted to do something.
	"That may be true." "You may confirm my identity with your case officer, if you wish." "May she rest in peace."
	What might be some possible differences between using the word 'can', the word 'could', the word 'might', and the word 'may'? To what extent might these differences vary culturally? How do we know which word(s) is/are able to demonstrate more certainty?
	Language
Meaning	A definition of a word, concept or action; significance or purpose. For example, we might talk about the 'meaning' of a poem (as in how we interpret it), or a family heirloom having a special meaning for you.
	How do we decide whether something is meaningful? Is meaning necessarily subjective, or can it ever be objective? How do we know?
	The Arts, Language, Human sciences
Meaning holism	Also known as semantic holism, this is the belief that the meanings of all words in a language are dependent on each other.
	According to meaning holism, only whole languages have meanings, so smaller units have to take their meaning from that larger one.
	How far are the meanings of individual words stable on their own (as opposed to part of the entire language)? To what extent might a more atomistic approach (taking the meaning of each word as totally independent from others) be a more valid approach? How far do we all share the same beliefs about what words mean and how they work together in our everyday speech and writing?
	Language

Measure	To work out the size, amount or degree of something, using standard units (eg inches, kilograms).
	How can we measure intangible qualities, such as teaching ability? How do we decide when something is valuable enough to measure, and who decides this? How do we know whether or not we gain from measuring something quantifiably (in numbers)? How else can measurements of quality be taken? How do we know whether our chosen measurement method is reliable? How do we decide which measurement methods or tools to use, as well as when and why they are used? Who typically decides when, where, and how things are measured? What are some possible implications of this?
	Mathematics
Memory	The processes that are used to acquire, store, retain, and later retrieve information; a way of knowing that is reliant on our recall of things that happened in the past.
	"Dad has a selective memory: he remembers the times he was right and forgets the times he was wrong."
	To what extent are our memories reliable? What would be some potential pitfalls of having a perfect (or photographic) memory? How far does our memory help us to preserve knowledge? What functions do working memory, short-term memory and long-term memory have in the development of personal and shared knowledge?
	Human sciences, Natural sciences
Memory distortion	When your memory of an incident is different from what actually occurred. (See also **false memories**.) False recognition is a type of memory distortion when people say they have encountered an object or event (believing that they really did) when they have not.
	How far are memories exact records of events? Are memory distortions the reflection of deficient cognitive processing? Is the architecture of memory fundamentally flawed, allowing false memories to arise?
	Human sciences
Memory implantation	A psychological technique used to study memory, in which researchers put a memory into subjects' heads which did not actually happen.
	A famous example of memory implantation is when researchers successfully induced subjects to 'remember' taking a hot air balloon ride, supported by altered photographs, when they had not. Memory implantation techniques were developed to show how easy it is to distort people's memories of past events.
	What are some possible ethical implications of memory implantation? How do we know whether a memory has been implanted by others, or whether it is real? What are the possible roles of language and technology in memory implantation?
	Human sciences, Language, Technology
mens rea	Meaning 'guilty mind' in Latin, this is the mental element of a person's intention to commit a crime; or, knowledge that one's action or lack of action would cause a crime to be committed.
	How can mens rea (when someone knows what they are doing and still break the law anyway) be proven? Do all crimes require mens rea as a factor for conviction? How do we know? What are some possible ethical implications of this? How far is it possible to be morally innocent but legally guilty?
	Human sciences
Mercator projection	A type of map projection from the 16th century that is now one of the standard ways of mapping the world (as seen in textbooks, and so on), as it preserves the shape of countries accurately. (See also **Hobo-Dyer projection**, **Robinson projection**.)
	The Mercator projection was immediately popular because it made navigation easier. However, it also distorts size and distances as you get closer to the two poles.
	How far is it mathematically possible to translate the surface of a sphere onto a flat surface? When creating a map projection, how do cartographers (map-makers) know which qualities to distort and which to preserve? Is there such a thing as a single 'correct' map projection? How do we know whether, for instance, Greenland is the same size as Africa?
	Human sciences

Metacognition

Thinking about thinking; awareness and understanding of one's own thinking and learning processes. Metacognition happens when you are critically aware of your own thinking and learning, and of what you are like as a thinker and learner.

How far can we objectively analyse and control our own cognition? To what extent can we truly 'know ourselves'? How far does self-knowledge advance the cause of collective knowledge?

Knowledge and the knower

Metacriticism

Criticism of itself, or criticism of criticism.

A piece of metacriticism might focus on the works of various academics, or just one. How can we decipher the motives inherent in metacriticism? How far does metacriticism advance our search for knowledge? To what extent can metacriticism be free of bias? How far can metacriticism be seen as a purification, or corruption, of knowledge?

The Arts, Language

Metadata

Data that describe other data.

If you have metadata, you can find relevant data much more easily. Most searches are done like a Google search – using text – so you need text metadata available so that people can also search for other data formats, such as audio, images, and video. In this way, metadata explains exactly what the data – whether document or image or video or audio file – is about.

What are the possible benefits of hashtags and keywords in search engine optimization? What are some possible implications if they are improperly used? How do we know whether file names are an effective form of metadata?

Language, Technology

Metaepistemology

The study of the methods, aims, and subject matter of epistemology. If epistemology involves questions about how we should process knowledge, believe, and enquire, then metaepistemology can be said to question this.

What does it mean to claim that someone should do or believe something? Do such claims express beliefs about independently existing facts, or only approval and disapproval? How do putative facts about what people should do or believe fit into the natural world?

Knowledge and the knower

Metaknowledge

1. Knowledge about knowledge.
2. In artificial intelligence, a piece of data that describes the knowledge present in the world of AI.

Research into metaknowledge finds regularities in scientific claims, and infers the beliefs, preferences, research tools, and strategies behind those regularities. Metaknowledge research additionally looks into the effect of knowledge context on content.

How do we know what we know about knowledge? How far does metaknowledge enable us to reshape disciplines?

Technology

Metaphor

An image used to compare something with something else, often using the verb 'to be' (either written or said out loud, or merely suggested). The images or ideas of a map or a tree are often used as metaphors for knowledge.

How far do you feel these ideas/images represent knowledge accurately? To what extent can metaphors help us to advance our knowledge? In what situations might they impede understanding?

The Arts, Human sciences, Language

Metaphysics

A field of knowledge dealing with the first principles of things, such as being, knowing, identity, space, and time; a branch of physics studying the fundamental nature of reality.

Some think that the question of the initial conditions for the universe is part of the realm of metaphysics; others think this is the domain of religion.

How far is metaphysics an appropriate tool to advance our knowledge of the basics of existence? How far can the reason for the existence of the universe be ascertained? To what extent can religious knowledge fill in some of these gaps?

Natural sciences, Religious knowledge

Metastudy	Also known as meta-analysis, this is a form of study compiling and analysing the results of a large number of previous studies. Metastudies try to use statistical approaches to create an estimate that is closest to the truth of the matter.

Metastudy

Also known as meta-analysis, this is a form of study compiling and analysing the results of a large number of previous studies. Metastudies try to use statistical approaches to create an estimate that is closest to the truth of the matter.

How can we judge the reliability of metastudies? How far can a meta-analysis of several small studies predict the result of one larger one? To what extent can metastudies correct for the design or biases of the original studies?

Knowledge and the knower

Methodology

A collection of methods, systems or rules that someone uses in order to find something out or to complete a task. For instance, two researchers might use completely different methodologies, even if they are researching the same thing.

How do we decide what methodology to use when researching? How do we know whether our chosen methodology is secure and does not contain flaws and loopholes? To what extent is it possible to develop a flawless methodology? How can we determine the respective value of different methodologies?

Human sciences, Natural sciences

Methods and tools

Ways of doing or achieving something; part of the IB TOK knowledge framework of four elements which helps you to explore the different themes and areas of knowledge.

How do we know which methods and tools help us to access different areas of knowledge? How do we judge if some methods and tools are 'better' than others?

Knowledge and the knower

Might

A modal verb indicating possibility or that one has not decided what to do yet. For example, we could say "It might rain tomorrow" or "I might go to the lecture."

Our TOK course might also claim that some or all of these are ways of knowing: faith, intuition, perception, and sensation.

How far can we judge whether or not this constitutes a complete list?

Language

Mind-dependent

The idea that everything we experience is dependent on our perception; that there is no such thing as an 'objective' reality; the idea that the existence of objects depends on the existence of minds. (See also indirect realism.)

Mind-dependent objects might also be described as sense-data, as they are the immediate objects of perception which we experience through our senses.

How far is truth itself mind-dependent? To what extent are values the products of the human mind? How far can mind-dependence and mind-independence be considered a spectrum, as opposed to a binary proposition?

Natural sciences

Mind-independent

If something is mind-independent, then it exists without depending on us thinking about it or perceiving it. (See also direct realism.)

Mind-independence argues that, for example, colours are qualities of things in our environment, whose essential nature is independent of our experiences as those who perceive them.

How can we judge whether any mind-independent objects exist? To what extent does reality exist independently of the mind?

Natural sciences

Minority

A smaller number or part, especially when representing under half of the whole; also, a small group of people within a country or community, differing from the dominant group in terms of culture, race, or native language.

For instance, you can win a minority of votes in an election (meaning that you lose the election overall). We could also, for example, say that ethnic minorities make up around 8% of a town's population.

How do we know whether minorities are statistically significant when working with data? To what extent is it ethical, or important, to ask questions about whether people are from an ethnic minority in surveys or censuses? How far is it possible, or desirable, to impose our own cultural norms on ethnic minorities?

Human sciences, Mathematics, Politics

Misattribution

1. Accidentally crediting the wrong person or group for information that has been received or produced; to incorrectly indicate the cause or creator of something.

2. In psychology, misattribution of memory relates to incorrectly designating where a memory has come from.

For example, you might see a meme online attributing a quotation to Oscar Wilde, only to learn later that it wasn't said by him at all – meaning that the meme was a misattribution. Art historians might also accidentally misattribute paintings to other artists before discovering who really created them.

How far does accurate attribution matter? What are some possible ethical implications of misattribution? Given our tendency as imperfect humans to misattribute memories (we remember information, but always not where it came from), how far can, and should, our memories be trusted?

The Arts, Human sciences

Misinformation

False or inaccurate information, which may or may not be intended to mislead us. (See also disinformation.) For example, there might be a lot of misinformation about a condition like AIDS that needs to be corrected so that sufferers do not face discrimination.

How can we tell where misinformation has originated from? How do we know if we have been misinformed? How can we establish whether there is malicious intent behind misinformation? How far can we distinguish between misinformation, disinformation, and fake news?

Language, Politics, Technology

Mislead

To deliberately cause someone to have a wrong idea or impression. (See also leading question.)

Misleading questions seem to ask one thing, but lead the respondent to answer another question entirely. We can also feel misled about something if we were initially made to believe that it happened for another reason.

How can we tell if we have been misled? What are some possible moral implications of asking misleading questions, particularly in the fields of journalism, law, the natural sciences, and the human sciences? How can we detect if we have just been asked one? How can we avoid asking misleading questions in our research?

Human sciences, Natural sciences

Misleading defeater

A statement which appears to undermine a theory, but then turns out to be untrue itself. (See also defeasibility theory, defeaters.)

We can believe that someone stole a book from a library, but then be told that person has an identical twin who was also at the library that day. The mother of the first person confirms they have a twin – but then we learn that the mother is a pathological liar. How can we decide whether defeaters are valid or misleading?

Knowledge and the knower

Misrepresentation

Giving a false or misleading account of what something is. For example, we might say that a documentary is a misrepresentation of the truth, bearing little resemblance to what actually happened.

Companies can also be charged with engaging in misrepresentation in their advertising, by organizations such as the ASA.

What are some possible moral implications of misrepresentation? How can we tell if something is being misrepresented? To what extent is it possible to accurately judge someone's motives for misrepresenting something or someone? In law, how do we decide if misrepresentation is innocent, negligent, or fraudulent?

Human sciences, Language

Misuse

To use something in the wrong way, or for the wrong purpose. You can misuse a variety of things, including drugs or public funds.

How far is it possible to prevent misuse? What methods could we use in order to try to do so? What might be some ethical implications of data misuse? How can we reliably judge what has caused misuse? In what ways do decision-makers misuse ethical expertise?

Technology

Mitigate	To make something less severe or painful. For example, companies need to mitigate risks to workers undertaking high-risk jobs; places may also wish to mitigate the effects of tourism if they feel like it is damaging the native environment.

Mitigate (continued)

"The judge said there were no mitigating circumstances."

To what extent is it possible to mitigate risks, or negative effects?

How can we decide if someone's personal circumstances are significant enough to reduce their punishment for a crime they have committed? How far does mitigation have moral obligation linked to it?

Human sciences

Modal verb

Modal verbs are words like 'can', 'may', 'might', 'must', 'will', 'could', 'would', and 'should'. They are a type of auxiliary verb that 'helps' another verb so that a sentence makes sense. Modal verbs are auxiliary verbs that show possibility or necessity.

"We should help the poor." "We can help the poor." "We will help the poor." "We might help the poor." "We could help the poor."

What are the differences between each of the modal verbs used here? What are their possible moral implications? How might modal verbs be used in IA prompts and TOK essay titles, and how might they affect your argument?

Language

Moderation

The process carried out by exam boards to check grades that have been awarded by examiners or teachers, to make sure they are fair.

Your school may have internal moderation processes to check that your exhibition grades have been given fairly, compared to others in your school. The IB has moderation processes in place when marking all of your external assessments to make sure your work has not been marked substantially differently to that of other candidates in your and other schools across the world.

To what extent can the moderation process be objective? How do we know whether academic work has been moderated correctly?

Knowledge and the knower

Modify

To make changes to something.

"She may be prepared to modify her views."

How do we know if our own opinions have been modified (either by our own thoughts, by others, or by events)? For what reasons might we wish to modify something, and how do we decide when and how to do this? To what extent is it possible, or desirable, to modify the views of others? What might be some possible moral implications of this?

Human sciences

modus operandi

Someone's methodology, or way of going about things; how something works. For instance, it could be said that every practitioner of a profession has their own modus operandi.

How might we establish the morality of someone's modus operandi? How reliably can crimes be linked through modus operandi?

Some may say that analysis is the prime modus operandi of the sciences, but that synthesis is the main objective of philosophy.

How can we judge whether or not this is the case?

Human sciences, Natural sciences

modus ponens

A method of logically proving or disproving an argument, in which the conclusion affirms the initial premise positively. Expressed mathematically as $p \rightarrow q$, $p \therefore q$

See also modus tollens.

"It is a sunny day today; therefore, I will wear my sunglasses." "You have a current password; therefore, you can log in to the network."

How can we judge the validity of a modus ponens argument? To what extent are such logical constructs useful in the real world, as opposed to just being a mathematical model of the real world?

Mathematics

modus tollens	A method of logically proving or disproving an argument, in which the conclusion proves the initial premise through negation. Expressed mathematically as $\dfrac{p \rightarrow q,\ \neg q}{\therefore \neg p}$ (See also modus ponens.)

"I will not wear my sunglasses; therefore, it is not a sunny day today." "You can't log on to the network; therefore, you don't have a current password."

How can we judge the validity of a modus tollens argument? To what extent are such logical constructs useful in the real world, as opposed to just being a mathematical model of the real world?

Mathematics

Monism

1. In religion, the idea that only one supreme being exists.

2. The more general view that reality is a unified whole, and that all existing things can be described using a single concept or system; that there is only a single material substance or object in existence (such as the earth itself).

(See also dualism, pluralism.)

Monism views man as a unified, varied, complex organism, and rejects any splitting of man into parts. Monism might also put forward that the mind and the brain are the same thing.

To what extent can two fundamentally entwined (linked) things, such as the body and brain, be separated? How do we know whether or not this is useful? What might be some pitfalls of a monistic worldview? How can we judge the possible implications of monism, within the natural sciences and religion in particular?

Natural sciences, Religious knowledge

Monty Hall problem

A probability problem which shows that things are often not how we think they are, and that we often make poor decisions based on this.

You are on a game show and can win a car, which is hidden behind one of three doors. The other two doors have goats behind them. You choose a door. The host reveals to you the location of one of the goats. Instinct tells us we should stick with the door we chose originally. In fact, this is wrong, as changing your door actually doubles your odds of winning (you increase your chances to 2/3, instead of 1/3, as your chances were originally). This video, among others, shows this problem visually: https://cutt.ly/MHPTOK

How do we know whether our choices are right or wrong? How might we manage the risks of switching versus sticking with our original choices? How far can we rely on our perceptions in terms of making choices and changing our minds?

Mathematics

Moore's paradox

The idea that something is occurring, and you recognize that it is, and yet you believe the opposite. (See also magical thinking.)

"I know Santa doesn't exist, but I still believe he does."

Another example of Moore's paradox would be going to a meeting believing yourself to be perfectly prepared for every eventuality when in real terms this simply cannot be the case, but still choosing to believe in your preparedness (despite this being false) because it helps you act confidently in the meeting.

How do we judge the benefits of Moore's paradox in our everyday lives, versus its potential pitfalls? How willing are we to admit to ourselves that sometimes we believe things that are false?

Knowledge and the knower

Moral

To do with ideas about 'right' and 'wrong' behaviour. For example, if you find some money in the street, you might hand it in to the police because you believe it is morally the right thing to do. Some people may also consider that certain films, books, TV shows and video games endanger public morals.

In what ways can we justify the moral rules we follow? What is the possible importance of scientifically explaining the origin and evolution of moral rules? How do we know if our morals are changing, or have changed, over time?

Human sciences

Moral imperative	When a person feels like they have to act on an issue because it is ethically the right thing to do. (See also categorical imperative, hypothetical imperative.)
	For example, we might say that protecting the human rights of refugees is a moral imperative; similarly, it is a moral imperative to analyse the cost-effectiveness of preventing or curing an illness, as the most effective use of funds can save more lives.
	Another example of a moral imperative would be returning a purse that you found in the street to the police station, even though you knew there was cash inside that you could have taken.
	How do we know whether we are acting because we genuinely believe something is morally right, as opposed to it being something society expects us to do? How far do we have a moral imperative to seek greater understanding of the world?
	Human sciences
Moral relativism	The idea that moral judgments are only true or false in relation to a particular standpoint (eg where we are in history), and that no moral standpoint is 'better' than any other. The idea that there is no one absolute set of moral principles that holds true across all time periods, places and cultures.
	"Moral relativism sees people examining the truth of moral judgments relative to their own beliefs, as well as possibly their culture's dominant beliefs."
	Even if there are ethical differences between cultures and time periods, how far does it logically follow that there is no universal moral truth? What problems may arise from imposing the morals of today on past individuals and societies? What are some possible links between moral relativism, no-platforming, and cancel culture? How can we judge whether moral relativism is problematic?
	History, Human sciences, Indigenous knowledge
Motivate	To provide someone with a reason for doing something. We might, for example, be motivated by our salary at work.
	How can we judge what somebody's motivations are? How do we know if someone's motivations are 'good' or 'bad', and how far can this be judged objectively? To what extent is our motivation to learn extrinsic (based on external rewards we gain from it), or intrinsic (what we gain personally or spiritually from it)? How do we know? Which of these 'should' it be?
	Human sciences
Motivated reasoning	Using emotionally-biased reasoning to justify our actions or help us to make decisions that are most desired rather than those that accurately reflect the evidence provided.
	Motivated reasoning arguably helps us to preserve a favourable identity, particularly in Western cultures. Motivated reasoning sees people (unwittingly) discounting unflattering or troubling information that may be seen as contradicting their self-image.
	How do we know whether we are engaging in motivated reasoning? To what extent is all 'reasoning' motivated reasoning – (ie not neutral)? How can we judge whether it is more important to defend our own beliefs or to see the world as clearly as we possibly can?
	Human sciences
Motive	A reason for doing something. For example, after a murder, police try to establish a motive (what the reason was for this person's murder; for example, revenge or a random attack).
	To what extent is it possible to objectively establish motive? How do we judge the ethical 'goodness' of someone's motives?
	Human sciences
Motte-and-bailey fallacy	A form of argument and an informal fallacy where an arguer conflates two positions which share similarities, one modest and easy to defend (the 'motte') and one much more controversial (the 'bailey'). The arguer advances the controversial position, but when challenged, they insist that they are only advancing the more modest position.
	One person might argue that homeopathic medicine can cure cancer. If told there's no evidence showing homeopathy is effective, they might back down, saying that, "Actually there are many ways for people to be healthy besides taking doctor-prescribed drugs." This argument started with a bold and controversial opinion that's hard to defend (homeopathic medicine cures cancer). But when challenged, they retreated to an uncontroversial argument that's much easier to defend: prescription drugs aren't the only route to good health.
	How far do motte-and-bailey fallacies stifle debate? How far do they enable it? How do we know?
	Language, Politics

Moving the goalposts	Changing the rules after they have been initially set; adding extra terms and conditions that were not there before, while a process or activity is still ongoing. For example, a government or company may waste years on negotiations before wanting to move the goalposts and hoping that the other party doesn't notice.

How do you know when the goalposts have been moved? What are some of the possible ethical implications of moving the goalposts? In what ways might moving the goalposts be problematic? How do we know?

Human sciences, Politics) |
| Multiperspectivalism | Also known as triperspectivalism, this is an approach to knowledge suggesting that in any given situation, we are in contact with at least three perspectives or things: ourselves (existential perspective), the object of knowledge (situational perspective), and how knowledge is attained (normative perspective). Multiperspectivalism also holds that all three of these perspectives are interrelated (that we cannot have one without the others).

According to multiperspectivalism, we therefore live in a universe which contains many – perhaps even unlimited – perspectives.

How useful is it to have potentially infinite perspectives through which to view a situation? How can we judge the validity of the perspectives with which we and others encounter objects, people, and situations?

Knowledge and the knower |
| Multiperspectivism | The idea that there are indefinitely many points of view to choose from on a single object or issue.

Consensual multiperspectivism means that voices and perspectives belonging to characters who basically agree, or at least believe in the possibility of consensus, coincide. In radical multiperspectivism, voices and perspectives belonging to enemies (eg victims and perpetrators) meet.

How might this approach enhance or frustrate our search for knowledge? How might multiperspectivism link to decolonization of curriculums and street names?

The Arts, History, Human sciences, Language |
| Multilateral | Agreed upon or participated in by three or more parties; having many sides. For example, we might try to use a multilateral approach to solve problems.

How can we assess whether multilateral thinking is likely to facilitate or frustrate our search for knowledge? To what extent are multilateral institutions able to build in sufficient safeguards to prevent their misuse?

Human sciences, Politics |
| Multiverse theory | The idea that there is more than one universe in existence, not just ours.

Multiverse theory holds that what we think of as 'the' universe could be just one of trillions of universes – that is, part of the multiverse.

How far is it possible that there are people just like us in a multiverse? What would be the criteria for something to be called a universe? To what extent would it be possible to empirically test this? How far might the multiverse theory be 'proof' of the existence of God?

Natural sciences, Religious knowledge |
| Mutual exclusivity | 1. Two events or ideas are mutually exclusive if they cannot occur or be true at the same time.
2. In psychology, this is the tendency to favour assigning one label/name to an object, as opposed to multiple names.

One example of mutual exclusivity is a coin toss: the coin can come up heads or tails, but not both. Also, in a standard card deck, it is impossible to draw a card that is both red and a club, because all clubs are black.

Mutual exclusivity theory in psycholinguistics means that if children already know the name of an object, they will be reluctant to accept a new, second name for it, and are more likely to disambiguate in favour of something they already know (eg calling a wolf a dog).

How do we know whether multiple ideas or events are mutually exclusive? In psychology, how reasonable an assumption is mutual exclusivity for children to make? To what extent might this bias be beneficial?

Human sciences, Mathematics |

Myth	A traditional story explaining the early history of a people or a natural phenomenon, often involving supernatural beings or events; also, a widely held but ultimately false belief or idea, or an idealised conception of a real person or event.

For example, allergists say that it is a myth that consuming honey can lessen the effects of hay fever.

How far is it possible to extract facts from myths? How do we know if a story is a myth, or history? How can the origins of myths be explained, and how do we know if these explanations are valid? How far is it problematic if the general public believe in myths? How do myths enable or frustrate the advancement of knowledge?

The Arts, History, Indigenous knowledge, Language, Natural sciences

Mythology

A collection of legends or supernatural stories, especially from a particular religious or cultural tradition; or, more generally, a set of beliefs or stories about a particular person or situation, usually believed to be exaggerated or untrue.

Many world mythologies have a myth about going down to an underworld, as well as a myth about a flood.

How far do mythologies deepen our understanding of the world? Does it matter if mythologies are reliable or can be verified, or not? How do we know? How far can artworks based on mythology accurately represent the myths themselves? How can we judge the claims mythologies make, and the reasons why those claims are made? Are some mythologies (eg Aboriginal, indigenous, Maori) – valued more than others? By whom, and for what reasons? How far can mythologies and religious narratives be differentiated?

The Arts, Indigenous knowledge, Language, Religious knowledge

Narrative

A spoken or written account of connected events; or, a story. (See also herstory, historiography, history.)

Who shapes the narratives which tell us what happened in the past or what is happening now? How do they do this, and how can we know why they might choose to do it in this particular way? To what extent are our narrative choices conscious? What are some possible ethical implications of reshaping past narratives? How can we detect differences in ways in which events from the past are told to us? To what extent are we morally obliged to seek out lots of different narratives of past events? Are all narratives equally valid? How do we know? How can we tell whether a narrative has been manipulated or altered in some way? How do we know, and decide, what is included and what is left out?

The Arts, History

Natural sciences

The study of the physical world, through subjects such as biology, chemistry, geology and physics.

How far does studying the sciences separately enable us to advance our knowledge of the world around us? Do we gain more knowledge, or less, by combining the natural sciences in a single course of study? How can we know whether the natural sciences are adequate tools to help us understand the phenomena of life and consciousness? How do we differentiate scientific endeavours from non-scientific ones?

Natural sciences

Naturalism

1. The idea that everything arises from natural causes and properties; spiritual and supernatural explanations are not considered.

2. Also, the study of nature. In the human sciences, naturalistic data are data relating to human activities that are neither requested nor affected by the actions of social researchers; naturalistic observations simply involve the researcher observing normal activity without getting involved themselves.

Some would argue that naturalism does still allow for the supernatural given that knowledge of it could be gained indirectly (as natural objects could be influenced by the supernatural in a detectable way).

How far can naturalistic observation methods prove reliable? What, if anything, do we gain or lose in our quest for knowledge by excluding religious viewpoints? To what extent should scientific methods be used to investigate all areas of reality, including the idea of the human spirit?

Natural sciences, Religious knowledge

Naturalized epistemology

The branch of TOK that emphasizes the role of scientific methods.

How far does naturalized epistemology enable us to reflect on the explicit norms we follow – including those related to methodology – and understand the circumstances in which we should continue to endorse those norms and methods? What are some possible limitations of naturalized epistemology? How can we judge its applicability across disciplines? Is a naturalized epistemology bound to leave unanswered some important epistemological questions?

Natural sciences

Nature

1. The phenomena of the physical world, including plants, animals, the landscape, and other non-human-produced features and elements of the earth.

2. The essential qualities or character of something.

For example, we can talk about the nature of a person (eg "It's not in her nature to listen to advice") or a piece of research (eg the qualitative or quantitative nature of a survey). We also talk about nature as meaning 'the natural world' – for instance, we can say that nature has given a particular species a specific ability.

How far can we understand the nature and scope of knowledge? How do we know what, if any, responsibilities we have concerning nature and the natural world? How do we know what is or is not 'in our nature'? To what extent can this be changed?

Human sciences, Natural sciences

Natureculture

A field of knowledge recognizing that nature and culture are not separable in our studies of ecology; the integration of humans, animals and plants to create one more equal and symbiotic culture.

Some would say that natureculture dissolves the boundary between nature and culture, mixing the arts, humanities, and the social and natural sciences.

How does our culture affect our interactions with nature? What might be some possible moral implications of this? How might considering nature in the context of culture advance our knowledge of both? How might this affect our studies of indigenous culture, and what such cultures can teach us about their knowledge of nature? To what extent is nature a construct of human observation and discussion? What knowledge is gained and lost when the human is decentralised as the ruler of nature and apex of evolution? How far is it possible to develop knowledge without an anthropocentric (human-centred) perspective?

Indigenous knowledge, Natural sciences

nemo iudex in causa sua

The idea that 'no one is a judge in his own cause'; this is designed to prevent people from making judgments in legal cases where they have a **vested interest** (stand to gain materially from the case) or know the people involved personally. The aim is to prevent **bias**.

For example, we can apply the nemo iudex in causa sua principle when legal decisions are made in favour of a company in which the judge is a substantial shareholder.

How can we assess the likelihood of biases interfering with justice? To what extent is it possible to prevent this completely? How do we know whether there is public confidence in the justice system?

Human sciences

Neutrality

Being on neither one nor the other side of an argument; in politics, when a country takes no side in particular in any wars or conflicts. Some countries famously retain their neutrality during wars. We could also say that the role of a judge is shaped by the obligation of neutrality.

How far is it possible to be truly neutral? How do we know when or if neutrality is necessary? To what extent does neutrality help us to advance our shared knowledge? What are some possible ethical implications of net neutrality (the principle that internet service providers should enable access to all content and applications regardless of the source, and without favouring or blocking particular products or websites)?

Human sciences, Technology

Nihilism

The philosophical view that everything is ultimately pointless. (Adjective: nihilistic; noun: nihilist). Nihilism states that society, and its morality, has no objective basis.

How do we know if we are nihilists? How far can it be argued that certain stages of life (eg youth, old age) are inherently nihilistic?

Nirvana fallacy	1. Comparing real things with unrealistic, idealised alternatives.
	2. The tendency to believe that there is a 'perfect' solution to a problem.
	Also called the utopia fallacy, the nirvana fallacy could be described as 'unattainable perfection', as it occurs when you criticize something because it's not perfect.
	How far is 'perfection' really possible? How do we know? To what extent is 'the perfect the enemy of the good'? Is it sometimes more important for things to be 'good enough' than 'perfect' in order for progress to be made? What, if anything, do grand conceptions of a perfect world do to advance our collective knowledge?
	Knowledge and the knower
No false lemmas	Meaning 'no false premises', it adds to the idea of justified true belief. In short, 'no false lemmas' states that we must not have obtained our information from anything or anywhere false. It shows that our beliefs are sometimes not knowledge.
	For example, if someone looks at a clock that says 12 o'clock, they are justified in believing that it is genuinely 12 o'clock. If the clock is in fact broken, but the person happened to look at the clock when it actually was 12.00, the belief that the clock is broken can be termed a 'false lemma', and so this situation does not show true knowledge.
	*How do we know whether our 'knowledge' is based on false assumptions? How can we judge whether the 'no false lemmas' condition always works? To what extent does 'no false lemmas' solve the **Gettier problem**?*
	Knowledge and the knower
nomen dubium	A term meaning 'doubtful name', used in the natural sciences when a scientific term is of unknown or doubtful use. (See also species inquirienda.) If there is a situation containing a nomen dubium, it might not be possible to decide whether a specimen belongs to a particular group or not.
	How can we judge what circumstances lead to a nomen dubium? How do we decide what actions, if any, to take thereafter? What are some potential (ethical, and other) consequences for the natural sciences (including extinction, and future breeding programmes), and indeed for our general knowledge, of a nomen dubium?
	Language, Natural sciences
non compos mentis	Not of sound mind; mentally incapable, due to an illness or disability. (See also compos mentis.)
	Some would argue that mere emotional instability or depression does not count as non compos mentis, and that this does not mean a person's intellect is completely destroyed.
	How do we judge whether someone is non compos mentis? What are some ethical implications of acting on behalf of someone who is non compos mentis?
	Human sciences, Natural sciences
non est factum	A legal clause which allows you to get out of doing something even if you signed a document saying you would, on the basis that you weren't aware of the meaning of what you signed. If you claim that you signed a contract by mistake, without knowing what it meant, this could be an example of non est factum.
	How can we judge whether someone is truly aware of the meaning of something? How can we assess whether a claim of non est factum is valid or not? What are some possible difficulties in making a claim of non est factum?
	Human sciences, Language
non possumus	A religious phrase meaning 'we cannot' in Latin. The phrase 'non possumus' was historically used to show an absolute moral determination to be faithful to the Catholic church; not to show that someone is incapable.
	How can we distinguish between whether something is physically possible or morally possible? To what extent is this a valid distinction to make? How do we know what our morals and faith oblige us to do?
	Religious knowledge

non sequitur	If something is non sequitur, it does not follow on in a logical way from what came before it. We can describe arguments as non-sequitur (both as an adjective and as a noun), especially if conclusions do not link up with what is said earlier on in a report or essay.

How do we know whether or not something is a non sequitur? How can non sequiturs contribute to, or frustrate, the search for knowledge? What are some possible motives for, and (ethical) implications of, the use of non sequiturs?

Language

Non-linear

Not arranged in an obvious sequence; not straightforward. In literature, some writers deploy a stream-of-consciousness, non-linear storyline. Some readers enjoy this, while others find it confusing. In mathematics or the sciences, we might expect there to be a relationship between two ideas, but may find that the apparent 'relationship' between the two is non-linear (or that they do not have an impact on each other).

How can we judge whether something is non-linear? If something does seem to be non-linear, how do we decide if this is useful to us? To what extent does non-linear data contribute to our pursuit of knowledge?

Human sciences, Mathematics, Natural sciences

Nonresponse bias

Also known as participation bias, this is when your results (especially of a survey or questionnaire) are affected in a way that may make them inaccurate, either because of participants' refusal to respond or participate for the whole length of the study, or because the participants disproportionately have a certain set of traits that change your results. This can occur when the subject of a survey is especially sensitive, but can happen for lots of different reasons. (See also response bias, selection bias, self-selection bias.)

For example, one study found that people who refused to respond to a survey about AIDS often attended church more frequently, were older, had a lower tendency to disclose their own sexual habits and preferences, and were less likely to believe that survey data was really kept confidential; this could affect the results of the survey.

Another example is that the results of the longitudinal 'Child of our Time' study (intended to last from 2000 to 2020) may have been skewed because of the child participants increasingly refusing to participate (this is known as attrition) as they grew older, for privacy reasons (the study was televised yearly from when the children were babies).

How can we test for non-response bias? Some people believe that incentives (eg payment) are a way of counteracting participation bias; what could be some problems with this?

Human sciences, Natural sciences

No-platforming

Preventing someone holding views regarded as unacceptable or offensive from contributing to a public debate or meeting. Some activists have protested against the no-platforming of controversial speakers at universities.

Are there any situations in which it is acceptable to no-platform someone? How do we know? What are some possible ethical implications of no-platforming? How can we counterbalance these against the potential moral implications of NOT no-platforming? To what extent does no-platforming stifle knowledge and its progress? To what extent is no-platforming a threat to free speech? How far should all values be promoted equally? To what extent is there a difference between freedom of speech and facilitation of speech? How far does no-platforming help to counteract extremism? How can we judge whether no-platforming, the creation of 'safe spaces', and the use of 'trigger warnings' enable the advancement of knowledge? How valid is it to equate no-platforming with cowardice?

Language, Politics

Normal

1. (Statistically) usual, typical or expected.

2. In a person, free of physical or mental disorders; developing and performing as expected.

How do we decide what 'normal' is? How do we judge the usefulness of the overall concept of normality?

Mathematics, Natural sciences

Normative	1. Relating to something that is standard or normal (especially behaviour); relating to what should have happened (as opposed to what actually did).

Normative

1. Relating to something that is standard or normal (especially behaviour); relating to what should have happened (as opposed to what actually did).

2. In the human and natural sciences, a normative sample provides a standard against which the performance of a particular individual can be compared.

(See also empirical evidence, is-ought problem.)

Normative questions ask what we should do or what we should have. Normative samples in studies are also representative of a general population, and enable us to compare individuals' performance to the average, usual or expected group performance.

How do we judge the usefulness of normative questions? How do we judge whether behaviour is normative (conforming to rules)? How can a normative sample be chosen reliably? In the human sciences, how do we know whether a normative model or process (showing what the answer to a problem should be) should be used, as opposed to a model that shows how the problem is solved?

Human sciences, Natural sciences

Novel

(Adjective) Interestingly new or unusual. For example, we can talk about a novel virus, or even about taking a novel approach to a problem.

How can we judge the validity of a novel idea?

Knowledge and the knower

Nuance

A subtle or small difference, especially in the meaning of something. For instance, actors are obliged to study the nuances of facial expressions, to help them show a wider range of emotions. Linguists also explore the nuances of language.

What impact might contextual nuances have on our search for knowledge? How do we know whether nuances are present, and how do we know which nuances are present? How do we decide how to interpret different nuances?

Knowledge and the knower

Null hypothesis

The idea in scientific research that our results are due to chance alone; the idea is to get results that are as far away from the null hypothesis as possible. (See also statistical significance.)

How can we establish a null hypothesis? How do we know whether we have proved or disproved a null hypothesis? How do we know whether something has caused our results, or whether they are just down to chance?

Mathematics, Natural sciences

Numinous

The sense of feeling very small on the realisation that we are part of something much bigger than ourselves (such as God's creation, or the universe); having a strong religious or spiritual quality. For example, when looking up at the night sky, or at an ancient landmark, we might feel a greatly spiritual sense of awe – that is to say, a sense of the numinous.

To what extent might a sense of the numinous be linked with religious knowledge? How far is the numinous applicable to non-believers? How do we know if we have had a numinous experience? How far can the numinous be understood?

Religious knowledge

Nut-picking

In politics, the act of intentionally seeking out extremely fringe, non-representative statements or individuals from members of an opposing group, and parading these as evidence of that entire group's incompetence or irrationality. Also known as the weak-man fallacy. (See also cherry-picking.)

Nut-picking might also be called guilt by association – those who nut-pick try to make a whole group look bad by linking it with what one 'nut' (what we might call a radical, extremist, or outlier) is doing or saying, knowing that what this one person says or does is generally viewed to be unacceptable. For instance, an unhinged racist appearing at a conference might be presented as evidence of a whole political party being racist.

What are some possible consequences of nut-picking? How do we know when or if nut-picking is occurring?

Politics

Object	A material thing that can be seen and touched. For example, newborn babies will automatically curl their fingers around any object placed into their palm, or any object they touch.

"Some would argue that objects should both have a useful function and be attractive to look at."

How far is this a valid assertion? How far do objects exist outside of the mind? How do we identify what objects are? How important is the classification of objects to our understanding of the world?

Natural sciences

Object permanence

The idea that objects continue to exist even once they have been hidden/have disappeared from view, or cannot be sensed in any other way (eg by hearing them).

Object permanence is usually acquired by age 2, and at this point a baby understands the idea of hiding objects in containers. If, for instance, you hide a toy in a matchbox, then put the matchbox under a pillow, and then, out of the child's sight, remove the toy and give them the matchbox, the child will usually look under the pillow for the toy. The child has developed a mental image of the object and tried to manipulate it to solve this problem.

How far does object permanence help us to understand reality?

Human sciences

Objective

Neutral; without interference from personal views, feelings or beliefs.

To what extent is it possible, or even desirable, to be objective and impartial in our professional and/or personal lives? How can we work out whether or not someone is truly objective? When do opinions become objective fact?

Knowledge and the knower

Objectivism

The philosophical idea that the proper moral purpose of one's life is the pursuit of one's own happiness, and that the only social system consistent with this morality is one that displays full respect for individual rights.

Capitalism, reality, reason and self-interest are all important to the concept of objectivism.

How far can true altruism (a sense of charity) be deemed to exist? To what extent is selfishness a virtue?

Human sciences

Obligatory

You have to do something; you have no choice. Compulsory. (See also optional.)

TOK is an obligatory component of the IB Diploma programme – everybody does it, whether they want to or not.

Does making something obligatory advance or stifle the search for knowledge? What are some possible motivations behind, and possible moral implications of, something being obligatory?

Knowledge and the knower

Obscurantism

Deliberately obscuring information, or keeping it from others. Also known as a cover-up.

Governments might be accused of obscurantism, for example. How do we know, or how can we investigate, whether obscurantism is occurring? How can we determine some possible motivations for obscurantism? What are some possible moral implications of obscurantism? What methods are used by obscurantists to keep information from others?

Language, Politics

Obscure

1. When something is not easy to see; when it is not certain, fully discovered, or known about.

2. Also, not clearly expressed or easily understood; vague or hard to define.

For example, if someone's origins and parentage are unknown, we can say these are obscure.

If something is obscure, how can we prove its existence? How far can obscurity be fully eliminated? To what extent can it be argued that life would be unfulfilling if everything was clear or known?

Human sciences, Mathematics, Natural sciences

Observable	When we can see, notice, perceive or discern something. For instance, if we have predicted that something will happen in an experiment, this needs to be easily observable.

If we cannot observe something to prove its existence, does it still count as knowledge? How do we know whether or not something is observable? What do we gain, if anything, from believing in unobservable things? How far can it be said that all observable events are caused by unobservable ones?

Human sciences, Natural sciences

Observer effect	When a system is disturbed because you are observing it. For example, a class of students may behave better because the headteacher is observing the class.

How far would this be an accurate observation of how the class really is all the time? What would be some more accurate methods of carrying out the observation? What might be some ethical implications of these?

The Heisenberg uncertainty principle is another good example of the observer effect – one video about this can be viewed here: https://cutt.ly/TOKHUP

Human sciences, Natural sciences

Obsolete	No longer used; old-fashioned; out of date.

"Some would argue, for instance, that technologies become obsolete faster these days."

How do we know whether a company has incorporated planned obsolescence (when the product is designed to break after a certain period of time so that you will have to buy a new one) into their product design? What are some possible consequences of this? How can we tell whether an answer to a question is now obsolete? How far should new knowledge always supersede (replace) old knowledge?

Technology

Ockham's razor	The idea that the simplest explanation is usually the right one. (See also heuristics.) An example of Ockham's razor could be to say that a doctor should reject rare or exotic medical diagnoses, when more common explanations for someone's symptoms are more likely.

How do we know if Ockham's razor is too extreme? How far does Ockham's razor diminish the variety of the universe? How do we know if the simplest, most likely solution is really the correct one? What are some possible weaknesses of simple-looking explanations?

Natural sciences

Omission	Something that is left out (deliberately or accidentally).

How do we know whether, and why, information has been omitted? How far is it necessary to know who has left out the information? To what extent can omission be considered the same as lying? Might simply not acting (this is called omission bias) – such as staying silent when your opponent in a sport orders food before an event that he is allergic to, and will make him ill – be more ethical than actively acting to sabotage something or someone (eg actively recommending the allergenic foodstuff to your competitor)?

Human sciences, Language, Politics

Omnipotent	All-powerful; having unlimited authority and influence. (See also God paradox.)

How far should citizens trust omnipotent institutions?

How far would an omnipotent being have an ethical responsibility to use their power wisely? To what extent is it necessary for a God or gods to be omnipotent? How far does omnipotence include the power to do something that is logically impossible?

Religious knowledge

Omnipresent	Always there; constantly encountered; widespread.

We could ask, for example, "Why do I need to go to church on Sundays? I mean, isn't God supposed to be everywhere (ie omnipresent)?" We can also talk about, for instance, the omnipresent threat of natural disasters.

What are some possible implications of God's omnipresence? How do we know what difference(s) it would make if God were not omnipresent?

Religious knowledge

Omniscient	All-knowing (particularly in relation to a God or gods, or a god-like person or entity). In literature, we might discuss the concept of an omniscient narrator – a character or 'voice' who knows everything about all the other characters and events in the story. God is also said to be omniscient.

How far is the idea of omniscience realistic? To what extent is this idea problematic in relation to religious belief? If an omniscient entity (such as a God or gods) knows everything, even about its own decisions in the future, does it therefore forbid any free will to that entity?

Religious knowledge

On paper	In theory, rather than in reality.

"The combatants were, on paper at least, evenly matched."

How far can we know whether something is true in theory? How do we judge whether theory and reality match up? Do they ever?

Knowledge and the knower

Ontology	The study of existence, and the nature of existence (ie what does 'to exist' even mean?).

Some would say, for instance, that only an incredibly permissive ontology allows for the existence of witches and leprechauns.

How do we decide whether we think something exists or not? To what extent does anything really 'exist' beyond the minds of those of us who believe in it? How far can the existence of anything be proven?

Knowledge and the knower

Open question	A question with many possible responses; a question that does not have a yes/no, right/wrong answer. (See also closed question.)

"Why did you decide to study Mathematics?" is an example of an open question, as it has many possible answers.

What do you have to consider when answering an open question? How do you know when a question is open or closed? How far do open questions help us to expand our knowledge? How can we judge whether open or closed questions are 'better' at this?

Language

Operant conditioning	A method of learning that uses rewards and punishments for behaviour, enabling us to associate negative and positive feelings with the consequences of the behaviour.

Operant conditioning relies mainly on reinforcement – actions that are reinforced by strong reactions, good or bad – are strengthened and so are highly likely to recur. For instance, if you tell a funny story in class and everybody laughs, you will probably be more likely to tell that story again in the future.

How far does operant conditioning account for our learning, and as such, our knowledge about and understanding of the world? What ethical issues may we need to consider in the practice of operant conditioning? How far does it teach the skills we require for life?

Human sciences

Opinion	A point of view, or thought on a particular subject, which may be well-informed or not.

How far can we judge if opinion is the lowest form of human knowledge? Are there instances in which an opinion might be valuable, and how would we decide if or when this is the case?

Knowledge and the knower

Optical illusion	Something that deceives the eye by appearing to be different from what it really is. One famous optical illusion looks like both a duck and a rabbit; another shows a man playing a saxophone when looked at one way, and a woman's silhouette when looked at differently.

How can we assess whether something we are seeing is an optical illusion? To what extent can we trust our senses? With the advent of technologies such as deepfakes, how far is it still valid that 'seeing is believing'? How far does experimenting with the limitations of our knowledge, through optical illusions and other methods, actually enhance our knowledge?

Natural sciences, Technology

Optional	You can do it, but you don't have to.
	"English is compulsory for all students, but art and music are optional."
	How do we decide what is optional and what is not? How can we judge the motives of those who decide this?
	Knowledge and the knower
Oral tradition	The process through which information and stories are transferred down the generations through speech and voice, particularly in pre-literate, prehistoric, and indigenous communities. Some tribes have strong oral traditions composed of group knowledge, legends, myths, and stories.
	How can the reliability of oral traditions be judged? To what extent can the embedding of biases in oral traditions be prevented? How far does this matter? What advantages might be present in not writing down oral traditions or histories?
	History, Human sciences, Indigenous knowledge, Language
Original	Existing from the beginning; the first or earliest; created personally by an artist/not a copy; not dependent on the ideas of others.
	To get the highest marks for your TOK essay and exhibition, you need to show evidence of your own original thoughts.
	How do we know whether we are showing original thoughts? Is an 'original thought' even possible? How do we know? How can we establish whether someone else is an original thinker? To what extent is this something we can learn, or is it an innate skill?
	Knowledge and the knower
Otherness	The quality or state of being 'other' or different, particularly in relation to minority groups.
	For example, the killing of George Floyd can be said to have transcended barriers of otherness unlike no other events before it. Those from minority groups with a public platform – such as LGBT journalists – can also find that using their 'otherness' for good can further their careers. Teenagers often feel a sense of otherness and alienation as they try to discover their 'true' selves.
	How can we find ways to co-exist with and relate to 'the other'? What methods can we use to negotiate (group or individual) identity? How are different group and personal identities constructed? How can we work out ways to use our own sense of 'otherness' (which might, for example, include a feeling of not fitting in one way or another)? How far has the process of 'othering' and identifying 'otherness' contributed to the development of knowledge? To what extent might defining yourself by your 'otherness' be limiting? To what extent should we define ourselves (as people or groups) by what makes us the same, as opposed to what makes us different? How do we identify what our or others' 'otherness' is?
	Human sciences, Politics
Ought	Another word for 'should', 'ought' indicates what would happen in an ideal or morally perfect world, if we could choose. It can also show if something is probable or likely.
	"Three minutes ought to be enough." "I ought to have told her." "You ought to believe what your evidence supports."
	How far, or how often, do people do this in reality? How can we judge whether we ought to do something, or whether something ought to happen? How do we know? How can we tell whether what ought to happen, or what you ought to do, has changed?
	Human sciences
Outcome	The result of a procedure or process; in education, the product or proof of your learning.
	"We're the only ones who can influence the outcome of this."
	How far can we influence outcomes? How do we know if an outcome is consciously calculated, or arises from intuition (or some other way of knowing)? To what extent do students develop critical thinking skills as an outcome of their participation in their TOK course? How far do the learning outcomes of the TOK course impact student learning in other subjects that are part of their IB Diploma?
	Human sciences

Overpowered	In research, if a study is overpowered, they use too many subjects in the sample, resulting in a waste of resources. (See also underpowered.)

Overpowered studies may detect statistically 'significant' differences which are not actually significant in real-life situations; researchers, therefore, have to ask if their results are relevant.

How might overpowered studies impact knowledge? What are some possible ethical and mathematical implications of overpowered studies? To what extent does an overpowered study enable additional important questions to be addressed?

Human sciences, Mathematics, Natural sciences

Oversimplification	The process of making something easier to understand (simplification), but when the idea is made so simple that the original idea is distorted or errors are introduced.

"It's an oversimplification to just blame the government – there are more factors than this."

How do we know if something has been oversimplified? To what extent is oversimplification dangerous? How far should we accept simple answers to complex questions? What consequences might oversimplification have for truth? How do complex situations of ambiguity and paradox, as opposed to oversimplified explanations, actually enhance our search for knowledge?

Human sciences, Language

Overt	Obvious, blatant, clear. (See also covert, manifest.)

We might describe someone's attitudes, motivations or behaviour as being overt; for example, someone might give no overt sign of knowing you, or a child can be overtly dependent on a particular adult.

How do we know if someone is being overt in their behaviour, attitudes or motivations? What advantages and disadvantages may exist in doing so?

Human sciences

Overton window	Also known as the window of discourse, this is the range of ideas acceptable to the politically mainstream public at a given moment.

The theory of the Overton window states that public officials, in particular, cannot enact just any policy they like; they have to pick from policies that are politically acceptable at that moment. The Overton window defines that range of ideas.

How do ideas in society change over time? How do we recognize the differences between Overton windows in different cultures? To what extent do these overlap? How can we tell when/if the Overton window has changed, and what causes this? How do we know whether something is politically possible within a particular society at a particular moment?

Human sciences, Politics

Ownership	The act, state, or right of possessing something; taking responsibility for a problem.

"Do you have any proof of ownership of this car?" "We need to take ownership of this issue."

How easy is it to prove ownership of an idea as opposed to a physical object? How do we know who is responsible (if anyone) for particular problems we face in the world? How far is it possible to take ownership of, and apologize for, events that took place hundreds of years ago?

History, Human sciences, Politics

Paganism	A pre-Christian religion encouraging the worship of multiple gods, as well as nature-worship.

Some hold that paganism was 'created' by the early Christian church, simply to describe others who were not part of their belief system. A broader definition of paganism has it that pagans put nature at the centre of their beliefs, believing that life cycles of birth, growth and death are spiritually meaningful, with human beings being seen as part of nature.

To what extent do pagans (and humans generally) derive identity from this kind of 'labelling' of 'otherness' (anything that separates us from a mainstream group)? How far can we judge the validity of others' religious beliefs, and to what extent does it matter from what standpoint we are judging those beliefs? If the main source of authority in paganism is shared and personal experience, how far is this problematic?

Religious knowledge

Pantheism	The idea that God and nature, or God and the universe, are one and the same. Pantheists believe that reality and divinity are one and the same, and so don't believe in a distinct or separate God. *If in pantheism God is taken as immanent – an integral part of all things – how far is this compatible with the belief in God as a transcendent being who goes over and above everything we know to exist? How can we judge whether attendance at a religious institution (theoretically not required as part of pantheist belief), such as a temple, is necessary to help shape our beliefs in a God or gods?* Religious knowledge
Paradigm	A typical/standard example or pattern of something; a world view underlying the theories and methodologies used in a particular area of knowledge. *How do we know who and what shapes existing paradigms, or the foundations of thought, in a particular subject? Are ontology (the nature of things that exist), epistemology (TOK!) and methodology all equally involved in shaping paradigms?* Knowledge and the knower
Paradigm shift	A fundamental change in approach or underlying assumptions. (See also Kuhn cycle.) Some would say, for instance, that the internet is an example of a paradigm shift in terms of the way we think about knowledge and communication. *How do we know whether a paradigm shift is taking place, or has already taken place? To what extent does the existence of the internet change how we think about communication and knowledge? What leads people to question the basis of our knowledge? How do we know what conditions might enable paradigm shifts to occur?* Knowledge and the knower
Paradox	When two contradictory/opposite ideas are true at the same time. One example of a paradox is: "The more you fail, the more likely you are to succeed." *How do we know if an idea constitutes a paradox? How useful are paradoxes in our search for knowledge? If paradoxes go against our intuition, to what extent can intuition be trusted as a way of knowing?* Knowledge and the knower
Paraphrase	Restating someone else's ideas in your own words, while still crediting them for the original information. "You can either quote from or paraphrase literary texts in the examination." *In what ways might paraphrase be more effective than direct quotation, or the other way around? How do we know? To what extent could paraphrasing be considered deceptive? How can we ensure that we avoid plagiarism when paraphrasing?* Language
Partial	Incomplete, or existing only in part; containing some, but not all, of the required information or parts. Also, biased or prejudiced in favour of one side or another. "This is a question to which we have only partial answers." *How do we know if the information we have received is only partial? What are some possible consequences of this? To what extent is all knowledge 'only partial'? How do we know?* Knowledge and the knower
Participant observation	Observing people as they go about their normal activities, in the name of scientific research. (See also ethnography, observer effect, triangulation.) Participant observation aims to enable researchers to become more familiar with certain groups of people (such as a religious group, or a group of people working in a particular profession, or even an individual family), by being intensely involved with people in their cultural environment, over a long period of time. *How far is it important that people know they are being observed? How might knowing or not knowing affect the results of an experiment? What are some possible moral implications? To what extent does this method of scientific research advance our knowledge?* Human sciences

Participate	Take part in. For example, participatory work can be said to be creative and to involve everyone.
	"It can be fun to participate in the local swimming event.
	How do we know whether mass participation is beneficial (for example, in learning?) How far should all people participate in all activities and all decisions (in the case of democracy)? What are some possible ethical implications?
	Human sciences
Pascal's wager	The idea that humans bet with their lives that God either exists or does not – and that you should probably believe in God anyway, since you have nothing to lose (the potential trade-offs perhaps seem minor in relation to a potential reward of eternal paradise).
	Pascal's wager essentially posits that believing in God is the better bet, as if you believe in a God and there turns out to be one, you are rewarded with salvation; if there is no God, your belief costs little.
	What possible arguments could be made in favour of, or against, Pascal's wager? How do we know whether to believe in God or not? If we believe in God as a result of Pascal's wager, is our belief sincere enough to convince God that we are 'true' believers?
	Religious knowledge
Patently	Clearly; without doubt. For instance, we might describe claims as being patently true or false, or even patently flawed.
	If something is patently flawed, wrong or false, how do we detect this? To what extent is it preventable? What may be some ethical implications of somebody being clearly wrong?
	Knowledge and the knower
Pathos	Persuasion through the use of emotions (usually urging people to contribute or act based on feeling sorry for a victim). (See also ethos, logos.)
	We might use pathos in a speech to persuade people to believe in the same cause that we do, or pathos may be evoked in a film, book or piece of music in order to move us emotionally.
	How far is pathos an example of manipulation? To what extent is it ethical to use the technique of pathos on others? How do we know?
	Language, Politics
Paywall	A system where only those who have paid to subscribe can access a website. Paywalls typically allow access to a small amount of content (for example, one article a week if the paywall is on a newspaper website), before asking you to pay or subscribe to access more.
	How far can, or should, access to high-quality information be completely free? What are some possible ethical implications for news providers, especially given that the goal of journalism is arguably to educate and inform? How far do paywalls enable a high quality of knowledge to be produced? To what extent can this be balanced with the need for access to information? How do we decide whether paywalls are necessary?
	Language, Politics, Technology
Peer review	An evaluation of academic work by others working in the same subject area (at least at the same level/stage and with similar competency), usually before research is published in a journal. Articles or findings submitted to an academic journal usually undergo a peer review process before they are accepted.
	How do we know whether the peer review system is accurate? How far can bias be removed from this process?
	Knowledge and the knower
Perceive	To realize; interpret, or understand; to become conscious of something. For example, it can be said that we frequently perceive women's magazines as being superficial publications; we can also perceive emotions in someone's voice or on their face.
	How far can we perceive information accurately? How might this affect the development of both personal and shared knowledge?
	Human sciences, Natural sciences

Perception	The ability to become aware of something through the senses; the way in which something is understood or interpreted; insight or deep understanding. For instance, we are often cautioned against the use of drugs, as they can change our perception of reality. A writer could also be praised for the high levels of perception conveyed in a novel they have written.
	In order to achieve high marks in your TOK essay and exhibition, you have to be perceptive.
	How do you know whether your ideas are perceptive? How do we judge whether somebody else's ideas are perceptive or not? How can we know if somebody's perceptions are accurate? What are some possible links between perception and reality? How do we know what sources of information are needed for accurate perception to occur?
	Human sciences, Natural sciences
Perceptual variation	The fact that not everyone sees things the same way. (See also indirect realism, sense-data.) Perceptual variation can be challenging, as it is difficult to say whose perceptions are accurate.
	How do we decide whose perceptions are accurate (if indeed anybody's are)? To what extent is accuracy possible?
	Natural sciences
Permanent	Everlasting; not temporary. For instance, it could be said that some aspects of our identity have greater permanence than others – they are present throughout our childhood and through into adulthood, as opposed to disappearing in, say, the teenage years.
	How do we know whether or not something is permanent? To what extent is knowledge permanent? How far is anything permanent, and what implications might this have for our search for knowledge?
	Knowledge and the knower
Permeate	To spread throughout something; to pervade. For example, we can say that the idea of celebrity has permeated the modern era, or that dissatisfaction with governments can permeate all parts of society.
	What conditions enable an idea to permeate a society or era? How do we know? How do social structures and social attitudes permeate our epistemic practices?
	Human sciences, Politics
Perpetuate	To make something continue (indefinitely/without end). For instance, we can say that the media perpetuate confusion, or that films perpetuate stereotypes.
	Thoughts perpetuate questions, further theories, and advance experiments – how does this impact our knowledge of the world? How do we know if the perpetuation of a particular idea is impacting our knowledge positively or negatively?
	Knowledge and the knower
Perspective	A particular way of considering something; a point of view. In visual arts, the way that objects are made to appear smaller when they are further away and the way parallel lines appear to meet each other at a point in the distance. Considered part of the knowledge framework in your TOK course of study.
	For instance, it can be said that different people have different perspectives on a country's problems depending on where they live, the jobs they do or the amount of money they have. We can also say that artists use perspective differently depending on what effect they want to have on the viewer.
	How far can artistic perspective manipulate our own vision and knowledge of the world? How do we know what shapes our perspectives on particular issues? How can we tell if our perspective has changed? What evidence for our perspectives might prove valid?
	The Arts, Human sciences, Natural sciences
Perspectivism	The theory that knowledge of a subject is unavoidably partial, and limited by the individual perspective from which it is viewed. Perspectivism holds that truth is a matter of perspective, not fundamental reality.
	How far can the world in which we live be represented neutrally? How stable is perspectivism as an account of knowledge?
	Natural sciences

Persuade	To convince someone that your ideas or viewpoints are correct, usually through the use of rhetoric. (See also ethos, logos, pathos.) For example, a defence lawyer can persuade a jury that their client is not guilty.

How do you know whether you are, or someone else is, being persuasive? To what extent can all communication be said to be persuasive? For what reasons might people hope to persuade others? How far does persuasion work without a clear moral stance?

Human sciences, Language, Politics

Pertinent	Relevant; applicable.

"She asked me a lot of pertinent questions."

In order to score high marks in your TOK essay and exhibition, your ideas must be pertinent to the topic at hand.

How do you know whether your ideas are pertinent?

Knowledge and the knower

Phallogocentrism	The privileging of the masculine in the construction of meaning. Phallogocentrism holds that historically men have had greater control over what things mean than women have had.

Does it make a difference whether a man or a woman came up with the term 'phallogocentrism'? Why or why not? To what extent is phonocentrism – the prioritization of speech over writing – part of phallogocentrism? How far is phallogocentrism problematic? To what extent is phallogocentrism overly binary? How might this idea affect our search for knowledge? How far can this symbolic order be weakened by providing alternative interpretations?

Human sciences, Language, Politics

Phenomenon	The plural is phenomena. A phenomenon is an observable and/or remarkable fact or situation which is existing or happening, especially one whose cause or explanation is in question. Also, an object of a person's perception. (See also phenomenology, sense-data.)

For instance, some people would describe glaciers as interesting natural phenomena.
A phenomenon can be seen by some as a vital problem to solve, whereas others may see it as an insignificant issue.

How do we know how we should interpret a particular phenomenon? How do we know if our perception of, or possible explanation for, a phenomenon is reliable? How far does a phenomenon equal truth?

Natural sciences

Phenomenology	The study of the outside world as it is experienced through human consciousness, as well as how reliable or distorted these experiences and consciousnesses are. It is the direct investigation and description of phenomena (remarkable or questionable things that happen in the world), without necessarily applying theories about how or why these have occurred. (See also direct realism, indirect realism, sense-data.)

For instance, phenomenology can involve studying the flash of light that sometimes occurs just after sunset or just before sunrise.

How far might our personal biases interfere with phenomenological inquiry? To what extent is reality independent of consciousness? How far is our (individual or collective) consciousness a product of the socio-historical context in which we are situated? How far are we able to make sense of phenomena?

For a further 3-minute explanation of phenomenology, go here: https://cutt.ly/MPTOK

Natural sciences

Philosophy	The study of knowledge, reality, and existence. Also, a theory or attitude that guides our approach to life.

"Don't expect anything, and you won't be disappointed – that's my philosophy."

How can we judge the usefulness of philosophy as a discipline? To what extent can the study of philosophy help us to understand the world?

Knowledge and the knower

Physical	Relating to things we perceive or detect through our senses, rather than our minds. (See also sense-data.)
	We arguably make assumptions about the physical world and its objects every day – their continuity and their behaviour – so as to avoid, for example, crashing our cars.
	To what extent do we access knowledge only through the physical world? How far is the physical world reliable?
	Natural sciences
Pitfall	A hidden or unsuspected danger or difficulty.
	How far can pitfalls be avoided? How do we detect what potential pitfalls may exist in a situation? To what extent is problem-solving an innate skill? How far is it something we can learn? What challenges may stop us from successfully solving a problem? How do we know if we have successfully sidestepped pitfalls?
	Human sciences
Plagiarism	The act of taking someone else's work or ideas, and presenting them as your own, without crediting the source or author. For instance, students may plagiarize from an article they have read online.
	How do others (such as your teachers) know when you have plagiarized? How do you know if you have plagiarized or not? What are some possible ethical and practical consequences of plagiarism?
	Language, Technology
Planning and progress form (PPF)	This is the form you must complete alongside your TOK essay, based on three interactions with your teacher before, during, and after the writing process. There is also a space for a teacher comment at the end of the form.
	The TOK guide states that "the completion of the PPF will support the process of writing the essay, and support the authenticity of a candidate's work."
	How will you use the form to prove that your work is really yours?
	Knowledge and the knower
Platonism	The theory that numbers or other abstract objects are objective, timeless entities, independent of the physical world and of the symbols used to represent them.
	Platonists think that actual things are copies of 'ideal' or 'perfect' versions of these things, which exist in our collective consciousness, and that these transcendent ideas are the objects of true knowledge. This is explained in Jostein Gaarder's novel Sophie's World *through the analogy of gingerbread men: the cookie cutter represents the 'ideal' or 'perfect' version, whereas the real-life version of the gingerbread man might be a bit singed or broken.*
	To what extent does this idea (also known as the theory of forms) seem plausible? On this basis, how far can 'true knowledge' be considered something accessible? What implications might Platonism have for, for example, mathematics?
	Knowledge and the knower, Mathematics
Plausible	Possible or believable; realistic. For example, we try to find plausible explanations for events in our lives.
	How do we know whether or not an occurrence or explanation is plausible? What are some possible criteria for plausibility?
	Knowledge and the knower
Plausible deniability	When people (especially those in a position of authority) deny knowledge of, or responsibility for, wrongdoing on the basis that there is a lack of information or evidence for their participation in that wrongdoing.
	If people within a political party keep political leaders uninformed on purpose about illicit or unethical actions, then the political leaders can realistically claim not to know about these actions if questioned; this is plausible deniability.
	In what ways can plausible deniability be created? How can we know when or if this tactic is being used? What degrees of visibility and acknowledgement actually exist?
	Politics

Pluralism

A theory or system that recognizes multiple ideas or principles at the same time; the idea that there are several ways of knowing things. (See also dualism, monism.) Pluralists might say, for instance, that we are all aiming to understand the same truth in equally valid ways.

What could be some possible problems with pluralism? How do we know where 'same' becomes 'different'? How do we distinguish a 'good' difference from a 'bad' one? To what extent does pluralism offer an equal opportunity for everyone to 'know' 'truth'? How far does pluralism mean accepting all views as equally valid? To what extent are we all capable (intellectually and socioeconomically) of pluralism?

Human sciences

Point of view

Opinion; a particular attitude or way of seeing a problem. Also, the position from which something or someone is observed. We can try to see issues from others' point of view; geographically, we also might be standing in the wrong place for something to be visible from our physical point of view.

How can our, or others', point of view highlight or hide knowledge? How far is it possible to change someone else's point of view? Are there any situations in which this might be a particularly desirable or undesirable course of action? How do we know whether our, or others', point of view is consistent or not? How do we judge where a point of view has come from? How far can we judge the validity of a particular point of view?

Human sciences

Polarisation

The division of two sharply contrasting sets of ideas, opinions, or groups. For instance, society can be polarised by political debate.

Is group polarisation best understood as a kind of cognitive bias, or rather in terms of epistemic vice? How does the increased polarisation of opinion, particularly online, contribute to or inhibit our search for knowledge? What are some possible consequences of polarisation, particularly for politics and language?

Human sciences, Language, Politics

Police

To make sure certain standards are followed. (Verb) For instance, the use of certain chemicals is carefully policed as they are extremely dangerous if misused. Some would also argue, for example, that it's the government's responsibility to police the financial markets.

What possible biases could come into policing? To what extent can these be prevented? Who decides who polices what? To what extent do we all have a responsibility to help police the societies in which we live? How far is it possible to police ideas?

Human sciences

Political science

The study of the state and of government systems, and the scientific analysis of political activity and behaviour. Political science might study, for example, public attitudes towards government, or the influence of party mobilization efforts on voter turnout.

How far can political science help us to solve global problems? What are some possible limitations of political science, especially when applied to non-Western contexts?

Human sciences, Politics

Politicize

To cause a non-political event to become political in character; to make a person or group politically active or aware. For instance, governments don't want to be accused of politicizing tragedies. We can also say that a whole generation of women was politicized when they were given the right to vote.

How might one go about politicizing people or events? What are some possible ethical implications? How might we judge the possible motives behind politicization of an event or people? How do we judge whether politicization is positive or negative?

Politics

Politics	The activities of the government, and those who try to influence how a country or local area is run; someone's opinions about how a country should be governed; the relationships within a group or organization and how these allow some people to have power over others.

Politics

The activities of the government, and those who try to influence how a country or local area is run; someone's opinions about how a country should be governed; the relationships within a group or organization and how these allow some people to have power over others.

We can talk about our own politics – for example, by saying that our politics have become more liberal as we have got older. We can also talk about politics as a whole system – for instance, by encouraging more people of colour to enter politics. We can also talk, on a narrower scale, about the politics of a particular place – especially workplace politics.

To what extent do philosophical topics have relevance to political debate? What standards, if any, guide us in learning about and developing political processes? How do we know what is required of politics and politicians in a given situation? What are the roles of knowledge, trust, and justification in politics? What are the possible epistemic values of electoral processes?

Politics

Popularize

To cause something to be liked or popular; to make an academic, specialised or technical subject understandable to the general public. For instance, books can popularize a niche concept, such as a particular sport.

How do we judge whether popularization is good or bad? To what extent does popularization diminish the search for knowledge, and to what extent does it enable it? What role might language play in popularization?

Human sciences, Language

Posit

To put something forward as a fact or as a basis for an argument or discussion. We can posit, for instance, that wage rises cause inflation.

How do we assess the validity of an idea being posited?

Knowledge and the knower

Positivism

The idea that only something that can be proved scientifically or mathematically is valid.

How far is positivism a useful approach? How do we know? For what reasons could, or should, non-scientific and non-mathematical knowledge be rejected? To what extent can positivism provide certainty? How might possible gaps between theory and practice affect positivism? How far is the positivist researcher able to detach themselves from their subject and approach it without prejudice?

Mathematics, Natural sciences

Possible

Able to be done or achieved; able to be or become; may exist or happen, but is not certain.

"He was a possible future customer." "Surely it was not possible for a human being to live for so long?" "We should pay careful attention to the possible effects of global warming."

How do we judge what is possible and what is not? What effects might the idea of possibility have on the production of knowledge, both for individuals and for groups?

Knowledge and the knower

post hoc

With the full name *post hoc ergo propter hoc*, this is an informal fallacy that states: "Since event Y followed event X, event Y must have been caused by event X." For example:

A new tenant moves into an apartment and the building's furnace develops a fault. The manager blames the new tenant for the malfunction.

How can such fallacious thinking be avoided? To what extent is avoiding this fallacy possible? How do we know if it is wrong to assume a causal relationship between two successive events? How can we judge what the best explanation is, based on the available evidence?

Knowledge and the knower, Mathematics

Postmodernism

Postmodernism rejects concepts of objectivity and universal truth. Instead, it emphasizes the diversity of human experience and multiplicity of perspectives.

Postmodernism is often associated with allegedly obscure, complex or contradictory aspects, such as allegory, allusions, fragmentation, pluralism, and quotations.

*How effective is postmodernism at showing the randomness of so many of our constructions or ideas? How far is it possible to define and remake society through the idea of deconstruction alone? How can we decide whether "without objective truths individuals are isolated in their subjective opinions"? To what extent is it an **absolute** truth, according to postmodernism, that there is no absolute truth? How far is reality produced by discourse? What ironies and problems may be present within the postmodernist approach?*

The Arts, Language

Post-structuralism	The idea that binary oppositions that can constitute societal structures should be criticized, and a rejection of the idea of interpreting media (or the world) within pre-established, socially constructed structures.

In literature, post-structuralism shifts the focus from the writer to the reader, with readers focusing on other sources beyond the author for meaning (such as cultural norms, other literature, and other readers). How far can these other sources have authority and consistency, compared to the author?

Historians who are poststructuralists might argue that people living in particular places think of history in different ways.

The idea of post-structuralism could be said to come from questioning core ideas of our existence, such as truth, reality, meaning, sincerity, good, and evil, with all of these being regarded as human constructions – and that, as such, there was no real authority, since everything is defined in terms of everything else, with that process of definition itself being relative and artificially constructed.

What might be some advantages, and some pitfalls, to a post-structuralist approach? What implications might this less binary, more pluralist approach have for the production and reception of knowledge? How do we decide if post-structuralism is a useful theory?

The Arts, History, Human sciences, Language |
| Post-truth | Relating to circumstances in which objective facts are less influential in shaping public opinion than appeals to emotion and personal belief. Some would argue that post-truth questions the very idea of truth itself – and that science is needed more than ever in this situation.

How far can we ascertain if science is the 'cure' to post-truthism?

Similarly, if the whole notion of objective truth is rejected, does this mean there can be no lies?

*What are some possible implications of this? What role does fake news play in a post-truth world? For what reasons might post-truth attitudes be dangerous? What implications might the post-truth era have for **accountability**, responsibility, human action, freedom, and knowledge itself? To what extent can post-truth politics be fought or reversed?*

History, Language, Politics |
| Postulate | To suggest or assume the existence, fact, or truth of something. For instance, scientists might postulate the existence of water on a previously unknown planet, or they can postulate possible explanations for a scientific finding.

In what ways might postulation advance our search for knowledge? In what respects might it be limited? How do you know if your postulates are true?

Human sciences, Natural sciences |
| Power | Strength or influence; the ability to do something. For instance, it can be asserted that democratic political processes allow people to have power over their own lives.

How could we judge whether or not this is the case? How do we know whether we have power or not, and what that power gives us? To what extent do the same groups in society have all the power? How can we judge the fairness of this? How might power affect the transmission of knowledge? What are some possible ethical implications of the intersection between knowledge and power, particularly in politics? How do we know what power our own knowledge has?

Human sciences, Language, Politics |
| Power differential | The greater power and influence that professionals have, as compared to the people they help or work with. For example, power differentials can have value, but also many impacts.

What can be some causes of power differentials? How can we tell if a power differential exists? What could be some possible moral implications of power differentials? How might this impact the ways in which we give and receive knowledge to and from others? To what extent are power differentials valid, applicable, and/or helpful?

Human sciences |
| Practicality | The aspects of a situation that involve actually doing something, rather than just theories. For instance, we can doubt the practicality of a proposal.

How do we know whether an idea is practical or not? How far should what we do in life always have practicality at the forefront?

Knowledge and the knower |

Practice	The actual application or use of an idea or method – not just the theories relating to it.

Practice

The actual application or use of an idea or method – not just the theories relating to it.

For example, it is important for a teacher to understand the real-life practice of teaching – not just the principles of educating children.

How can we distinguish between principles and practice? How do we judge when it is important to do so? How far can theories actually inform our practice? How do we know if a theory has a practical application or not?

Knowledge and the knower

Pragmatic test

An experiment that proves how well an idea works when applied to the real world, because it is related to facts in discoverable ways. Pragmatic tests might reveal the consequences of applying a concept to real life, for example.

How do we know if a pragmatic test has worked well? To what extent might pragmatic tests yield false positives, and how far can this be avoided? To what extent do pragmatic tests make a difference to our understanding of the truth?

Human sciences, Natural sciences

Pragmatism

1. Being practical.
2. In philosophy, seeing words and thought as practical instruments for prediction, problem-solving and action, and evaluating theories or beliefs in terms of how successful they are practically.

Businesses might prefer to take a pragmatic rather than an idealistic approach to problems, for instance. Someone might also make a pragmatic decision to settle a lawsuit because it would ultimately cost more to try it in court.

*How far can, or should, thought mirror, describe or represent reality? To what extent can thought serve a practical function? How far should our knowledge and actions always be based on pragmatism? How can we properly define usefulness (if indeed we even can)? If a theist finds usefulness in believing in god, who is an **atheist** to say that they are wrong?*

Human sciences, Religious knowledge

Precise

Exact; accurate; pays attention to detail.

While accuracy refers in the sciences to how close a measurement is to the true or accepted value, precision might refer to how close measurements of the same item are to each other.

To achieve the highest marks in your TOK exhibition or essay, you need to show that you have been precise in your argument.

How do you know if you have done this? How will you show this? What problems might arise from being overly precise?

Human sciences, Language, Natural sciences

Predetermined

1. Decided in advance.
2. In religion or philosophy, established outside of our own decision-making by a higher power (such as fate or God) – this is also known as predestination.

For instance, nurses might use a predetermined assessment tool (PAT) to help them handle telephone calls, as these guide them through a flowchart of questions and possible answers.

*What are some possible problems with the use of predetermined assessment tools in medical or emergency situations, or with predetermined interview questions when deciding who to hire? What biases may be inherent in these? How do we assess the usefulness and limitations of such methods? How do we know whether the courses of our lives are predetermined by a higher power? To what extent does the religious or philosophical idea of predeterminism exclude the idea of **free will**?*

Religious knowledge, Technology

Prediction

A statement about a possible future event; a forecast.

How far is it important to be able to test a prediction? How far is it ethical for anybody to be allowed or able to make a prediction? What are some possible implications of this? How do we know if our predictions are accurate? To what extent is this important?

Knowledge and the knower

P

Predilection

A preference, special liking, or bias in favour of something. For example, it could be said that children demonstrate predilections or abilities in particular subjects or areas from a young age.

How far can we judge if this is really the case?

What problems might our own predilections pose in our search (personally or collectively) for knowledge? What might be some other possible consequences?

Human sciences

Prehistory

The period of time before written records existed. For example, prehistoric instruments and human skeletons can be dug up by archaeologists. Anything from before a celebrity's official career could also count as 'prehistory' (such as demo tapes or home recordings).

How far can we reliably know what was done, and why, in prehistoric times? To what extent is it important to establish an exact chronology/timeline for prehistory?

History

Prejudice

An unfair and unreasonable feeling or opinion, formed without enough thought or background knowledge, especially when directed towards a particular person, place, or group. (See also bias.) For example, it can be reasonably argued that laws against racial prejudice should be strictly enforced.

How far is it possible to legislate against prejudice? How do we decide which anti-prejudice methods might be most effective? To what extent is it possible to completely suppress prejudice?

Human sciences, Politics

Premise

A statement or proposition from which we infer another; or, a fundamental idea on which a whole theory is based.

"If the initial premise is true, then the conclusion must be true."

One example of a premise might be: 'All mammals are vertebrates [major premise]; whales are mammals [minor premise]; therefore, whales are vertebrates [conclusion].'

We can also say, for instance, that we agree with a report's fundamental premise (or main idea on which it is based).

How do we find the premise in an argument? How do we know if a premise is true or not? In what situation can a logically true conclusion be drawn from false premises? What implications might this have for the idea of truth itself? What might be some differences between logical and semantic truth? How can we tell what these are?

Mathematics

Preposterous

Absurd or ridiculous; going against common sense. For example, we might say someone's idea is preposterous.

How do we judge whether or not an idea is preposterous?

Knowledge and the knower

Prescribed titles

The six essay titles that are released by the IB for every exam session, for students to choose from to write their TOK essay (you just choose one).

How do you know what the 'right' prescribed title is for you? How do you assess what issues your chosen prescribed title might want you to address?

Knowledge and the knower

Prescriptive knowledge

Knowledge that is dictated by experts, as opposed to being allowed to evolve naturally based on how knowledge and information is actually used. (See also descriptive knowledge.) For example, the Académie Française is often accused of being too prescriptive and of trying to police the French language, as they regularly issue new French phrases to replace English-language phrases that are already in popular use in French.

How realistic is it to try to control how language is used? How do we wish to create, manage and protect the information that people should conform to? To what extent should linguists be prescriptive in how language should be used? How do we know whether this should be or is the case? What are some possible advantages, and moral implications, of only having experts contribute to a field of knowledge? How do we judge the effectiveness of a prescriptivist approach?

Language

Preserve	To keep something in its original or current state; to keep safe from harm or injury; a sphere of activity being regarded as only for a particular person or group. For instance, we may try to preserve records of the past, or endangered species.

When using 'preserve' as a noun, we could say, for example, that something is the preserve of the middle classes – meaning that it is an area or activity that only they can, or do, participate in.

*How far can historical **artefacts** really be preserved in their 'original' state? How far should such artefacts be kept in the place that can best preserve them, as opposed to the place they 'belong to' or came from originally? How do we know whether life should be preserved at all costs? To what extent should all professions be open to everyone, rather than being the preserve of a particular group? How do we know?*

History, Human sciences, Natural sciences, Politics |
| Presumption | 1. An idea that is taken to be generally or likely to be true.

2. Behaviour that is arrogant, disrespectful, inappropriate or beyond the limits of decency.

For example, we can make presumptions about what people want, or be angered by someone's presumption.

How do we know whether our presumptions are accurate or appropriate? How do we know what to base our presumptions on? When might presumption become fact?

Knowledge and the knower |
| Pretest | 1. A preliminary test or trial, carried out ahead of or as part of the main experiment. (Noun)

2. To test something before it is used more widely. (Verb)

A pretest might, for example, assess a child's knowledge of a subject before they are placed in different groups at school, or a questionnaire can be pretested to be sure it is fit for purpose before being disseminated among the general public.

How do we know if pretests are free from bias? To what extent is this preventable? How far are pretests effective? How do we know what effects pretests might have on results?

Human sciences, Natural sciences |
| Prima facie | At face value; based on our initial first impressions.

"There is strong prima facie evidence that she perverted the course of justice."

How far should we make judgments prima facie? How do we know what a prima facie judgment, or piece of evidence, looks like?

Human sciences |
| Primacy | 1. The fact of being most important.

2. In psychology, the fact of an idea being presented earlier to someone, increasing the odds of them remembering it.

For example, a government might insist on the primacy of citizens' rights. An example of the primacy effect might be when companies deliberately release information about a new product before it is even available.

How do we decide what is most important to us? How far can we alter our initial reactions to situations? How can we assess the extent of impact of the primacy effect on our choices? How far does it matter in what order we receive information? Who chooses in what order we receive that information, and how do we know? What are some potential ethical consequences of the primacy effect?

Human sciences |
| Primary quality | A quality which really exists, as something 'embedded' within an object, and which really exists outside of our perception, such as mass, number, shape, and motion. They are knowable by means of mathematics. (See also primary/secondary quality distinction, secondary quality.)

How do we know what a primary quality is? How far do primary qualities matter?

Natural sciences, Mathematics |

Primary/secondary quality distinction	The difference between primary qualities (which can be determined by mathematics, such as number and mass), and secondary qualities (such as colour, which are in theory just the effects of primary qualities in the mind). (See also direct realism, indirect realism, mind-dependent, mind-independent, sense-data.)

How do we know whether secondary qualities – tastes, colours and so on – really exist? How reliable are our sense-data? How reliable are mathematical or primary qualities such as mass?

Natural sciences, Mathematics

Primitivism	An artistic mode that tries to recreate primitive experiences (= relating to a stage early in evolution or human development), or a sense of the primitive.

Primitivism may be seen as borrowing from non-Western, prehistoric, or indigenous people, seen by broader societies as being 'primitive'. Some examples of primitivist art include works by Paul Gauguin, Henri Rousseau, Frida Kahlo, and Pedro Figari.

What could be some problems with primitivism, or the idea of the primitive in general? To what extent might primitivist art be considered cultural appropriation, stereotypical, or perpetuating a colonial past, even if it is portraying imagined rather than real situations? Would portraying real examples of 'primitive' (or what some may describe as being close to indigenous) cultures make primitivist art 'better' or 'worse'? How do we know? How can we judge whether primitivist art is respectful? To what extent does the principle 'art for art's sake' apply to primitivist art? How far does our perception of the primitive matter? To what extent can, or should, ethnographic objects be viewed as art?

The Arts, Human sciences

Principle	A principle is a basic foundation of a bigger idea, or a rule or belief that drives our own behaviour. Not to be confused with 'principal' (an adjective meaning 'main' or 'authoritative'). For example, you might act in line with your principles by going to the police about a crime.

How do we know what a principle is, and when and how it applies? To what extent are basic principles of concepts such as justice timeless and invariable? How far should they be subject to revision?

Human sciences

Principled	If you are principled, it means you have strong morals and values and try your best to apply them in your day-to-day actions, as well as expecting others to also conform to high ethical standards. According to the IB learner profile, principled learners act with a sense of fairness, justice, equality, honesty, and respect, and take responsibility.

How do we know whether somebody is highly principled or not? How far might this characteristic be considered innate and how far is it learned? How far does being highly principled affect our pursuit of knowledge?

Human sciences

Prioritize	Designate or treat something as very/the most important. Some might say, for instance, that age affects the way people prioritize their goals.

How do we decide what to prioritize and what to let go? How do we know when/if our priorities have changed? How can we assess whether our priorities have changed for valid reasons?

Knowledge and the knower

Probability	Probability attempts to give the likelihood of future events based on past events. If the first coin you take from a bag is a penny, and so is the second and third, we could use inductive probability to state that all the coins in the bag are pennies.

To what extent is probability subjective? How far is probability conditional on the knowledge of the individual making the prediction about how likely something is?

Mathematics

Probability theory	A branch of mathematics concerned with analysing statistically random events. The outcome of a random event cannot be determined before it occurs, but it may be any one of several possible outcomes. The actual outcome is considered to be determined by chance.
	Probability theory tries to help us quantify uncertainties, and in 'real life' we come into contact with uncertainties all the time, such as (more spontaneously) trying to work out how long your journey will take you based on how bad you think the traffic is, or (more deliberately) managing your financial portfolio of investments.
	How do we know whether we have correctly assessed the likelihood of something occurring (or happening the way we want it to)? What is the relationship between truth and probability? How far could we make decisions without probability theory?
	Mathematics
Problematic	Causing difficulty; hard to deal with; presenting a problem.
	The Covid-19 pandemic was problematic for teachers, as they could not teach their students face-to-face – and in some cases, not at all.
	How do we know whether or not something is problematic? In what ways might the relationship between the past and the present prove problematic? How do we know if our approach to our research is flawed or problematic?
	History, Human sciences
Procedural knowledge	Also known as 'knowledge-how', procedural knowledge deals with our knowledge of step-by-step processes, or how to do things. (See also propositional knowledge.) You have procedural knowledge when you know how to do something, like riding a bike.
	To what extent is the knowledge-that/knowledge-how distinction useful? Is knowing how to do something just the same as knowing lots of facts (of the right sort)? How far can someone's procedural knowledge be assessed?
	Knowledge and the knower
Process	A series of actions or steps taken to achieve a particular goal; a natural series of changes. For example, we might talk about a peace process (in politics) or the ageing process in (biology).
	What processes help us to acquire knowledge? How do we know whether a particular research process is robust or reliable? How can we judge whether or not a process is working well?
	Human sciences, Natural sciences, Politics
Production	The creation of a product, or the process of it.
	For instance, we might talk about the production of a film or chemical weapons, or even the production of knowledge itself (for example, feminist epistemologies argue that the voices of women have historically been removed systematically from the production of knowledge). How can we judge whether one method of knowledge production is 'better' than another? How far does it matter who produces knowledge, or how it is produced? What are some possible moral implications of this? How can we assess whether or not particular groups have been silenced in the production of knowledge? How far should everyone have an equal role in the production of knowledge?
	Human sciences, Language, Politics
Progressive	1. Happening gradually or in stages.
	2. Favouring social reform.
	For example, we can talk about a progressive decline in popularity, or an innovative leader might be described as progressive.
	How far can progressive change be detected? How do we know if a person or idea is progressive? How far does progressive ideology alleviate the problems it claims to address? What biases might exist within progressivism, and how far are these dependent on cultural context?
	Human sciences, Politics
Propaganda	Biased or misleading information used to promote a political cause or point of view. For example, during a war, government propaganda is likely to push the view that the country is doing well.
	How do we know if something counts as propaganda? What are some possible ethical implications of propaganda? How does propaganda manipulate language in order to manipulate thought? How do we assess the possible dangers of propaganda? How do we know what effects the digital age might be having on propaganda?
	Language, Human sciences, Politics

Proportionality

1. The idea that a punishment for a particular crime must relate to how serious the crime is; being proportional in size, or corresponding in terms of ratio.

2. In maths, if something is directly proportional, then one thing increases at the same rate as another (eg height to weight). If something is inversely proportional, then as one thing increases, another thing decreases at the same rate (eg speed and travel time – the faster we go, the less time we spend travelling).

For example, courts can overturn cases on proportionality grounds.

In mathematics, an example of proportionality could be something like: if you are paid $30 an hour, the constant of proportionality is 30, as your earnings equal 30 x hours worked.

How do we know whether or not the punishment 'fits the crime'? How far are such decisions made through intuition, and how far are they made through reason? How might ideas about proportionality affect our search for knowledge about the world? How far can proportionality reflect value?

Human sciences, Mathematics

Proposition

A statement or assertion that expresses a judgment or opinion; a project, task or idea viewed in terms of how likely it is to succeed; or, in logic, a statement expressing an idea that can be true or false (but not both).

For example, we can deem a proposition undesirable, such as high taxation, or attractive, such as setting up your own business. In mathematics, an example of a proposition could be 'All students at this school wear glasses.' Also, value propositions ask why we should care about differences between what different people and businesses offer others.

How can we make such decisions? How do we test the validity of a proposition? To what extent is this possible?

Human sciences, Mathematics

Propositional attitudes

Beliefs about experience, or propositions. (See also qualia.) Examples of propositional attitudes might be believing that you have won a race, or fearing that your ice cream is melting.

How do we know whether something is really occurring, or whether we just believe that it is (or could be)? How far does this matter in terms of navigating our everyday lives? Are propositional attitudes always subjective? Are there such things as non-propositional attitudes (eg "I love my best friend")? How do we know?

Knowledge and the knower

Propositional knowledge

Also known as 'knowledge-that', or descriptive knowledge, propositional knowledge is knowledge that a proposition (or claim) is true. (See also procedural knowledge.)

An example of propositional knowledge would be "Paris is the capital of France", or "x+y > 20".

Some would argue that only propositions that are beyond all doubt can be considered knowledge.

Do you agree with this? Do we know things that are not beyond all possible doubt? To what extent is propositional knowledge changeable?

Knowledge and the knower

Protocol

A set of rules and procedures to follow within a certain environment or with a particular organization. For example, royal protocol explains how to act around a king or queen. Protocols for academic studies (ie how these studies are carried out) might be approved by ethics committees.

Who decides what a protocol for a particular place is? How is that protocol decided, and why? How far do decision-makers' methods and motives matter? How far is a protocol consciously decided?

Human sciences, Natural sciences, Politics

Protohistory

A period between prehistory and history during which a culture or civilization has not yet developed writing, but other cultures have already noted its existence in their own writings. Protohistory could describe times in the past where texts offer only an incomplete view of the time period.

How can we assess the reliability of protohistory? How do archaeologists know how best to construct narratives about protohistoric time periods? How can evidence for protohistoric periods be collected and used effectively? How far are new terms or concepts needed to flag the connections between different evidence streams? How might the ways in which different cultures think about time affect the study of protohistory?

History, Indigenous knowledge, Language

Prove	To demonstrate the truth, evidence, or existence of something through reason, logic and argument. If we can do this, we arguably then have proof.
	How do we know when something has been proved? What methods might we use in order to do so? What proof do we need in order to definitively establish whether something is the case, and how do we know what type(s) of proof we are looking for? How far does it matter what 'ways of knowing' we use in order to prove something?
	Knowledge and the knower
Provenance	Where something came from, or its earliest known history. For example, both scientists and religious experts might try to understand both the provenance and fate of the universe. In a more day-to-day sense, we might use 'provenance' to describe where something was made (eg "The vase is of Iranian provenance.").
	How far can the true provenance of ideas or objects be established? What are some possible ethical and legal implications of unknown or withheld provenance, especially when it concerns artworks or historical artefacts? How far is it important for provenance to be clear? How strong a proof is documentation of provenance? What counts as sufficient evidence of legal ownership? If the provenance of an object is found to be dishonest (eg plundering), how far is the owner obligated to return the object in question? How does provenance affect our knowledge and perceptions of a particular object or idea?
	History, Human sciences, Politics
Provisionally	Subject to further confirmation; for now/for the time being. For instance, we can say that a film has a provisional title, which could be changed before it actually comes out; similarly, we might make provisional changes or decisions, or provisionally accept a work contract or business deal, but can still go back on these if new information comes to light or if we change our minds.
	How far can or should we trust provisional information? To what extent are all scientific claims provisional? How do we know whether or not information is provisional?
	Knowledge and the knower
Provocative	Deliberately causing anger (or any strong reaction). Provocative words can fuel an argument further, for example; some people are also deliberately provocative because they like to see how other people will react to what they do or say.
	How do we know whether someone is being provocative or not? How do we assess the motives of somebody acting provocatively? How far do these motives matter? To what extent does the release of provocative information or viewpoints advance our knowledge?
	Human sciences
Pseudoscience	Statements, beliefs, or practices that claim to be both scientific and factual but are incompatible with the scientific method.
	Some people would say that acupressure, conversion therapy, faith healing, homeopathy, hypnotherapy, and neurolinguistic programming are all examples of pseudoscience. It could also be argued that pseudoscience seeks confirmations and science seeks falsifications.
	How can we tell the difference between science and pseudoscience? To what extent are pseudosciences testable? How far is pseudoscience able to provide justification for knowledge claims? How do we know whether pseudosciences provide people with any benefits? For what reasons might people continue to practise pseudosciences?
	Human sciences, Natural sciences
Psychodynamics	The study of the links between unconscious and conscious mental and emotional forces that determine personality and motivation.
	Also known as psychoanalytical theory, psychodynamic theory tries to explain personality based on unconscious psychological processes (such as wishes and fears that we're not fully aware of). Psychodynamic theory also asserts that events in our childhood deeply influence our adult lives and shape our personalities.
	What assumptions might the psychodynamic approach make? How far can we attribute our current behaviours to childhood experiences? How far can our personalities be explained?
	Human sciences

Psychology

The scientific study of the human mind and its functions, especially those aspects affecting behaviour; also, the mental state or faculties of a particular person or group.

Crowd psychology, for instance, can help us to understand the behaviour of large groups (for example, by observing shoppers during the sales). Documentaries might also examine the psychology of mass murderers, for example.

To what extent is psychology an exact science? How far can psychology and logic be considered separate disciplines?

Human sciences

Publicise

To make something widely known; to advertise or promote. Charities might wish to publicise human rights abuses, for instance.

How can we judge whether the possible consequences of publicising something are 'good' or 'bad'? How far do or should the motives behind a publicised person or event matter to us? To what extent do media outlets have a duty to publicise particular causes? How do they decide what to publicise?

The Arts, Language, Human sciences, Politics

Purportedly

Supposedly; allegedly; as something appears or is stated to be, even if this is not necessarily true. For example, companies might be purportedly guilty of antitrust offences.

How do we know whether or not something is really the case? What are some possible ways of checking whether or not information we have received about something or someone is true?

Knowledge and the knower

Purpose

The main reason or function of something; a person's sense of resolve or determination. If you do something 'on purpose' then you have done it deliberately/planned to do it.

For example, your purpose at work can be to make a profit, or we can do something on purpose to get someone else into trouble.

How do we determine our purpose in life? How do we know whether something has been done on purpose? How can we tell whether something is purposeful/meaningful? How far does identifying our purpose in life (if indeed this is possible) help us in our search for knowledge?

Human sciences

Pursuit

A search, quest, act of following, or chase. We might, for example, travel the world in pursuit of our dreams.

How do we know whether or not to pursue a particular dream or goal? How do we know what is useful to our individual or collective pursuit of knowledge?

Knowledge and the knower

QED

Short for the Latin phrase "quod erat demonstrandum", this translates as "that which was going to be proved", or, more concisely rendered in English, "it is proved".

For example, if someone is asked to examine a document which they allegedly signed (even if they knew they didn't sign it), and yet still find their name there, they are then obliged to confirm their name is in fact on the document. We could then reasonably say, "Then you signed it. QED."

In mathematics, we can also use QED at the end of a mathematical proof, to show we have solved it.

How do we know whether or not we have proved something to be true? What methods can we use to check?

Mathematics

Qualia

The plural of 'quale', qualia are qualities or properties as experienced by an individual person; individual examples of subjective, conscious experience. (See also propositional attitudes.)

Qualia can be, for instance, the perceived pain of a headache; the taste of chocolate; or the colour of an evening sky. Qualia are often described as being private, indescribable, and yet directly detectable in our own consciousness.

How do we judge the importance of qualia? How do we know whether qualia are reliable? How can you be sure that your subjective experiences (material or not) actually exist in your brain? How do we know whether qualia are consistent? How far do qualia increase our knowledge?

Human sciences, Natural sciences

Qualify

To be entitled to something by fulfilling a necessary condition; to become eligible for something; to become officially recognized to practise a particular profession; to further explain something you said or wrote previously.

For example you can qualify as a solicitor, qualify your answer, or find out if we qualify for a bursary. You can also qualify a claim. For instance, "Mammals cannot fly, except for bats."

How do we know whether we qualify for something? How can we tell whether we need to qualify our initial thoughts or writings? How do we know if a professional qualification should be recognized in another country?

Human sciences, Language

Qualitative

Measuring or analysing something according to its quality, rather than quantities or numbers. Qualitative research may consist of conducting in-depth interviews, for example.

To what extent can qualitative research be carried out objectively? How do we know what an ideal sample looks like (in terms of size and demographic) for qualitative research? How far is it useful to use qualitative data in isolation, as opposed to with quantitative data?

Human sciences, Mathematics, Natural sciences

Quantitative

Measuring or analysing using quantities or numbers rather than the quality of something. For example, in some professions it is common for quantitative data to be generated based on the dollar value of their sales, or the number of hours spent with a client. Some people might also think that quantitative studies are more concrete and scientific than qualitative studies.

An example of quantitative data might be if people participating in an experiment overwhelmingly choose blue cups over red ones.

What might be some possible problems with the system of generating quantitative data based on dollar value of sales or hours spent with clients? How far would it prove that you were good at your job? How could we judge whether quantitative studies are really more concrete than qualitative studies? How can we be sure that the quantitative data we have collected is reliable? How do we know how to interpret quantitative data? How can we tell whether our quantitative results are replicable?

Human sciences, Mathematics, Natural sciences

Questioning

1. Interrogating someone or asking them questions. (Noun)

2. Curious or inquiring. (Adjective)

How do we know whether questioning is required? How can we tell if someone is asking good questions? How far can biases be avoided during questioning? How far does questioning help to advance our knowledge? What might be the role of inquisitiveness in our daily lives, as well as some possible moral implications?

Human sciences, Language

Quid pro quo

An exchange of goods or services, in which a favour is done in exchange for another. If you cover for your friend by lying for him, and he repays you by doing the same for you at a later date, this is an example of quid pro quo. Similarly, someone might give money, and in return receive something of similar commercial value.

How far can quid pro quo be used honestly? What could be some possible repercussions of a quid pro quo arrangement (whether legally or ethically)? How do we know whether a quid pro quo arrangement has taken place?

Human sciences

Quotation

A group of words taken from a text and repeated by someone who is not the original writer, while crediting their original source. Similarly, in music or art, a passage or segment taken from one piece of work and used in another.

We might, for example, see a quotation from a famous person at the beginning of a book; composers may also quote others in their musical compositions. For example, Schönberg quotes Puccini in the *Les Misérables* soundtrack.

How do we determine the purpose of quotation in a particular context? How do we know whether the quotation's attribution – the person alleged to have said or created it – is reliable or accurate? To what extent does the use of quotation enhance our knowledge?

The Arts, Language

Radical translation	The translation of a completely unknown language with no historical or cultural links to familiar languages. Radical translation can neither assume any prior understanding of the language in question nor resort to a bilingual interpreter.
	During the process of radical translation, linguists might rely on native speakers' behaviour to aid their understanding.
	What is the role of knowledge and lack of knowledge in interpretation and translation? To what extent is meaning fixed (or determined) by empirical data (such as body language)? How far is it possible to determine meaning as a non-native speaker of a language? How far is a behaviourist approach, involving complete immersion in the language, but without any means of translation, an effective way to understand and learn languages? What knowledge can help us to interpret others' languages? How can we judge the reliability of linguistic interaction?
	Human sciences, Language
Randomized	Mixed up in no particular order; in randomized trials, including a wide range of participants of lots of different backgrounds. For instance, one piece of research might involve a randomized study of thousands of people.
	How far is it always possible to carry out a randomized trial in the natural sciences? To what extent is bias eliminated through randomization? What other problems may randomization cause for a study? To what extent can such problems be diminished?
	Human sciences, Natural sciences
Ranking	Putting things in a particular order according to a particular scale or hierarchy. 'Rank' can be used as a noun or a verb. For example, if someone is ranked number one in the world at the game of chess, this is good evidence of their expertise.
	Survey participants might also rank product names in order of preference. In a school setting, your scholastic rank (ie if you are academically top of your class, somewhere in the middle...) can help school officials to see what level of classes you should take.
	How far is the process of ranking useful? How do we know whether we have ranked people or items accurately? To what extent can we rank our beliefs and revise their importance to us over time?
	Human sciences, Mathematics, Natural sciences
ratio decidendi	Latin for 'the reason for the decision'. In law, these are the essential elements of a judgment which create binding precedent, and must therefore be followed by inferior courts, unlike obiter dicta, which do not possess binding authority.
	Ratio decidendi might refer, for instance, to the moment or key idea in a legal case that ultimately decides its outcome.
	How do we know what the reasons for our decisions are? On what basis do we make decisions? How can the ratio decidendi of a legal case be established? How might our perceptions differ in terms of which reasons are more important than others?
	Human sciences
Rationalism	The view that reason is the main source and test of knowledge. Rationalism has been linked for a long time to the use of scientific methods. Most rationalists are also atheists or agnostics (see under agnosis).
	To what extent is rationalism incompatible with religion? What role, if any, do sense-data play in rationalism? What do we gain, or lose, by relying only on reason as a way of knowing?
	Mathematics, Natural sciences, Religious knowledge
Reading	An interpretation, especially of a text or situation. (Noun) For instance, stories from religious texts can be open to multiple readings. We can also have situations where a piece of technology, such as a weighing scale or a digital thermometer, gives two very different readings in a short space of time.
	How do we assess whether one reading is more valuable or valid than others? How far do different readings contribute to, or frustrate the development of, knowledge?
	The Arts, Language, Natural sciences, Technology

R

Real life situation (RLS)	Also known as an RLE (real life example), these are everyday, down-to-earth moments or objects that can be used to link to wider ideas in the TOK essay or exhibition.

Real-life situations are important to the writing of the TOK essay; for instance, in an essay about labels, a good real-life situation relating to this could be the discovery of how fungal networks connect the roots of different trees to share resources. Translated poems could also be used as a relevant RLS.

How do you know which real-life situations or examples apply to your essay or exhibition prompt?

Knowledge and the knower

Realism

The idea that abstract concepts have an objective or absolute existence, or 'perfect' versions of themselves, independently of our own minds; this is sometimes known as the theory of forms. In art or literature, the representation of people or things as they really are. Also, the attitude or practice of accepting a situation as it really is.

Some people like watching soap operas due to their gritty realism, for instance; artistic realism will also typically avoid the use of supernatural elements in paintings.

How far is a realistic approach satisfying in art if a painting looks exactly like a photograph? How can we judge whether facts exist outside of our minds? How far can we be realists about some things and not others?

The Arts, Politics

Reality

The state of things as they actually exist (not a romantic or idealised notion of them); a thing that is actually experienced or seen; the quality of being lifelike; a thing that exists in fact (ie not just in your mind).

For example, we can say that someone refuses to face reality, that we want to make someone's dreams reality, or that a documentary explores the harsh realities of a particular situation.

How far do virtual reality technologies enhance, or frustrate, our search for knowledge? How far can we distinguish between appearance and reality? Should real possibilities be regarded as part of reality? How do we know if our, or someone else's, perception of reality is disordered? How far does reality change when theories do? How far can we prove that there is such a thing as reality? To what extent is 'objective' reality really just the subjective agreement of a given group?

Natural sciences, Technology

Reasoning

The act of thinking about something in a logical, sensible way. We might, for instance, be asked to explain the reasoning behind our decision-making.

How do we know whether somebody's reasoning is valid (or, conversely, faulty)? To what extent can all knowledge be formed through, or based on, reasoning?

Knowledge and the knower

Rebut

Claim or prove that a piece of evidence, or an accusation, is false. A lawyer may attempt to rebut a witness' testimony, for example.

How do we know whether a rebuttal is valid? How do we know what makes a good rebuttal? How do we know if a rebuttal is sincere?

Human sciences, Language, Politics

Reciprocity

Exchanging things with others for mutual benefit, especially privileges granted by one country or organization to another.

We could argue, for example, that mature relationships are based on respect and reciprocity. The reciprocity norm is when people feel obliged to return favours after people have done something for them. Some traditional cultures might have strong relationships of reciprocity between humans and other animals.

How far might the reciprocity norm be considered cultural? To what extent does reciprocity exist in terms of knowledge transfer? How far is it possible to achieve reciprocity in international relations? How do we know? What knowledge is gained when cultures treat animals as reciprocal partners in their relationship with the earth? How do we know whether we are obliged to reciprocate when someone has done something for us?

Human sciences, Indigenous knowledge, Politics

Recognize

To identify or know something/someone again from when you have seen it/them previously. Also, to acknowledge the existence, validity or legality of something. For instance, marriage between two people of the same sex is recognized by law.

We also might not recognize someone we know when we pass them in the street if they are bedraggled by heavy rain or if they are wearing clothes that they don't normally wear.

How do we know whether we recognize a person or not? How do we know whether to recognize a subject as a completely new/separate area of knowledge? How can we tell whether we should recognize somebody's qualifications or other legal certificates? What are some possible methods of recognition and how do these contribute to the development of knowledge?

Human sciences, Natural sciences

Reconceptualize

To conceptualise, or form an idea about, something again or in a new way; to rethink. Some have argued that due to the Covid-19 pandemic, we as a society now need to confront ideas such as universal basic incomes, or reconceptualize what we consider 'work' means.

What does the reconceptualization of ideas mean for knowledge? How far does it matter who is doing the reconceptualizing? How might this alter our perspective of the new version of the idea?

Knowledge and the knower

Reconcile

To make compatible, to make someone accept; to restore friendly relations; to make one account consistent with another.

For example, you can be reconciled to the fact that you have to move house, or you and your friend can be reconciled after an argument. If accounts have been reconciled, this means that the accounts have been confirmed to be accurate, complete, and consistent.

How far is it possible to reconcile sources and make sure they both contain the same information? What might be some difficulties with this process? How does mutual agreement contribute to the progress of knowledge?

History, Human sciences, Mathematics

Record

1. A piece of evidence about the past, especially written. (Noun)

2. To set down in writing or some other permanent form to refer to later; to make public or official. (Verb)

For instance, you might record everything that you eat for a week. A coroner may also record a verdict of accidental death when trying to decide how somebody died. In *The Handmaid's Tale*, Offred records her memoirs onto a cassette for future generations to listen to.

How do we know whether records are trustworthy? To what extent can they be altered? For what reasons may records be altered, and what are some possible ethical implications of this? How do we know if people are honest in the process of recording information? How far does it matter what method(s) we use to record information?

History, Language, Politics, Technology

Red herring

A clue or piece of information which intended to be misleading or distracting; a believable but ultimately irrelevant diversion. For example, we can say that certain issues were 'red herrings' in an investigation.

How do we know if something is a red herring? How can we tell if we are being distracted by issues which appear to be important but in fact are not? What consequences might red herrings have for the development of knowledge?

Language, Politics

reductio ad absurdum

Taking an argument to extremes; reducing the argument so far that you get to the point of silliness (or absurdity). For example, arguments that resort to generalities, such as 'always', 'everyone', 'never', or 'nobody', are prone to reductio ad absurdum – that is, they are prone to being reduced to absurd conclusions.

Another example of reductio ad absurdum would be, "Your friend can't stay because we don't have house guests. If I could afford the rent, I'd get rid of you too. PLUS we only have emergency earthquake supplies for two people. If there's an earthquake tomorrow and she's here then we'll run out of supplies faster and might resort to cannibalism!"

How do we know if someone's argument is absurd and extreme?

This link shows the above example in more detail: https://cutt.ly/TOKRAA

Knowledge and the knower

Reductionist	Analysing something complex in terms of its simple or fundamental parts. It can be argued that if we are reductionist about our personal identity, this can lead to moral bankruptcy (a lack of morals).

Reductionist

Analysing something complex in terms of its simple or fundamental parts. It can be argued that if we are reductionist about our personal identity, this can lead to moral bankruptcy (a lack of morals).

We can also distinguish between a reductionism of methodology (simplifying, or even oversimplifying, how we carry something out), and reductionism of concepts (simplifying, or oversimplifying, ideas).

How far is knowledge advanced through a reductionist approach? How can we tell what the possible advantages and disadvantages of reductionism are?

Knowledge and the knower

Reductive materialism

The view that only the material world (matter) is truly real, and that all processes and realities observed in the universe can be explained by reducing them down to their most basic scientific components, such as atoms and molecules.

Reductive materialists might view a supposedly terminally ill cancer patient miraculously and unexpectedly healing as just a random biological coincidence, to do with the person's physiological processes, while others might view such an instance as coming from other factors, such as prayer or meditation, which can subsequently influence biological reactions.

To what extent can purely material elements explain everything? How far are the natural sciences the only 'valid' area of knowledge? What do we gain or lose from this approach? How do we know?

Natural sciences

Reference

Mentioning or referring to something; in an essay, citing a source. For example, we can say that each chapter in a book is fully referenced, citing research up to the year 2000. We can also make reference in a conversation to a particular idea.

How do we know whether we have referenced sources correctly? How do we choose which sources or ideas to make reference to? How can we tell whether our references are reliable or true?

Knowledge and the knower

Reflection

1. A sign or result of something.

2. Serious or careful thought.

3. The return of light, sound or heat from a surface.

For example, the presence of soldiers on the streets may be a reflection of how scared people – or even governments – are.

Scientifically speaking, the reflection of light through ice crystals can make snow appear to be white, even though it is actually translucent.

You can also decide that you were wrong after a period of reflection.

As part of the preparation for your TOK essay, you have to write three reflections on the planning and progress form (or PPF). These reflections should show your thoughts when deciding on your essay topic, during the writing of your essay, and after you have finished your essay, showing how your ideas and feelings have developed over time.

How do we know whether our reflections are effective or helpful?

Human sciences, Language, Natural sciences

Refutation

The act of proving a theory to be wrong or false. (See also falsifiability.)

Some would say that scientific theory is characterized by its tentative nature, and the idea that it is open to refutation.

How far is all knowledge open to refutation? How do we know when an idea has been conclusively refuted? What methods can we use to refute an idea?

Language, Natural sciences

Regress argument

The argument that any proposition requires a justification. However, any justification itself requires support. This means that any proposition whatsoever can be endlessly (infinitely) questioned, resulting in infinite regress.

Infinite regress can see us going round in circles, meaning we can't always see where a process begins or ends.

How far can the regress argument be solved? What are the implications of the regress argument for the development of knowledge? To what extent can infinite regress be described as a barrier to thought?

Mathematics

Regression fallacy	The assumption that something has returned to normal because of corrective actions taken while it was abnormal. This fails to account for natural fluctuations. (See also post hoc.)

The regression fallacy can be explained as follows. Examples of quantitative data, like golf scores, or the earth's temperature, as well as qualitative experiences, like chronic back pain, fluctuate naturally, usually regressing toward the mean. However, it would be wrong to expect exceptional results to continue as if they were average. People are most likely to take action when the most extreme results are present. After this, when results become more normal, they think their action caused the change, when in fact it didn't.

How do we know whether there is a cause-effect relationship at work when something changes?

Human sciences, Mathematics, Natural sciences

Regressive

1. Returning to a former or less developed state/condition; representing a backward step, or the opposite of progress.
2. In philosophy, this can refer to a process of tracing effects back to causes, or particular cases back to more general or universal ideas.
3. In psychology it refers to a return to a previous way of reacting to situations.
4. In medicine, it means a condition is getting better.

For example, trauma may manifest itself through regressive behaviour, such as bed-wetting, throwing tantrums, or waking in the night. It could also be said that burning waste products, rather than recycling them, would be retrograde or regressive.

How do we know whether or not an action or condition is regressive?

Human sciences, Natural sciences

Relative

Not objective or absolute; considered in relation or comparison to others, or in connection with other ideas.

For example, your parents might discuss the relative merits of each school in a particular area before deciding which one to send you to. We could also look at data and decide that relatively speaking, when looking at numbers as a percentage of a population, the rate of disease is not very high, even if the numbers seem big in absolute terms.

How do we decide whether to look at absolute or relative data or numbers? How far can relativism act as a neutral strategy? To what extent is truth itself relative? What might be some possible advantages and drawbacks of relativism?

Knowledge and the knower

Relevant

Closely connected; appropriate. It can be argued that political parties need to work hard to stay relevant in a fast-moving world, for instance, or that old stories still have relevant messages for us in the 21st century.

How do we judge whether or not something is relevant? How far does what is relevant change, for both individuals and groups? To what extent does something have to have a practical function in order to be relevant?

Knowledge and the knower

Reliabilism

The theory that a belief is justified if and only if it is produced by a reliable psychological process, meaning a process that produces a high proportion of true beliefs. (See also direct realism, Gettier problem, indirect realism, sense-data.)

Reliabilists think that beliefs can constitute knowledge, even if the believer does not know about or understand the process making the belief reliable. For example, if you see a bird outside your window, and thereby believe there is a bird there, you might not understand the cognitive processes enabling you to correctly perceive this – and yet these processes still worked reliably.

What are some possible limits of reliabilism? How far can we assess our psychological or rational reliability? What does the fact that all humans engage in irrational behaviour (from falling in love to buying a lottery ticket) tell us about our reliability? How do we know what counts as a (reliable) method of acquiring belief?

Human sciences, Natural sciences

| Reliability | The quality of being trustworthy and performing consistently well; how far something can be depended on to be accurate. For example, we could argue that the reliability of our family car is without question, as it has been used without problems for years. |

To what extent, and by what measures, can reliability be assessed? If something has been reliable for the past ten years, how can we be sure that it will be just as reliable tomorrow? How can we ensure that our research methods are reliable? Are some areas of knowledge and ways of knowing more reliable than others? How do we know? To what extent is reliability concerned with the replicability of scientific findings? How far should reliability be understood as a matter of agreement between researchers?

Human sciences, Natural sciences

| Religion | The belief in and worship of a superhuman controlling power and/or a set of teachings, especially in relation to a God or gods. While some people don't believe in any religion, others find strength in religious belief; some would say that the ultimate test of religion is behaviour. |

How far can the sincerity of religious belief – or faith – be tested? What knowledge of ourselves, others, and the world around us do we gain from religion? How far can the answers to scientific questions be found in religion? To what extent is religious belief reasonable and rational – and is it important if it is not? What evidence would convince you that God does/doesn't exist? How do we decide between the competing claims of different religious systems? How might a connection between a believer and his god(s) be tested? How far is it possible to 'know' God? How can we assess the likelihood of religion completely disappearing from the world? How do we know whether or not to accept the knowledge that religion proposes to us?

Religious knowledge

| Replication | The act of copying or reproducing something. |

For instance, computerization allows information to be replicated very quickly. Modern buildings might also be cheaper than a replication of what was there previously. In the natural sciences, DNA replication happens in all living organisms, as it is needed for biological inheritance. If a scientific experiment's results are replicable, it means that someone else could do the same experiment and get the same results.

How far does replicating a scientific experiment validate a theory derived from the initial results? If we replicate or share information online, recreate old buildings as they were in the past, or clone DNA to create a new animal, how far do these processes of replication advance our knowledge? How far does it enable us to create new knowledge, as opposed to just copying existing knowledge? What are some possible ethical repercussions?

Human sciences, Natural sciences, Technology

| Repository | 1. A place in which things are kept physically, or a digital space in which data is kept and managed. |

2. A person or thing regarded as an excellent source of information, or in which a particular quality can be found.

For example, data can be aggregated in a repository, or people's minds can even be described as repositories. Some might argue that libraries are both repositories and guardians of knowledge.

How can we decide if libraries are both repositories and guardians of knowledge? Who decides what a repository contains? What are the possible limitations of repositories as physical spaces, and how does this affect the ways in which we acquire knowledge? In terms of digital repositories, they are theoretically infinite in terms of the amount of data they can hold: what are some possible advantages and disadvantages of this, and again, how do the qualities of the digital space affect our search for knowledge? Who decides what data is held in digital repositories, and for what reasons? How far can this data be truly erased ('the right to be forgotten')? What are some possible moral implications of data being held in this way, especially about children (think of parents who post pictures of their babies on social media)?

Human sciences, Mathematics, Technology

Representation

The description or portrayal of something in a particular way, or the depiction of something in a work of art. Some artists strive for a true representation of reality in their paintings, while others are more expressionistic. People might also disagree with the ways in which particular groups are represented in the media.

How far can art represent reality? Who decides how a particular social group is represented to the wider public? How and why are such decisions made? How far does this matter? How do we know what art represents? To what extent can language truly represent thought? How do we know if a media representation is harmful? How does the media influence our beliefs? What are some possible moral implications of this?

The Arts, Language, Politics

Reproducible anomaly

An oddity in research results that doesn't fit the norm, which can be seen again and again if the experiment is repeated or if another person does the experiment.

Programming bugs are examples of consistently reproducible anomalies that anyone can repeat. One example of a reproducible programming bug might be a cosmetic error in the update time displayed, which could make it seem like an update had occurred before it had been created.

What are some possible advantages and disadvantages of reproducible anomalies? How might these affect our search for knowledge? How do we know whether an anomaly is reproducible?

Mathematics, Natural sciences, Technology

Research

Investigation and study of materials in order to establish facts and reach new conclusions. For example, we can research our family history, or how cancerous tumours form.

How do we know whether our research methods are reliable? What unanswered questions might our research raise, and how might this affect our search for knowledge? How do we know whether a topic is worthy of research?

Knowledge and the knower

Response bias

Also known as respondent bias, this is the tendency for participants in research studies to respond inaccurately or falsely to questions.

Response bias might be particularly prevalent in surveys investigating socially unacceptable or embarrassing behaviours.

To what extent can response bias be prevented? What impacts might response bias have on knowledge? How do we know if a survey participant is not telling the truth in their responses? How far can language choice influence respondent bias?

Human sciences, Language

Responsibility

Duty; being accountable for, or to blame, for something; a moral obligation.

How far do we have a responsibility to control our behaviour? Who is responsible for the production and dissemination of knowledge? How do we know? How far do we have a duty to share what we know? How far are we morally responsible for our actions?

Human sciences

Restitutive history

A history that does justice to those whose suffering previously lay hidden.

People might support the idea of restitutive history if they believe that past historical accounts have failed to do justice to subjugated peoples, and/or have supported imperialist projects.

How far should our study of history take on moral responsibilities of this kind? How can we judge the value of a restitutive approach?

History, Politics

Restrictive

Imposing limits on someone's activities or freedom. For example, some countries have very restrictive immigration policies.

How far is being restrictive necessary in order for knowledge to develop? What are some possible moral implications of being restrictive? How do we decide when it is necessary to be restrictive?

Human sciences

Revelation	A surprising and previously unknown fact or idea that has been revealed to others; a remarkable quality; in religion, a divine or supernatural disclosure from a god to a human being about something to do with human existence.
	Celebrity memoirs can contain many revelations about their personal lives, for example.
	In religion, receiving a revelation from a god is seen as a divine source of knowledge, which is then often disseminated through religious texts and places of worship.
	How far is the nature of knowledge dependent on who reveals it, and how it is revealed? How can we judge whether revelations are valid or reliable? How important is the act of divine revelation to the development of religious knowledge?
	Religious knowledge
Revisionism	Revising attitudes so that they will be accepted; in historiography; the re-interpretation of an historical account.
	Revisionism can be seen as an updated or revised version of history, showing new discoveries of evidence, interpretation, and fact. In dramatic cases, revisionism reverses older moral judgments.
	How can we assess whether revisionism is necessary? What are some possible moral implications? How do we know whether the version of history we are receiving has been revised?
	History, Language, Politics
Rhetoric	Methods of persuasion, especially in speech, but also in writing. Rhetoric includes techniques such as ethos, logos, and pathos, as well as inclusive language and rhetorical questions.
	For example, people often want to see if politicians are able to translate their campaign rhetoric into action. If we feel like someone's response is stylish but ultimately meaningless, we might accuse them of using empty rhetoric rather than properly answering our question.
	To what extent does rhetoric advance the development of knowledge, and how far does it obscure or damage it? How far does rhetoric create knowledge?
	Language, Politics
Rigour	Thoroughness; carefulness; severity or strictness; harsh and demanding conditions. For instance, we might say that someone who has broken the law will face the full rigour of the court; we can also say that someone's analysis lacks rigour.
	How do we know whether a curriculum or argument is rigorous? What effect does rigour have on our search for knowledge?
	Human sciences, Language
Risk-taker	Someone who is prepared to put themselves into new and/or dangerous situations in order to expand their knowledge or gain a thrill.
	Risk-takers typically want to try new things.
	To what extent does all new knowledge start with risk-taking? How do we know whether we should avoid risk? How do you know if you are an effective risk-taker?
	Human sciences
Ritual	1. A ceremony, often religious. (Noun)
	2. Done out of habit. (Adjective)
	For example, football players might gather in a ritual – or traditional – huddle before a match. In religious terms, archaeologists can use artefacts to help decode how ancient rituals may have been carried out.
	How far do rituals, or ritual behaviours, contribute to or inhibit the development of knowledge? How far do religious rituals help us to know God, others, and ourselves? To what extent can rituals be judged to have benefits, or to be valuable?
	Indigenous knowledge, Religious knowledge
Robinson projection	A compromise map projection, showing the poles as lines rather than points, and more accurately portraying high latitude lands, as well as the water to land ratio, but at the expense of countries' shape and land mass. (See also Hobo-Dyer projection, Mercator projection.)
	The lines of altitude and longitude in the Robinson projection are evenly spaced across the map.
	How far should art, and how far should mathematics, be considerations in cartography (or map-making)? How do we know whether countries on a map are accurately represented?
	The Arts, Human sciences, Mathematics

Role

The function assumed by a particular thing or person in a certain situation. For instance, the newest and most advanced equipment can play a vital role in medical treatments.

How do we know whether something or someone has an important role or not? Who decides?

Knowledge and the knower

Romanticization

A portrayal of something as ideal.

For example, films can be accused of romanticizing particular ideas or settings.How do we know if something has been romanticized? How far does romanticization damage our development of knowledge? What role does social media play in the romanticization of ideas? Here's an article to help you think more about this: https://cutt.ly/TOKRMHSM

The Arts, Language, Technology

Sage

Wise; a wise person. A self-styled sage might be described as self-taught, rather than having received official training. A book's insights can also be described as sage.

How do we know who, or what, is sage or wise?

Knowledge and the knower

Sample

A sample is a group of people or objects used in an experiment that you think might represent the wider population of people or objects. In statistical testing, samples are used when it would not be possible for the test to include all possible observations or members (for example, when populations are very large).

How do we know whether our sample is representative? How far can this be ensured? How do we know if we have made a sampling error or if the sample is biased? How can samples influence research outcomes, and thus the development of knowledge?

Human sciences, Natural sciences

Sample size

Sample size is the number of completed responses your survey receives, or the number of samples you have included in an experiment. If wanting to make inferences about a population as part of a wider study, for example, the sample size can be an important feature.

How do we know whether our sample size is big enough? How do we know if our sample size has negatively affected our results?

Human sciences, Natural sciences

Sampling frame

In statistics, the source material or device from which a sample is drawn. Sampling frames list everyone within a population who can be sampled; this can include households, individuals, or institutions.

How do we know whether or not we have been included in a sampling frame? What are some possible moral implications of sampling frames? How far can sampling frames be judged to aid research, and thus the advancement of knowledge? How do we know whether a sampling frame is representative of the population? How might sampling frames also lead to sampling bias (also known as the selection bias)?

Human sciences, Mathematics

Sanitization

The act of changing something in order to make it less strongly expressed, less harmful, or less offensive. (See also bowdlerisation.) In medicine, this involves the thorough cleaning of an object or surface.

For example, films might be praised for not sanitizing history. In medicine, sanitization is important to help maintain good hygiene and to avoid the spread of disease.

How do we know if something has been sanitized? What effects might the sanitization of ideas have on the overall progress of knowledge? How can we tell if ideas or knowledge have been sanitized for the wider public? What might be some ethical implications of sanitization? How can we practise good 'epistemic hygiene' so that accurate knowledge can be allowed to spread in a community? To what extent is this realistic? To what extent is 'good cognitive citizenship' a more appropriate description?

Human sciences

Scale	A graduated set of values to help us measure something; a full range of different levels; the relative size or extent of something. For instance, we might need to assess the scale of a disaster, or we may need to know where on our workplace's salary scale we have been placed so that we know how much we will be paid in our jobs.

How do we decide where something falls on a scale? How do we know if a particular scale we are using is accurate? How far does it matter who has determined or invented the scale? What methods can we use to assess the scale of impact of an event? How might the time scale of knowledge transfer (how long it takes to transfer knowledge) affect our development as thinking individuals? How far can personal, local, national and global scales of knowledge interact to advance, or frustrate, the development of knowledge?

Mathematics

Scaremongering — Also known as fearmongering, scaremongering is when information is disseminated to deliberately scare a population into thinking or acting a certain way. Sometimes anecdotal evidence can be presented as an analysis even when it is clearly partial, and this could count as scaremongering.

What might be some differences between anecdotal evidence and analysis? How far is scaremongering always irresponsible? What role does the press play in scaremongering? How far do social media exaggerate or downplay this?

Politics

Scepticism —
1. Doubt; a questioning attitude.

2. In philosophy, the theory that certain knowledge is impossible.

(See also evil demon problem, regress argument.)

For example, conservationists might view a company's environmental claims with scepticism. Separately, the principle of radical scepticism claims it's impossible to know anything – including that we cannot know about knowing anything.

How far is scepticism a useful approach in terms of developing knowledge? To what extent is truth knowable? How far is scepticism the most rational standpoint?

Knowledge and the knower

scientia potentia est — Latin for 'knowledge is power'.

To what extent do higher forms of knowledge correlate with greater power? How do we know if we have power? How can we use our knowledge powerfully?

Knowledge and the knower

Scientific — Systematic, methodical, or relating to science. For example, someone might be engaged in the scientific study of earthquakes.

How do we know when a scientific approach is appropriate? How do scientists know what they know? How far are there only particular philosophies of certain scientists, as opposed to an overall 'philosophy of science'? How far can all ways of knowing be considered 'scientific'? To what extent can scientific writing be considered the ultimate authority or form of knowledge? How do we know what constitutes scientific knowledge?

Natural sciences

Scope — The extent or breadth of the area or subject matter that something deals with or is relevant to. Also, the opportunity or possibility to deal with/address/solve something. Considered part of the knowledge framework in your TOK course of study.

For instance, the scope for change may be limited by pragmatic concerns. We can also widen the scope of our investigation.

How can we judge the scope of a particular theory (ie which and how many phenomena can they account for)? How can we define the scope of knowledge itself (if indeed we can)?

Natural sciences, Politics

Scrutinize	To examine or inspect thoroughly. For instance, it may be useful to scrutinize the small print of a contract when you purchase a good or service, or sign a contract for a job.

What forms might scrutiny take, and how do we know if these forms are reliable? How do we know when or whether scrutiny is needed? What are some possible ethical implications of a lack of scrutiny? How far does scrutiny advance, or frustrate, our search for knowledge? How do we know what questions to ask in order to effectively scrutinize somebody's actions or motives?

Politics

Second-order knowledge	Knowledge, or claims about, knowledge itself. (See also first-order knowledge.)

"How do we know that mammals cannot fly?" would be a second-order question, as opposed to the first-order question "Can mammals fly?'

How far does second-order knowledge enhance humanity? To what extent do we require definite answers in order to say that second-order questions and claims (eg "Mathematical knowledge is certain") contribute to our knowledge?

Knowledge and the knower

Secondary quality	Secondary qualities might be judged as subjective qualities – such as colour, taste, and smell – which are merely the effects of real properties (or primary qualities) on the mind.

A number of conditions can affect our perception of secondary qualities, including how well our sense organs and nervous system work; our distance from the object or its motion relative to us; lighting; or intervening factors, such as fog.

How far can we all agree that the standard alleged examples of secondary qualities – colours, sounds, tastes, smells, touch – are really correctly classified as such? How can we know if things really are as we see them? How far can we distinguish between primary and secondary qualities? Given that these ideas date from 1689 (or maybe earlier), how far can we judge that they are valid ideas?

Natural sciences

Seek	To look for, or attempt to find, something. Also, to try. (Irregular past participle alert: 'sought', not 'seeked'!) For example, it can be said that someone sought medical help immediately, that someone sought to reassure us when we were upset, or that a new database is useful to anyone seeking information on a particular topic.

In seeking knowledge individually, how far do we advance the knowledge of our wider communities? What are some of the big questions we seek to answer about life, and about knowledge itself? How far do we alter the ability to find what we are seeking just by changing our method? What other elements does a successful search for knowledge depend on?

Knowledge and the knower

Selection bias	Also called sampling bias or the selection effect, this is when a choice of research method or selection of study participants is biased towards a specific subset of the population, meaning it doesn't represent the population as a whole.

For instance, selection bias could occur if you decided to carry out in-person interviews at health food stores and gyms to test overall brand awareness of your health food products. The data would be biased, as you would be targeting people who are already likely to want to buy your products, and who might already know about them, as they clearly frequent health-related venues regularly. This might make you think that a lot more people are aware of your brand compared to how many really are.

How do we know whether selection bias has occurred? To what extent is selection bias conscious? How far can it be avoided?

Human sciences, Natural sciences

Selective	Relating to careful choice; or, affecting some things and not others. For instance, you can be selective in your reading, or modern chemical compounds (such as pesticides) can be adapted to be more selective in their effects.

What are some possible advantages and disadvantages of selectiveness? How can we detect whether being selective in a particular scenario might have ethical implications? How far does it matter who is doing the selecting? How do we know who is doing the selecting, and for what reasons?

Knowledge and the knower

Self-actualization	The complete realisation of one's potential, and the full development of one's abilities and appreciation for life. Some studies indicate that self-actualization is linked to higher levels of stability. Examples of self-actualization could be being creative, searching for spiritual enlightenment, pursuing knowledge, or giving back to society.
	How do you know if you are self-actualized? To what extent does self-actualization contribute to the development of knowledge? How far is it possible or desirable to 'complete' the process of self-actualization?
	Human sciences
Self-awareness	The experience of your own personality, individuality and identity. Self-awareness of one's faults is a valuable skill, for instance.
	To what extent is self-awareness necessary in order to 'know' others? How can we judge whether or not self-awareness is an advantage? How do you know if you are self-aware? How are you supposed to tell if you need more self-awareness if you don't have self-awareness?
	Human sciences
Self-censorship	Deliberately controlling what you say and do in order to avoid being criticized by others. Some authors in certain countries are obliged to practise self-censorship to avoid persecution from the authorities.
	How do we know whether self-censorship is necessary? What is its possible impact on the development of knowledge? What are some possible risks, and ethical implications, of self-censorship? How far is self-censorship important to society?
	Human sciences, Language
Self-deception	Allowing yourself to believe that a false or unvalidated feeling, idea or situation is true.
	Self-deception can, for example, help us to block out facts that trouble us, or even to feel more confident at work or at school (we can tell ourselves, for instance, "you've got this" as a motivator, even if we really don't think we have the ability to complete a task, or someone might tell us to "fake it 'til you make it" if we're not feeling confident in a new role or situation).
	How do we know if we are deceiving ourselves? How far can we truly deceive ourselves when we so often know the truth 'deep down'? How far can you trick yourself into believing the truth even if you are not 'feeling' it enthusiastically to be the case? How far is self-deception beneficial?
	Human sciences
Self-evident	Obvious; does not need to be demonstrated or explained.
	"We hold these truths to be self-evident: that all men are created equal, that they are endowed by their creator with certain unalienable rights, that among these are life, liberty and the pursuit of happiness."
	How do we know whether something is self-evident? How far are self-evident truths sufficient?
	Knowledge and the knower
Self-selection bias	A bias that is introduced into a research project when participants choose whether or not to participate in the project, and the group that chooses to participate is not equivalent (in terms of the research criteria) to the group that opts out.
	For instance, students may not apply to study at a particular university if they don't believe they can get a place, even if this is more to do with the attitudes and background of those around them as opposed to their real abilities. This means the outcome (applying/ not applying, being accepted/not being accepted) is skewed by this self-selection bias. Similarly, thrill-seeking individuals are more likely to take part in certain studies; this could skew the ensuing data if it is examining those personality traits.
	How far is it possible to take research participants from a sample that is not self-selecting? How do we know if this is desirable? How can we assess whether self-selection bias has occurred? To what extent can we correct for or prevent self-selection bias (whether via statistical means, or by using other methods)?
	Human sciences, Mathematics, Natural sciences

Semantic	Relating to meaning in language. If someone says "That's just semantics" they are accusing you of unnecessarily picking apart the meaning of a word to draw a different conclusion, but that it all means the same thing.
	"One legal case was based on the semantic question of if a langostino could legally be considered a lobster."
	How do we know whether semantics are important? How can we ensure that the intended meaning of something we say aligns with the received meaning? How far can we successfully interpret semantics in written contexts (such as online), as opposed to when words are spoken? To what extent can tone indicators online deepen our understanding of semantics in the real world?
	See this article for more ideas on this topic: https://cutt.ly/TOKTIS
	Language
Semantic illusion	Also called the Moses illusion, this is when people fail to spot an inaccuracy or inconsistency in information they are given.
	Semantic illusions contain words or phrases that appear to fit the general context of a sentence, despite not actually making sense. Examples of semantic illusions are "After a plane crash, where should the survivors be buried?" "How many animals did Moses take onto the ark?" and "Can a man marry his widow's sister?".
	How do semantic illusions affect how we process knowledge?
	Language
Sensation	A physical feeling or perception resulting from what happens to, or what comes into contact with, the body. Also, an awareness or impression. For example, you can have a sensation of being watched, or lose sensation in one of your limbs.
	To what extent is sensation the only way of establishing truth? How far do sensations rely on consciousness? To what extent is the perceived reliability of sensation culturally dependent?
	Natural sciences
Sensationalism	1. The presentation of news stories in a way that is designed to provoke an emotional reaction or public interest, often at the expense of facts or accuracy.
	2. In philosophy, a theory that limits experience as a source of knowledge to sense-perception.
	For instance, newspapers might be accused of sensationalism in their coverage of a murder. According to the philosophical theory of sensationalism, everything we know about the world comes through our senses.
	How do we know whether information has been sensationalized? What are some possible ethical implications of this? How far are our senses a reliable source of knowledge? What do we lose or gain, knowledge-wise, from relying solely on our senses? How does sensationalism affect our thought processes?
	Language, Natural sciences, Politics
Sense-data	Our direct perception of objects. (See also direct realism, indirect realism, qualia.)
	Examples of sense-data can be the sound of our fingers tapping on a table, feeling the hardness of the wood that the table is made of, and seeing the colour of the table (which we know, under any paint or varnish that has been used, to be 'really' the brown of wood) changing as the sun goes down.
	Sense-data 'appear' in our brains after being filtered through our potentially unreliable senses, and yet before we have a chance to make mistakes through analysing the sense-data.
	To what extent are sense-data therefore incorrigible (unfailing or completely reliable)? Are the real objects in front of us more or less reliable than the sense-data (are we more inclined, for example, to mistake the actual object for something else?). How far do sense-data really have the properties that they appear to have? How do we know? How do we determine the possible relationship between sense-data and physical objects?
	Natural sciences
Sense perception	Understanding gained through the use of one of the senses such as sight, taste, touch or hearing. Sense perception is arguably the source of belief in which we place the most confidence.
	What are the limitations of sense perception as a source of knowledge? How far is our sense perception affected by language? How can we judge the objectivity of our senses?
	Language, Natural sciences

Senses	1. Faculties through which the body perceives external stimuli; the faculties of sight, smell, taste, touch, and hearing.
	2. Feelings that something is the case. If something 'makes sense', it seems reasonable.
	For instance, you can have the distinct sense of being an outsider, or an excellent sense of smell.
	How can we judge whether or not our senses are reliable? How do we know how many senses we have (some say five, others say seven, and others more than this)?
	Natural sciences
sensus plenior	A Latin term meaning 'fuller sense' or 'fuller meaning', used when interpreting the Bible to describe the supposed deeper meaning intended by God but not by the human author.
	The main idea of sensus plenior is that the religious text's original meaning is not lost, but that we can infer additional meanings on top of this.
	How far is it possible that more meaning can be found within scripture than the original human authors intended? How do we know what the 'real' meaning of a text is (if indeed we can know)? What implications does sensus plenior have for religious knowledge? How far are sensus plenior interpretations reproducible and verifiable? Do they need to be? What are some possible links between sensus plenior and the field of translation?
	Language, Religious knowledge
Sentient	Aware of feelings or sensations. For example, some people consider fish to be sentient beings while still cognitively primitive compared to humans.
	How do we determine whether or not a particular being is sentient? What are some possible implications of this decision for other decisions that we make? How far can all sentient life forms be deemed equal?
	Human sciences, Natural sciences
Serial-position effect	The idea that people tend to remember the first and last items in a series better than the items in the middle of a series. Some people explain the serial position effect by saying that the recall of the first and last items in a list originates in our long-term memory, while remembering the other items is dependent on our short-term memories.
	How far does sequencing affect the consolidation and recall of knowledge? To what extent can we improve our long-term and short-term memories?
	Human sciences, Language, Natural sciences
'Ship of Theseus' paradox	A thought experiment that raises the question of whether an object that has had all of its components replaced, remains fundamentally the same object.
	For instance, given that different human cells last different lengths of time (eg colon cells last only about four days, whereas skin cells last two to three weeks), the body you are in now is not the same as it was last week, last month, or last year, although it feels the same.
	So, are you truly the same person? How do we know what the 'real us' is composed of?
	Natural sciences
Should	Indicating obligation/duty or correctness; also, showing a desired or expected state; indicating what is probable; or offering advice or suggestions.
	For example, we can say that someone should have told their friend if they overheard someone else saying something bad about them, or that by the age of seven, children should be able to read independently. We might also advise someone who is ill by saying "You should go back to bed", or, if estimating, we can say "This should be enough to buy him out".
	How do we know what we should do, or be able to do? To what extent is this culturally dependent? How do we know what is the 'best' choice, or what might be possible? How far does considering what we should do, or should have done, advance our search for knowledge?
	Human sciences

Significant	Important; likely to have an influence or effect; noticeably or measurably large.
	"Studies have shown that women typically suffer a significant decrease in satisfaction and self-esteem after viewing images of models, regardless of their own physical size."
	Someone's choice of clothing might also be significant, or we can perhaps see if significant progress will be made today on a project that we are working on.
	How do we know what is significant? How might this change over time, and what are some possible implications for knowledge?
	Knowledge and the knower
Silencing	To prevent from being heard; to suppress dissent. For instance, it may be in the interests of corporate bosses to silence workers' voices.
	*In what different ways, and for what reasons, are oppressed groups silenced? How do we know? In what ways might this affect the acquisition and development of knowledge? What are some possible ethical implications? To what extent might strategies such as **no-platforming** and **cancel culture** count as silencing? How do we know what the similarities and differences between these are?*
	Human sciences, Indigenous knowledge, Politics
Similarity	Being alike or resembling each other. For example, the similarity of symptoms can make diseases difficult to diagnose.
	How can we distinguish between two very similar things? How far can we know about some entities' unrealised possibilities by extrapolation from knowledge about some other, similar entities' realised possibilities?
	Knowledge and the knower
Simplicity	The quality of being easy to do or understand; the fact of being plain and uncomplicated. (See also **heuristics**.) For example, for the sake of simplicity, a chapter of a book may concentrate on only one theory, as opposed to several.
	How far does a simplistic approach advance the development of knowledge? What are some possible dangers of being overly simplistic? How do we know when simplicity is appropriate to the situation and goal? What are the possible limits of simplicity as a strategy?
	Language, Human sciences, Politics
Situationism	The theory that changes in human behaviour are factors of the situation rather than the traits a person possesses permanently/had originally. Situationism holds that our dispositions, feelings, and past behaviours and experiences and behaviours do not dictate what we will do in a given situation; rather, the situation itself does.
	How do we know whether situationism is a valid explanation for people's actions? How far can we judge or assess the motives of human behaviour?
	Human sciences
Skew	A bias towards a particular group or subject; especially in a way that is seen as unfair, inaccurate, or misleading. For instance, some schools skew their curriculum more towards practical subjects than arts subjects, or vice versa.
	How can we tell whether or not our priorities are skewed? How can we judge the reasons for this?
	Human sciences
Slippery slope argument; slippery slope fallacy	An argument asserting that a small first step will lead to a chain of related events, culminating in a much more significant effect – often a disastrous or unlikely one. For example, some might say that assisted dying laws put us on a slippery slope to people murdering their own relatives.
	A slippery slope fallacy assumes wrongly that there is no middle ground between the two points (the 'reasonable' end of the argument and the more 'extreme' possibilities it could lead to). This can also be referred to as 'the thin end of the wedge' or the 'domino fallacy'.
	How can we decide if slippery slope arguments are weak or strong? How do we know if action X will actually lead to consequence Y? How can we avoid the slippery slope fallacy in our own work? What could be wrong with a slippery slope argument?
	Human sciences, Knowledge and the knower

Social constructivism	How social groups construct knowledge. (See also consensus.) According to social constructivists, all knowledge develops through social interaction and language use, meaning that knowledge is therefore a shared endeavour, not an individual one.
	How far is collectively constructed knowledge reliable? To what extent does social constructivism enable independent, individual learning and development of knowledge? How do we judge whether social constructivism is an efficient method of learning?
	Human sciences
Social epistemology	The idea that human knowledge is a collective achievement and that individuals learn mainly through social interaction.
	Social epistemology holds that we need a collective understanding of how the world is before we can talk about it.
	How far can we determine the relevance of communities to the development of knowledge? When does a belief that x is true, which resulted from being told by someone else that 'x is true', constitute knowledge? When and how should I revise my beliefs in light of other people holding beliefs that contradict mine? What does it mean to attribute knowledge to groups rather than individuals, and when are such knowledge attributions appropriate? To what extent would it be possible for a human who is completely isolated from others to have knowledge?
	Human sciences
Sociology	The study of the development, structure, and functioning of human society. Some would argue that a particular area's sociology and ecology cannot be separated from its political history. Sociological studies might investigate changes in public attitudes.
	How can we tell the difference between social facts and social constructs? How far can we objectively establish facts about human interactions and societies? Sociology is based on a set of categories forming intellectual structures; to what extent are these structures themselves social facts? How far is the individual shaped by society? How do we know whether our social class, gender or ethnicity affects our life chances? Is there such a thing as a social structure that constrains individual action, or is society nothing more than a figment of our imaginations?
	Human sciences
sola scriptura	The view that the Christian scriptures are the sole infallible source of authority for Christian faith and practice.
	The principle of sola scriptura rests on the idea that everything we need to know to be 'saved', or everything we need to know for our spiritual life, is taught in the Bible.
	How can we decide the validity of the sola scriptura principle? Not all branches of Christianity accept sola scriptura – how do we decide which viewpoint is correct? If Scripture is divinely inspired but interpreted by flawed, fallible men, then how do we know that we have the right interpretation and not some heretical misinterpretation? If Scripture is the true revelation from God, how do we deal with competing interpretations of the Bible? To what extent is it dangerous or desirable for each individual person to become their own authority on Scripture? How far is a unifying voice (such as a priest) needed to help develop religious knowledge?
	Language, Religious knowledge
Solipsism	The view or theory that the self is all that can be known to exist; self-centred or selfish.
	"Some might equate solipsism with short-sightedness or laziness."
	How far is the self the only thing we can be sure of? To what extent can a solipsistic view aid the development of knowledge?
	Human sciences, Politics
Somewhat	Rather; a bit; moderately. We can say, for instance, that things have improved somewhat since changing jobs.
	Survey questions often ask participants to rate or rank things based on a scale like Strongly agree; Somewhat agree; Neither agree nor disagree; Somewhat disagree; Strongly disagree.
	For what reasons might the 'somewhat' option be included? How informative is it to indicate that you somewhat agree or disagree? How far do these 'halfway houses' enable us to develop our knowledge?
	Language

Sound	1. Reliable, sensible, and will probably give good results or a good judgment. (Adjective)

2. A noise; vibrations that travel through the air or another medium and can be heard when they reach a person's or animal's ear. (Noun)

For example, we might say that someone has given us sound advice, or that they have a sound knowledge of theory appropriate to their job.

How do we know whether our knowledge, our work, or someone's advice, is sound? How do we know whether language is just a series of random sounds?

Language, Natural sciences

Source

1. A place, person or thing from where something originates or can be obtained.

2. Something or someone which is used to provide evidence.

For instance, we can say that oily fish is a good source of vitamins and omega-3, that historians need to use both primary and secondary sources, or that government sources have announced a reduction in the use of nuclear weapons.

How do we know whether our sources are reliable? How is information affected by who gives it to us? How can we identify the sources of our problems? When researching, how do we choose which sources to use?

History, Natural sciences, Politics

Species inquirienda

In zoology, a species of doubtful identity requiring further investigation. (See also nomen dubium.) For example, a zoologist might consider that eight new specimens belong to a particular species, while the two remaining specimens are species inquirienda.

What implications does species inquirienda have for taxonomy? How far is labelling and categorization needed in order for us to have knowledge? How do we judge the possible consequences of species inquirienda for the natural sciences generally?

Language, Natural sciences

Specific

Clearly defined or identified; precise and clear; belonging or relating to a particular subject. Specificity is also used in the sciences to evaluate a clinical test.

For instance, pharmaceutical companies may develop booster shots of vaccines that are specific to new variants of a virus. In the natural sciences, we might talk about the sensitivity and specificity of quantitative tests (such as pregnancy tests) – these are dependent on a particular cut-off value (eg hCG levels), above or below which the test is positive. In general, the higher the sensitivity, the lower the specificity, and vice versa. In physiotherapy, different exercises might work a big group of muscles, whereas isolation moves work only one specific (often very small) muscle.

"Some online forums, such as subreddits, have their own specific vocabulary, which can be quite extensive and will almost never be explained to newbies."

How far is specificity important to the development of knowledge? If a clinical test only has 53% specificity, how do we know if it is reliable?

Natural sciences

Speculation

A form of prediction or educated guessing.

For instance, we can speculate about someone's motives, or about what could happen in the months to come. We can also speculate about past events (for example, would the Brontë sisters have been successful if they had published their novels under their own names from the outset?).

How useful is speculation as a way of knowing? How far is speculation dangerous? How do we know whether our speculation has proved correct? How far should we seek to eliminate speculation in favour of proof and certainty?

Human sciences

Spin
: To give a news story a particular emphasis or bias. (See also propaganda, vested interest.) For instance, political ministers might spin news stories in their favour. A spin doctor advises politicians on how to present their actions and policies to the general public.

How far does political spin subvert the public's ability to make independent, rational judgments? What are some possible ethical implications of political spin? How do we know whether spin is harmful to the political system? How do we know where emotion stops and reason begins? How much detail does the public need to know to consider themselves informed? To what extent do we rely on politicians' rhetoric to inspire us – or to scare us about things we should genuinely fear? How do we know which facts are relevant or important to a political debate? How do we know when to believe what a politician says?

Language, Politics

Spirituality
: Concerned with the human soul or spirit, rather than physical or material things. Studies have proven that spirituality and religion are linked to better physical health, as well as better mental health.

Some might argue that we cannot understand material knowledge until we understand spiritual knowledge; how far can this be proven? How do we know what is meant by spiritual knowledge? What methods can we use to enhance our spiritual knowledge? How far is it useful to do so? To what extent does spiritual knowledge prevent confusion? How do we know whether spiritual knowledge is important or not? How far can we be satisfied with our lives if we prioritize material knowledge?

Indigenous knowledge, Religious knowledge

Stance
: An attitude or standpoint. For example, different authors in the same book may still take different stances on a subject.

How do we know what somebody's stance on an issue is, or if their stance has changed over time? How do we know if somebody's stance is morally problematic? What stances, or approaches, can we take towards knowledge itself?

Knowledge and the knower

Standards
: Levels of quality or attainment; something used as a measure when making comparisons; used or accepted as normal or average.

For instance, we can say that in the past, wages were low by today's standards, or that children's toys need to comply with European safety standards before they can be sold. We can also say that there are standard procedures for the handling of radioactive waste, or that someone has high moral standards.

How do we establish what certain standards are (be they moral or otherwise)? How do we know when or if standards have changed? How far can we apply present standards to the past?

Human sciences, Politics

Static
: Lacking in action, movement, or change; a fixed or stationary condition.

Someone might criticize a particular political approach for being static or conservative, for instance; the myth of 'traditional' cultures and identities being fixed and static was also debunked long ago.

How far is truth static? To what extent are our individual beliefs static? How far do we require some ideas to be static in order to develop our knowledge of the world? To what extent is culture static?

Human sciences, Indigenous knowledge

Statistical evidence
: Evidence which uses numbers to support its main point. (See also logos.) For example, you can use various types of statistical evidence in an assignment, such as data from your own research or surveys you have conducted, or percentages from government reports or peer-reviewed studies.

Why do people tend to disregard statistical evidence when non-statistical evidence is available? How do we know how strong our statistical evidence is? To what extent can statistical evidence prove causation? In what ways might statistical evidence be abused?

Mathematics

Statistical significance	Statistical significance refers to the claim that a result from data generated by testing or experimentation is likely to be attributable to a specific cause. (See also null hypothesis.) Statistics with high significance are more reliable, though the calculation of statistical significance is subject to a certain degree of error.
	How do we know whether our results are statistically significant? How far does statistical significance translate into practical significance? How do we know what factors may affect statistical significance?
	Human sciences, Mathematics, Natural sciences
Status quo	The current state of affairs; how things are at the moment.
	Antidisestablishmentarianism means you are fine with the status quo, and don't wish to disrupt it. We can also say that student movements have historically risen up against the status quo. We can also talk about the status quo bias, which shows that the burden of proof lies with the person who is attempting to overturn the current theory, rather than on the current theory to justify itself.
	How far should the status quo be confronted? In what ways can this be achieved (if at all)? How far is the status quo bias necessary to advance our understanding? How do we know if the status quo is problematic?
	Politics
Stimuli	The plural of 'stimulus', stimuli are things or events that provoke specific reactions; a spur or incentive; something which arises; energy or activity.
	For instance, one day my students were instructed to write an essay based on the stimulus that I wrote on the board. It read 'I don't care about people in poor countries'.
	In economics, abolishing a certain tax might act as a stimulus to exports; in neurology, it can be said that some areas of our brains respond to auditory stimuli.
	How do we know whether stimuli are effective? How far is failure the stimulus of innovation?
	Knowledge and the knower
Straw man	A 'straw man' argument consists of Person A making a claim, Person B creating a distorted version of the claim (the 'straw man'), and then Person B attacking this distorted version in order to refute Person A's original assertion. An example of a straw man argument could be:
	Senator A says that the nation should not add to the defence budget. Senator B says that he cannot believe that Senator A wants to leave the nation defenceless.
	What implications does the straw man argument have for the development of knowledge? How do we know when/if it has been used?
	Human sciences, Language, Politics
Structuralism	The idea that one may understand human culture by means of a broader structure (such as language).
	The structuralist school emerges from theories of language and linguistics, and it looks for underlying elements in culture and literature that can be connected so that critics can develop general conclusions about the individual works and the systems from which they emerge.
	How far is knowledge based on structure? How far can it be determined that because of these underlying structures, human agency and free will is an illusion? To what extent do structures enable us to 'make sense from chaos'?
	The Arts, Human sciences, Language
Subconscious	Of or concerning the part of the mind of which one is not fully aware but which influences one's actions and feelings.
	For example, users of prosthetic limbs should be able to operate them subconsciously after a short period of time. We can also talk about subconscious desires, or subconscious biases; these can be very difficult to counteract, as we are hardly aware of their existence.
	How far can subconscious feelings be proven? How might our subconscious affect the ways in which we process knowledge?
	Human sciences

Subjective	Based on or influenced by personal beliefs, feelings, tastes, or opinions.
	For instance, we could say that the value of art works is entirely subjective, or that the right parietal lobe in our brains is responsible for the subjective experience of time.
	How do we know whether a question or statement is subjective? How far do subjective claims or queries advance human knowledge? How far can the standards of rational belief be based on those of individual believers? How far can we only know truth from a subjective perspective?
	Knowledge and the knower
Subjective idealism	The idea that only minds and mental contents truly exist.
	According to subjective idealism, objects are mere bundles of sense data in the person perceiving them.
	How far is subjective idealism a necessary viewpoint to study psychology? How might subjective idealism account for things that exist and happen when nobody is around? How far do our minds define existence? How can we know about the existence of things we can't immediately perceive?
	Natural sciences
Subliminal messaging	Auditory or visual stimuli that the conscious mind cannot perceive, usually deliberately inserted into advertising and other overt messaging.
	Advertisers can use subliminal messaging to help make their advertisements more persuasive, or even to convey an entirely different message. Other examples of subliminal messaging include embedding messages in songs, either at a different frequency or by singing something backwards; flashing words and images briefly between frames of a film; or hiding subtle images in drawings or photos, such as a word spelled out in clouds in the background.
	How do you know whether or not subliminal messaging has been used? How do we know whether subliminal messaging really works or not? What are some possible ethical implications of subliminal messaging?
	This episode of a popular TV series gives good examples of subliminal messaging: https://cutt.ly/TOKSNKB
	Language, Technology
Subsample	In research, a sample taken from a larger sample.
	"From an initial sample, a further subsample of participants can be recruited to participate in a study."
	How do we know whether our chosen subsample represents the population accurately? What could be some possible implications if they do not?
	Human sciences, Natural sciences
Substantiation	Supporting an idea with factual backup; showing that a claim is true. For example, companies can produce receipts to substantiate their claims for expenses. Criticisms can also be deemed substantiated or unsubstantiated by facts.
	How do we know whether our ideas are sufficiently substantiated?
	Knowledge and the knower
Subtle	Delicate or precise, in a way that can be difficult to detect; deliberately complex or understated; ingenious, elaborate, and indirect. For instance, a plan can be clever, yet subtle; language can also express rich and subtle meanings if its vocabulary is extensive.
	How do we know whether something is subtle? How far does subtlety advance our search for knowledge?
	The Arts, Language
Subvert	To undermine or overthrow the power or authority of an established institution. For example, artists often subvert the meanings of familiar objects through their work, so as to challenge how we interpret particular imagery. In order to protest, people can also subvert, ignore, or flout particular laws.
	How do we judge the value of subversion (whether legal, artistic, or other)? How do we know whether our chosen methods of subversion are effective? How far is subversion necessary to advance the development of knowledge?
	The Arts, Politics

Sufficient	Enough; adequate. For instance, we can talk about needing sufficient resources to survive, giving particular skills sufficient weight, or there being a sufficient level of evidence to support analysis and review of the results of an experiment.
	How do we judge whether information is of sufficient value, validity or level of detail?
	Knowledge and the knower
Suggestibility	The quality of being inclined to accept and act on the suggestions of others.
	Examples of suggestibility are the placebo effect, hypnotic suggestibility, and interrogative suggestibility. The placebo effect is when we attribute our recovery to a particular medication or course of action, when this recovery can't be attributed to the treatment. For example, doctors or pharmacists may prescribe a placebo if they perceive that it's mainly a change of mindset that's required: sometimes just the feeling of doing something about a problem can be sufficient to trigger recovery. Hypnotic suggestibility shows how far people respond to suggestions while under the influence of hypnosis. Interrogative suggestibility is how far someone will give in to a suggestive question, and how much that person will change their answers after the person in control exerts pressure on them.
	What are the possible consequences of being (too) willing to accept information given to you by others?
	Human sciences, Natural sciences
Superficial	Cursory; lacking in depth; implying a concern only with surface aspects or obvious features.
	If changes are superficial, then the situation appears outwardly or for a short time to have changed, but long term it proves to not be the case. Serious flaws in a plan might also be revealed after even a cursory or superficial inspection.
	How do we know whether or not something is superficial? What implications does superficiality have for knowledge? How can we show that our understanding goes beyond the superficial?
	Knowledge and the knower
Superimposed	Placed or laid over something else, typically so that both things are still visible or evident. Palimpsests have multiple texts superimposed onto each other, for example.
	How far does superimposed, or overlapping, knowledge impact our general search for information? How far does the superimposing of images and sounds impact how we process information and ideas? How do we know whether one culture has been superimposed onto another? What are some possible consequences of this? The concept of 'make-perceive' suggests that human beings have the capacity to 'augment' reality by superimposing mental imagery on the visually perceived scene; how can we tell whether this is possible?
	The Arts, Human sciences, Natural sciences
Superior	Higher in rank, status, quality or size. For instance, one might be chosen for the job because you are the superior candidate. Some people also believe that acoustic recordings are superior to digital ones.
	How do we know whether one thing is superior to another? How do we know, for instance, whether reason is superior to existence as a way of knowing?
	Knowledge and the knower
Supernaturalism	Belief in a supernatural power and order of existence. Supernaturalism is associated with religion by some; some also believe that supernaturalism erodes democracy, as it potentially promotes a dualism between religion and science which degrades the social values that religion originally promoted.
	How can we judge the extent to which this is the case? How far does supernaturalism reveal what is morally good or bad? How far is supernaturalism verifiable?
	Religious knowledge
Support	To give approval to something; to suggest the truth of something. For example, other scientific studies can support our findings, or members of an ethics committee might support our research proposal.
	How do we know whether to support an idea? How do we know whether our ideas are supported? In research, how can we ensure that our ideas are well-supported? How do we know whether a person's evidence supports a proposition or not?
	Knowledge and the knower

Supposition	A belief held without proof or certain knowledge; an assumption or hypothesis. We can, for example, work on the supposition that somebody's death was an accident.
	How do we know when it is useful to make a supposition? How far can supposition be described as a state of imagination?
	Knowledge and the knower
Suppress	To forcibly put an end to something; to prevent the dissemination of information; to inhibit. (See also silencing.)
	For instance, some drugs can suppress the body's natural immune response; uprisings can also be suppressed. We can attempt to suppress a feeling of panic within ourselves, or we can describe certain voices as being historically suppressed (such as those of people of colour).
	How do we know whether something or someone has been suppressed? What are some possible ethical implications of this? How do we know whether a drug successfully suppresses the body's natural response? How do we know in what situations this might be desirable?
	Language, Human sciences, Natural sciences
Survey	1. To look closely at, or examine; to investigate people's views by asking them questions. (Verb)
	2. An investigation into people's experiences or opinions, based on a series of questions. (Noun)
	For example, a survey might only be concerned with interviewing those of a certain demographic. We can also survey the damage to our car after a crash, or write a book surveying the history of feminism.
	How do we know whether a survey we have devised is free of bias? How far can this be avoided? How do we know whether surveys are an effective way of obtaining and developing our knowledge?
	Human sciences, Natural sciences
Survivorship bias	The logical error of concentrating on the people or things that made it past some selection process and overlooking those that did not, typically because of their lack of visibility.
	Survivorship bias can be seen, for example, if three of the five students with the best college grades went to the same high school: some might believe, as a result of this, that the high school must offer an excellent education when maybe it is just a larger school than others attending the same college came from.
	What are some possible effects of survivorship bias? How far can survivorship bias be avoided?
	Human sciences, Mathematics, Natural sciences
Susceptible	Likely to be influenced or harmed; easily influenced by emotions. For instance, patients with a particular disease may be susceptible to infection, or con artists can persuade susceptible individuals, such as the elderly, to part with their money.
	How do we know if we are susceptible to something? How far is knowledge itself susceptible to analysis?
	Human sciences, Natural sciences
Syllogism	When a conclusion is drawn from two given or assumed propositions (premises); a common or middle term is present in the two premises but not in the conclusion, which may be invalid (eg all dogs are animals; all animals have four legs; therefore, all dogs have four legs).
	An example of a faulty syllogism could be: "All men have brains. All humans have brains. Therefore, all humans are men."
	Advertisements sometimes contain syllogisms, as they skip major or minor premises in order to persuade quickly (eg "Women love men who drive Lincoln MKZs.").
	How do we know whether syllogisms are useful? How do we know if a syllogistic fallacy has taken place? What possible effects do syllogisms, and syllogistic fallacies, have on knowledge and how we process information?
	Language

Symbol	A mark, image or character representing an object, function, idea, or process. In cognitive science and *semantics*, the symbol grounding problem concerns how it is that words (symbols in general) get their meanings, and hence is closely related to the problem of what meaning itself really is.

Symbol — A mark, image or character representing an object, function, idea, or process. In cognitive science and *semantics*, the symbol grounding problem concerns how it is that words (symbols in general) get their meanings, and hence is closely related to the problem of what meaning itself really is.

For instance, a limousine in a novel might symbolize a character's wealth and authority. In a research report, we might refer to a symbol being used in a particular figure and what this might represent (eg "R, as seen in Figure 5, represents an ineffective gene.").

How do we interpret a symbol's meaning? How far can this be done accurately? How do we know if symbols have any meaning at all? To what extent is the meaning of symbols culturally dependent? How far do symbols help us to advance our knowledge, and how far do they frustrate it? How do we know if the use of symbols is necessary? How do we know whether symbols aid the transmission of knowledge? How reliable are symbols as mirrors of reality? To what extent do we say that a symbol is a true representation of the ideal or **absolute** *knowledge?*

The Arts, Language, Mathematics, Natural sciences

Syncretism — The combining of different beliefs, while blending practices of various schools of thought. In religion, syncretism is when multiple belief systems are blended into a new system. It could even be said that few religions are completely free of syncretism or encounters with other religions.

How do we know whether syncretism has occurred? How might syncretism enhance, or frustrate, the development of knowledge? What conditions make a mingling of religions possible? To what extent does contact from missionaries enable syncretism to occur? How do we know under what circumstances syncretism will result in a functional religion? How do we know whether similarity between doctrines is accidental, or an example of deliberate syncretism?

Religious knowledge

Synthetic — Artificial; made to imitate a natural material; or, insincere/not genuine. In logic, being able to determine whether something is true or false based on experience.

For instance, we can say that the car tyres were made of synthetic rubber, or that speech-writers often use synthetic personalization to persuade listeners (making the speech seem personal to them, or like it is addressing them directly, when of course it is not).

How can we distinguish a natural material from a synthetic one, or synthetic behaviour from genuine emotional reactions? How far does this matter in relation to the development of knowledge?

Human sciences, Natural sciences, Technology

Systematize — To arrange according to an organized system; to make systematic. For instance, some scientists try to systematize life and its origins.

How do we decide how to systematize ideas? How do we know which systems are 'best' for classifying, categorizing and organization of knowledge? How do we know whether systematization is needed?

Knowledge and the knower

Taboo — Prohibited or restricted utterances or actions, according to social customs. For example, sex can be considered a taboo subject.

How can we judge whether or not something is taboo? How can we tell whether or not the designation of something as taboo is justified? How far is the idea of taboo useful or necessary in terms of the advancement of knowledge?

Human sciences, Language

Tabula rasa — An absence of preconceived ideas or predetermined goals; literally a 'blank slate'. Also, the theory that individuals are born without built-in mental content, and therefore all knowledge comes from experience or perception.

How far can humans be considered a 'tabula rasa'? How do we know whether the development of the human mind is entirely controllable? What are some possible advantages of, and problems with, this theory? How do we know whether a newborn's mind is 'blank'?

Human sciences

Tacit knowledge	The kind of knowledge that is difficult to transfer to another person by writing it down or verbalizing it; intuitive knowledge that is transferred to others through socialisation and mentoring.
	Tacit knowledge might also be considered 'unwritten rules' that are well-known in an organization or society, but never documented, pointed out or discussed. Other examples of tacit knowledge could be leadership, innovation, aesthetic sense, salesmanship, body language, humour, or emotional intelligence.
	How far are individuals aware of what they know (and as such, of what they can pass on to others, even if only implicitly)? How far can explicit knowledge be converted into tacit knowledge, and vice versa?
	Human sciences, Language
Tangible	Perceptible by touch; substantially real; obvious or easily detectable. For instance, baking can be considered a rewarding pastime as it yields immediately tangible results. Your teachers might also say you have made tangible progress this school year.
	How can we tell if something is tangible or not? How far is reality made up of tangible things?
	Natural sciences
Tautological	Needlessly repetitive of an idea, statement or word. In mathematics, a formula or assertion that is true in every possible interpretation.
	For example, the phrase 'water baptism' is tautological, as baptism is always with water. In mathematics, an example is "x=y or x≠y".
	If a statement appears to impart new information, how can we tell if it is really doing this, or just giving us information that is already known? What are some possible limits of mathematical tautologies?
	Language, Mathematics
Taxonomy	The branch of science concerned with classification, especially of organisms. For example, a scientist might revise the taxonomy of groups of bacteria that are important in the field of medicine. We can also say that a taxonomy of a particular group of organisms (eg Cuban birds) is still in flux if it has not been finalised or completed.
	How do we know whether a particular classification system (or taxonomy) is effective? How far can we decide how to partition life? How far do taxonomies help us to organise and expand knowledge? In what ways might taxonomies limit our knowledge?
	Natural sciences
Teachings	Ideas or principles taught by an authority. For example, we might talk about the teachings of the Koran.
	How do we know what different teachings are based on? How do we decide which teachings to follow, trust or believe?
	Religious knowledge
Technology	The application of scientific knowledge for practical purposes; machinery and equipment developed from the application of scientific knowledge. For instance, it can be argued that science and technology improve our lives, and that the technology of the world wide web, in particular, has transformed how we receive news and information.
	How do we know what the limits of technology are? How do we decide whether technological presence in our lives is a good thing? What are some possible ethical implications of the use of technology? How do we know that technology is being used in a moral way? How far does this matter?
	Technology
Teleology	The study of the end purpose or overall goal of something, as opposed to its cause. (See also aetiology.) Teleologists might argue that we can, and should, judge how good or bad something is by how good or bad its result is. Teleological explanations of evolution also claim that all changes happen for a reason, or definite purpose.
	How far is it valuable to consider the reason or end result of something? What may this approach contribute to knowledge? What may it be leaving out? How might this approach impact our decision-making?
	Knowledge and the knower

Temporal	1. Relating to time.
	2. Relating to worldly/non-spiritual matters.
	For example, it can be argued that a particular political or environmental crisis should be analysed from different temporal perspectives.
	How do we know whether we should view a problem or situation in its temporal context, or whether this does not matter?
	Natural sciences, Religious knowledge
Temporary	Not permanent; lasting only for a short time. For instance, prescription drugs can temporarily relieve pain, or a company can seek extra temporary workers in busy periods (eg in the run-up to Christmas or Eid).
	How far can it be foreseen whether a situation is temporary or permanent?
	Knowledge and the knower
Tenable	Able to be maintained or defended against attack or objection. For example, scholarships can be awarded based on a student maintaining a particular GPA; if this happens, then the scholarship can be considered tenable. If a situation is deemed untenable it means that the speaker thinks the situation cannot continue in the same way.
	How do we know whether a situation, system, idea, or conclusion is tenable or not? How far might whether something is tenable or untenable be culturally dependent?
	Human sciences
Tension	1. A mental or emotional strain; a strained political or social state or relationship.
	2. A relationship between ideas that have conflicting demands or implications.
	For instance, tension between governments and the military can result in a coup d'état. Also, if you suffer a lot from stress or tension, it can be difficult to think clearly. If there is a lot of tension between two sometimes competing parties or fields – such as medicine and the media – it may not make for an easy relationship.
	How might tensions between different beliefs enable knowledge to develop, or frustrate this process?
	Human sciences, Politics
Tentative	Not certain or fixed; provisional; hesitant or without confidence. For instance, scientists may form tentative conclusions about specimens that they have discovered.
	How do we know whether or not we can be secure in our conclusions? If the nature of knowledge is tentative, how far can any of us really say we know anything at all?
	Knowledge and the knower
Testable	Able to be trialled or tried. Some would argue that if a theory is truly scientific, then it should be testable.
	To what extent are theories testable? How do we know whether an idea is testable or not?
	Human sciences, Natural sciences
Testify	To give evidence based on your personal knowledge and belief, especially as a witness in a court of law. For example, you can testify in court that you saw someone leaving an area at the time of an incident; new managers may also testify that managing people is not easy.
	How might group testimony differ from individual testimony? To what extent can we reliably testify how things are in the world? What responsibilities (both epistemic and other) come with testifying? How far can we ensure that people testify competently, conscientiously, and honestly? How do we know whether someone has the knowledge, skills, or abilities to testify competently?
	Human sciences, Language
Testimony	A formal written or spoken statement, especially in a court of law, explaining a point of view on an incident; the intentional transfer of a belief from one person to another; also, evidence or proof of something. For instance, an eyewitness' testimony may be read out loud in court.
	How do we judge the epistemic value of testimony (is it reliable, and when and how does testimony become fact)? Is someone's word alone sufficient to justify the beliefs a hearer acquires from those assertions? How far can testimony give us knowledge if we have no reasons of our own?
	Human sciences, Language

| Theme | A subject, topic, or recurring idea. The TOK course has one core theme (knowledge and the knower) as well as five optional themes: knowledge and language, knowledge and technology, knowledge and politics, knowledge and religion, and knowledge and indigenous societies. |

How might teachers decide which two of the five optional themes you are to study in class? How might these decisions affect the development and dissemination of knowledge? How useful is it to separate knowledge into themes?

Knowledge and the knower

Theory

A system of ideas intended to explain something, usually based on general principles that are not obviously or directly connected to the thing you are trying to explain. Also, an idea used to account for a situation or course of action. For example, the theory of evolution is based on all species being related and gradually changing over time.

How far can theories be deemed simplifications of reality? How do we know whether or not our theories are correct? How can we tell if a theory has been misapplied?

Natural sciences

Thesis

1. A statement or theory that is put forward to be proved or disproved.

2. A long essay written as part of university studies (also known as a dissertation), usually running to at least 8000 words.

For example, your experiments in your chemistry class might help you to formulate a thesis to share with your teacher and classmates. When writing an essay, it can also be a good idea to include a thesis statement in your introduction, where you state your opinion on the topic directly, in one or two sentences. This can also include an overview or preview of your essay's structure and what you will discuss.

How do you know if you are putting forward a valid or well-argued thesis (or thesis statement)?

Language, Natural sciences

Thinker

A person with highly developed intellectual powers, who considers things deeply and seriously. For instance, some would argue that we are not entitled to rewrite past thinkers in the light of current concerns.

How do we know whether someone is a great thinker? Is it more important to be a great thinker or a great doer, and how do we know? How far do such standards of 'greatness' change? To what extent is this innate, and how far is it a skill that can be learned?

Human sciences

Thorough

Detailed; careful and complete. For example, you need to be thorough in your research, and apply and analyse it judiciously, to receive a good grade.

How do we know whether we have been sufficiently thorough? In what situations might it be possible to be too thorough? What implications might this have for our knowledge?

Language

Thought experiment

A hypothetical situation in which a hypothesis, theory, or principle is laid out for the purpose of thinking through its consequences.

One famous thought experiment is Mary's Room: if Mary is brought up only with black and white pictures, and raised in a black and white room, with a computer that has a black and white screen, and has never seen any other colour, yet becomes a colour researcher who knows everything about colour, does Mary learn anything if one day her computer breaks and only shows a red screen?

What questions do thought experiments raise about the nature of knowledge? How do we know what a 'good' thought experiment is? How can we judge whether thought experiments are useful for the development of knowledge? How far can we trust our intuitions we have about problems set in non-existent worlds, or that postulate the existence of impossible creatures?

Human sciences

T

Time-lag argument	The idea that there is a delay between our perceptions and the external things we seem to directly perceive; these external things happen in the past; thus, what we directly perceive must be something else (for example, sense-data) and we can only at best indirectly perceive other things. (See also indirect realism, sense-data.)

When we see the sun, what we are actually seeing is how the sun was 8 minutes ago; the sun might not even exist now, but we are still seeing what we see – which is not at all identical with the sun. This is essentially what the time-lag argument presents to us.

How do we know whether what we see is a past or current image? How far is the time-lag argument compatible with the idea that the brain and eye appear to have a mechanism that helps us 'predict' future events?

See https://cutt.ly/TOKBSF for more on this topic.

Natural sciences

Tool

A thing used to help perform a job; a person who is used or exploited by another. (Not to be confused with the slang word 'tool', meaning 'idiot'.)

For example, early humans made tools out of stone, or laws can prove effective tools in fighting poverty. If wanting to show that we think someone is being exploited, we can say, for instance, that the government is a tool of an organization like the ERG or NRA.

In archaeology, how do we know what primitive societies used tools for? How can we tell whether a person is being used as a tool by another person or organization?

Human sciences, Politics

Topical

Of immediate relevance, interest, or importance owing to its relation to current events. Late-night chat shows often contain topical discussions, for instance, as well as celebrity interviews and political debates.

How do we know what is topical? How do we know when or if what is topical has changed? How might the decision as to whether something is topical or not affect the development of knowledge? To what extent does what is topical organically evolve?

Human sciences, Politics

Totemism

A system of belief in which humans are said to have kinship or a mystical relationship with a spirit-being, such as an animal or plant.

For individuals, totemism might represent a relationship of friendship and protection between a person and animal (or other natural object), whereas for groups, totemism might involve multiple features, including a mystic association between animal and plant species, natural phenomena, passing down totems within families, group and personal names based on the totem, and the use of totemistic emblems and symbols.

How far is totemism represented in Western society? How might this differ from its representation amongst indigenous peoples? How far is a traditional way of thinking and structuring of social relations within the community, and its relationship with nature using the totemic system, viable in modern times?

Indigenous knowledge

Trade-off

A situational decision that involves diminishing or losing one quality, quantity, or property of a set or design, in return for gains in other aspects. Trade-offs may exist, for example, between the level of accuracy of a particular scientific method and the cost of undertaking it.

How far can we assess or predict the value of possible trade-offs? What are the possible effects of trade-offs on the development of knowledge?

Knowledge and the knower

Traditional ecological knowledge

Also known as TEK, this refers to indigenous and other traditional knowledge of local natural resources. TEK might be particularly important, for example, in terms of understanding the impact of changes within ecosystems.

How far should indigenous populations retain intellectual property rights over traditional knowledge? If TEK is most often preserved by way of oral traditions, how far can these methods be validated without documentary evidence? If methods of acquiring and collecting knowledge in TEK are different from those used to create and validate scientific ecological knowledge from a Western perspective, how far can we decide which are 'most' valid or valuable?

Human sciences, Indigenous knowledge, Natural sciences

Trajectory	The pathway an object or trend is following, or is predicted to follow. For example, a missile may deflect from its intended or expected trajectory, or we can say that someone's career or a country's politics is on an upward or downward trajectory. It can also be argued that valid trajectories ought to correspond to patterns of change in other variables.
	How far can we estimate what a trajectory might look like?
	Human sciences, Mathematics, Natural sciences
Transcendental idealism	The idea that fundamental aspects of experience are contributed by the person doing the perceiving, rather than by the perceived objects themselves. (See also indirect realism.)
	For example, if a bartender asks you for ID, they are comparing your appearance in your photo to the appearance of your actual face at that moment, and wondering if this is an informative, accurate portrayal of reality. This real-life situation is an instance of transcendental idealism, as the bartender – who is perceiving you – is contributing to their fundamental aspects of experience more than your photo or your actual face at that moment when they ask you for ID. (Whether the bartender gets it right or not depends on how experienced they are; that is, many years of experience of IDing people, or just a few weeks).
	How do we know whether space and time exist 'in themselves', as opposed to being dependent on our perceptions? How far is appearance a reasonable reflection of reality?
	Knowledge and the knower
Transcendentalism	The belief that at heart people are truly good, along with a belief in the goodness of nature and the belief that people are at their best when truly self-reliant and independent.
	Transcendentalists would say that individuals can generate completely original thoughts and insights, with little attention paid to past masters, with subjective intuition emphasized over objective empiricism.
	How far are we reliant on others' past knowledge to build our own present knowledge? To what extent can intuition be said to be a more important way of knowing than experience and scientific experiment? How far do society and its institutions corrupt the purity of the individual? How far could transcendentalism be described as 'beyond reason'? How can we tell if this is a positive or negative thing? How do we know whether we are truly independent or self-reliant, and what implications does this have for knowledge?
	Human sciences
Transformation	The act or process of changing completely. For example, the Covid-19 pandemic has seen a transformation of the music and theatre industries, who have ramped up their provision of streaming services at a time when face-to-face gigs are no longer possible.
	To what extent is knowledge transformed by technology? How do we know if we are transformed by new knowledge?
	Human sciences, Knowledge and the knower, Technology
Transient	Lasting only for a short time; impermanent or ephemeral. For instance, scientists might report transient differences of only a few degrees Fahrenheit from one spot to another within a cell, even though this is a space ranging from only about five to 120 microns in diameter in humans.
	We can also talk about emotions as transient (as in fleeting and untrustworthy), or even populations (for example, Antarctica is home to a transient population of about 4,000 scientists and support staff, as well as around 20 million penguins).
	How do we judge whether something is transient or more permanent? To what extent is a transient diversity of beliefs necessary for good inquiry?
	Knowledge and the knower
Translation	1. The process of rendering a text into a different language, and the end product of this process.
	2. The conversion of something from one form or medium into another.
	For instance, it can be considered vital that research findings are translated into clinical practice.
	How do we know whether ideas and theories have been translated into real-life practice? How far does translation enable the transmission of knowledge? And how far does it inhibit it? How do we know what the 'best' translation of a text is? Why might there be a need for multiple translations of a text into the same language? How can we assess whether or not translation is a reliable process?
	See this link for a specific example: https://cutt.ly/TOKDFF
	The Arts, Language

Transmission	The act or process of transmitting something (or, 'passing it on'). For instance, drugs can be used to prevent the transmission of a disease.
	In the natural sciences, how do we know how or if a disease has been transmitted from one person to another? More generally, how do we know whether our ideas have been transmitted in the way we intended? How far can we obtain knowledge through the written and spoken words of others?
	Language, Natural sciences
Transparency	(Literally) see-through; (figuratively) operating in such a way that it is easy for others to see what you have done and why.
	If you are being transparent, this means you are being open; this implies communication, and accountability. In philosophy, pain is considered strongly transparent, as people know immediately if they are in pain or not.
	How far can, or should, transparency be fully achieved in social contexts? What implications does transparency have for knowledge as a whole? How do we distinguish between transparency, confidentiality, and privacy? How far does our subconscious make full transparency possible? What are the possible relationships between revealed and concealed knowledge? What are the possible connections between transparency and power?
	Human sciences, Language, Natural sciences, Politics
Transrationalism	The idea of phenomena occurring within the natural universe where information and experiences do not readily fit into the typical cause and effect structure; the kinds of experiences often dismissed as superstitious.
	Transrational experiences might include people seeing or sensing evil or blessed omens which later come true, or feelings of dread which save an individual from catastrophe, even without prior context or knowledge (for instance, having a 'feeling' that you shouldn't board a plane, and then the plane later crashes).
	How do we know whether transrational experiences are based on truth? How far does transrationalism equate to faith? Is instinct the same thing as transrationalism?
	Human sciences, Religious knowledge
Trend	1. A general direction in which something is developing or changing.
	2. A fashion, or a topic that comes up on social media many times within a short period.
	For example, we might detect a steady upward trend in profits. 'Trend' can also be used as a verb.
	How can we tell if a trend exists? In what ways might we be able to manipulate the presentation of data to show a trend? How far can we predict a trend's cycle (in the case of fashions) or trajectory (in the case of data)? How far do trends create opportunities? In what ways might only showing recent trends be problematic?
	See https://cutt.ly/TOKMDT for more ideas on this topic.
	Human sciences, Mathematics, Natural sciences
Trial and error	A method of problem-solving, characterized by repeated, varied attempts which are continued until success is achieved. Learning to crawl as a baby is an example of trial and error.
	How do we know if trial and error is the 'best' way to solve a problem? To what extent is scientific research a trial-and-error process?
	Human sciences, Mathematics, Natural sciences
Triangulation	Using more than one method to collect data on the same topic. It can be reasonably argued that triangulation increases the credibility and validity of the results of qualitative research.
	How far does the use of triangulation increase the accuracy of the knowledge we produce? If there are four types of triangulation (1. data, involving space, time, and people; 2. investigator – using multiple researchers; 3. theory – using more than one theory to interpret the phenomenon; and 4. methodological – using more than one method), how do we decide which method(s) of triangulation to use, and which might be more reliable?
	Human sciences

Trolley problem	A **thought experiment** involving ethical dilemmas of whether to sacrifice one person to save a larger number.
	If the trolley problem asks us to sacrifice different individuals each time, such as a fat man or a young child, how does this affect our responses? How far does the trolley problem (and thought experiments generally) apply to the real world and as such contribute to the development of real-life knowledge? To what extent can trolley problems, and other thought experiments, be used to judge our moral fibre? How far is the trolley problem too extreme to be useful? To what extent can the trolley problem be described as a mathematical problem rather than an ethical one? What implications might the trolley problem have for modern technologies, such as self-driving cars?
	For a short video explanation of the trolley problem, go here: https://cutt.ly/TOKTP
	Human sciences, Mathematics, Technology
Trope	1. The use of figurative language, via a word, a phrase or an image, for artistic effect, such as using a simile or metaphor.
	2. Also, referring to commonly used themes, motifs, or clichés.
	For example, TV shows might try to avoid the trope of being unmarried meaning that you are unfulfilled – or deploy this trope deliberately to create comedy. Metaphysically, tropes are qualities, such as the redness of a particular rose, or the specific nuance of green of an individual leaf.
	How far can we distinguish between one trope and another? To what extent can tropes contribute to the development of knowledge?
	The Arts, Human sciences, Language, Natural sciences
Trust	Firm belief in the reliability, truth, or ability of someone or something; faith or confidence; accepting the truth of a statement without further investigation or requiring more evidence. For example, we might trust in the powers of justice, or trust only in primary sources when researching.
	What are some possible risks of trusting others for information? How far is this necessary? How far is it valuable to trust others for information, as opposed to relying on oneself? How far does trust enable the dissemination of knowledge? How far does trust also involve responsibility? To what extent is self-trust an intellectual virtue? What are some possible relationships between trust and power, and what might be some possible implications for knowledge?
	Human sciences, Politics
Truth	That which is true, or in accordance with fact or reality. We might check to see if something is true using the correspondence test (by checking to see if it corresponds with reality), the coherence test (seeing if the piece of information is clear and logical, and consistent with what we already know), and/or the pragmatic test (checking to see if something is practical/actually works or not).
	Is truth 'made', or 'found'? How might we be able to distinguish between these two ideas? How important is it to discover 'the truth'? To what extent is truth discoverable?
	Human sciences
Truthiness	The belief or assertion that a particular statement is true based on the intuition or perceptions of some individual or individuals, without regard to evidence, logic, intellectual examination, or facts. (See also **knowledge claim**.)
	Truthiness can be said to refer to statements that feel true but are actually false. For example, climate change deniers may make some very strong, authoritative sounding statements which appear to be true, but which are actually not.
	For what reasons might truthiness feel or seem plausible? What are some possible implications of truthiness for the development of knowledge?
	Human sciences, Politics
Tu quoque fallacy	Also known as the 'you too' fallacy or 'look who's talking' fallacy, this tries to discredit the opponent's argument by attacking the opponent's own personal behaviour as being inconsistent with the argument's conclusion(s).
	One example of tu quoque would be a teenager saying to his parents, "How can you punish me for experimenting with drugs? You did the same thing when you were younger!"
	Why might the tu quoque fallacy be seen as 'more reasonable' than other fallacies? How far can this fallacy be avoided?
	Human sciences

| Two-eyed seeing | The idea that we should learn to perceive things both from the viewpoint of indigenous knowledges and ways of knowing, as well as from the standpoint of mainstream knowledges and ways of knowing, for the benefit of all. |

Two-eyed seeing arguably helps you to always look at things from different perspectives.

How far can non-indigenous populations understand indigenous knowledge and ways of knowing? To what extent is it possible to deploy a mainstream and indigenous viewpoint simultaneously?

Indigenous knowledge

Uncertainty

The state of not knowing; involving imperfect or unknown information; doubt, scepticism, suspicion or mistrust. For example, there may be a degree of uncertainty over the future of a company.

To what extent can uncertainty be overcome? What implications does uncertainty have for decision-making? What are the possible consequences of aleatory uncertainty (uncertainty related to random events involving probability) for the area of knowledge of mathematics, and in general?

Mathematics

Uncertainty principle

The idea in maths and physics that the position and the velocity of an object cannot both be measured exactly, at the same time. The uncertainty principle essentially states that merely looking at a quantum system disturbs it unavoidably.

For a video explanation of the uncertainty principle, go here: https://cutt.ly/TOKUP For a joke about the uncertainty principle, go here: https://cutt.ly/TOKUPBB

How far does the uncertainty principle place limits on what can be known? How far can we be specific about what is meant by 'uncertainty of position' and 'uncertainty of momentum'?

Mathematics, Natural sciences

Unconscious bias

Unconscious biases are social stereotypes about certain groups of people that we form outside our own conscious awareness. For example, white people may have an unconscious bias for other white people. Research into unconscious bias also shows that blonde women are paid around 7% more than brunettes at work.

How far can unconscious bias be understood or reversed? How far can we identify our own unconscious biases? What are some possible ethical implications of unconscious bias?

Human sciences

Unconscious mind

Feelings, thoughts, urges, and memories that are outside of our conscious awareness. The unconscious contains contents that are unacceptable or unpleasant, such as feelings of pain, anxiety, or conflict. For instance, our dreams can be manifestations of our unconscious minds, with conflicts being worked out in dreams and this process preparing us for oncoming challenges.

How far can our unconscious mind be 'unlocked' or accessed? How do we know the extent of the unconscious mind's influence? How do we judge whether or not the unconscious mind even really exists?

Human sciences

Underlying

Significant as a cause or basis of something but not necessarily manifest or obvious. For instance, statistics may or may not tell us about underlying trends; the flu can also be very severe for those with underlying health conditions.

How would we know whether we have an underlying condition or not, if by its nature it is not obvious? How do we know what constitutes an underlying condition? How far can underlying trends or themes be detected, and their significance assessed? How far does the idea of knowledge being multilayered enable us to advance our knowledge?

Natural sciences

Underpowered	In research, an underpowered study does not have a sufficiently large sample size to answer the research question. (See also overpowered.)
	How can we establish what the design of a study is underpowered for (ie what we would like the design of the study to detect)? If a study is underpowered, how can we judge the possible impact on the statistical significance of the results of the study?
	Natural sciences, Human sciences
Unfairness	A lack of equality or justice. For example, one might protest at the unfairness of a trial.
	How do we know whether something is fair or unfair? How far is it possible to act unfairly without knowing it?
	Human sciences
Uninterested	Not concerned about something. (See also disinterested.) For instance, someone can appear uninterested, and look as if they would rather be elsewhere, during an occasion that bores them. Ancient Greek statesman Pericles famously stated that 'Just because you do not take an interest in politics doesn't mean politics won't take an interest in you.'
	How do we decide whether or not something is interesting? What impact does being interested in something – or not – have on the development of knowledge? How do we know if being interested in something is enough to make it worthy of attention? What implications are there of being uninterested?
	Human sciences, Politics
Unilateral	Performed by or affecting only one person, group, or country involved in a situation, without the agreement of another or the others. For example, a world leader could unilaterally withdraw their country from an international agreement.
	What implications does unilateral thinking have for the advancement of knowledge?
	Knowledge and the knower
Unique	One of its kind; unlike anything else in existence; remarkable, special, or unusual. For instance, a situation might be described as being unique to a particular country's politics.
	How do we know if something is unique? To what extent is true uniqueness possible? What implications might this have for the production of knowledge?
	Knowledge and the knower
Universality	The quality of involving or being shared by all people or things in the world, or in a particular group; timelessness; true in, or appropriate for, all situations. For instance, a non-governmental organisation may affirm the universality of human rights, or mathematicians may find universality in electrons' mathematical pattern when materials conduct electricity.
	To what extent is mathematics a universal language? How can we judge whether universality (or what some might call 'relatability') is important in the arts? What implications does universality have for knowledge?
	For more on mathematical universality, take a look at this video: https://cutt.ly/TOKUM
	The Arts, Mathematics
Universe	All existing matter and space considered as a whole; the cosmos. For example, the universe has been expanding since its inception around 13 billion years ago, and is thought to be at least 10 billion light years in diameter.
	How do we know where or if the universe starts or ends? How do we judge the odds of intelligent life existing elsewhere in our universe? How far can the shape of the universe be measured? How do we know how fast the universe is expanding, and how far is it a problem if we don't know the answer to this?
	Natural sciences

Unmistakable	Distinctive; cannot be mistaken for anything else; evident or obvious. For instance, an actress may be said to have unmistakable red-carpet style, or that the Covid-19 pandemic has driven unmistakable suffering.

To what extent can something be proved to be unmistakable? Does it matter if the quality of being unmistakable is intangible? What implications does the idea of something being unmistakable have for our knowledge? To what extent can meaning be unmistakable? How do we know if we have correctly identified something or someone?

Knowledge and the knower

Unobservables

Entities whose existence, nature, properties, qualities or connections are not directly observable by humans. Examples of unobservables could be causation, desire, gravity, or religious belief.

How far can unobservables be controlled during experiments? What other ways might there be to account for or adjust for them? How do we know whether or not these methods of adjustment are reliable? How far can we make valid claims about unobservables?

Natural sciences

Unresolved

When a solution to a problem has not been reached.

To what extent must all questions be answered or all problems be solved? What are some possible implications for knowledge? How might this also affect general satisfaction with our lives? How far is epistemology itself unresolvable? How far can something be deemed functional if it is unresolvable?

Knowledge and the knower

Unsupported

Not borne out by evidence or facts.

What would count as adequate support for a belief? How far do beliefs need to be supported by evidence? What are some possible implications of this for Religious knowledge in particular?

Human sciences, Religious knowledge

Urban legend

A humorous or horrific story or piece of information circulated as though true; it may originate as having allegedly happened to a friend or family member. Urban legends can be circulated orally, or via media, such as newspapers, email, and social media. One such urban legend is that of Slender Man, which has gained something of a cult following.

How far does technology facilitate, and how far does it debunk, urban legends? What implications might this have for knowledge? How do we know whether something is an urban legend or not? How do we decide whether or not to believe in them? For what reasons might people believe in urban legends? How far is it possible or desirable to suppress the spread of urban legends?

Human sciences, Language

Usefulness

The quality or fact of being helpful or useful. For instance, a book's usefulness can be added to through the use of a bibliography and references; trials also have to confirm treatments for new diseases before they can be prescribed to the general public.

How do we know when or if something has outlived its usefulness? What factors may affect the usefulness of something?

Knowledge and the knower

Utilitarianism

The theory that all actions should maximize happiness and wellbeing, and avoid causing unhappiness or harm. Utilitarianism ultimately aims for the betterment of the whole society, and this is particularly important when making social, economic, or political decisions.

How far can we decide if an action is right or wrong based on its effects? What might be some problems with this theory? How far is it possible to always act in a way that causes no unhappiness or harm? How do we decide what 'happiness' and 'wellbeing' might consist of? How far is utilitarianism effective as a 'one-size-fits-all' policy? To what extent does utilitarianism enable a society to function well?

Human sciences

Vacuum	1. A space entirely devoid of matter.
	2. A gap left by the loss, death, or departure of someone or something significant.
	3. The idea of a context-free space.
	For example, the death of a particularly prominent political leader may be said to leave a vacuum in society. It can also be said that no artists work 'in a vacuum' as everyone is inevitably influenced by others and what is going on around them.
	How far can ideas be considered in a context-free space?
	The Arts, Language, Politics
Vagueness	Lacking certainty or precision.
	For example, the vagueness of the terms used in a document, or the vagueness of someone's plans, may give us cause for concern. Some might also argue that the predicate 'is tall' is vague as nobody can say definitively at what point someone becomes 'tall'.
	How far can reality and knowledge themselves be vague? What implications does vagueness have for knowledge? To what extent can vagueness be prevented? In what situations might vagueness actually be desirable?
	Language
Valid	1. Based on fact or logic; reasonable.
	2. Legally acceptable.
	For instance, a visa can be valid for 30 days, or someone can put forward a valid argument.
	How do we know whether an idea or explanation is valid? How far might what is considered valid change over time? What implications might this have for knowledge? How far does it matter who decides what is valid?
	Human sciences
Validate	To check or prove the accuracy of something. For example, trials can validate scientific claims, and courts can validate contracts.
	How far can something be fully validated? How do we know what processes are necessary in order to validate something? For what reasons do ideas need to be validated? What judgments are we making when we validate an idea, and how do we know if we are correct to do so?
	Human sciences
Value judgment	A judgment on the rightness or wrongness of something. Such judgments vary from person to person (and also within people over time).
	"That vase is really ugly." "He did a very good thing there." "The decision was completely wrong." "She is beautiful!" "It was right that he took the purse to the police station." "It was a bad time in her life, but she has bounced back from it well." All of these statements are examples of value judgments.
	How far can values be objective? How do we know what our and others' value judgments are based on? How far could it be said that value judgments are always wrong? To what extent do value judgments have a practical purpose or application?
	The Arts, Human sciences, Language
Value-free	Purely objective; free from criteria imposed by subjective values or standards. It can be argued, for instance, that science could and should be value-free.
	What would be some potential risks of being value-free? To what extent should academic disciplines be value-free? What are some possible ethical implications of freedom from values? How far can research be neutral if researchers (as human beings) cannot be value-free? How far are texts value-free? What implications might this have for power and its connections to knowledge?
	Human sciences

Values	The importance, worth, or usefulness of something; principles or standards of behaviour, based on what you think is important in life.
	For instance, children can internalize their parents' values and rules. Someone's support can also be of great value; financially, a book priced at €10 might be perceived as good value if it contains high-quality content, is printed using sustainable materials, is supported by well-designed graphics, and so on.
	How do we know what our ethical and social values are? To what extent can we consciously decide what these are? How do we know if our values have changed? How can we tell if something has epistemic value (or adds to our knowledge)? To what extent are values objective?
	Human sciences, Politics
Vantage point	A place or position giving us a good view of something, or the circumstances or context from which we approach an idea.
	In a literal sense, we can say, for instance, that from a particular vantage point it is possible to see into the garden of the house next door. More metaphorically, we can say, for example, that we should not view problems from the vantage point of a single political party, or that in our research, we are approaching ideas from a different vantage point to previous researchers.
	How do we know whether our chosen vantage point is valuable, correct, or useful? How far is our vantage point something we can consciously choose?
	Human sciences
Veridical	Truthful; coinciding with reality. It is possible, for instance, that our perceptual experience is not veridical, due to things like illusions or hallucinations.
	How do we know whether or not something is veridical, especially our sense-perception? How far does language enable us to conceptualise what is veridical?
	Language, Natural sciences
Verificationism	The idea that only statements that are empirically verifiable (ie verifiable through the senses) are cognitively meaningful. As such, verificationism rejects statements specific to entire fields, such as aesthetics, theology and ethics, as these are not verifiable through the senses.
	How far can we judge whether or not something is meaningful? To what extent does it matter if something is not scientifically verifiable? To what extent is meaningfulness in the sense of influencing emotions of behaviour different to meaningfulness in the sense of conveying information or facts? What are some possible implications of verificationism for different areas of knowledge, including science itself?
	Natural sciences
Verify	To make sure, demonstrate or check that something is true, accurate or justified. For example, conclusions can be verified by experiments.
	How far can we verify the truth of a claim? How do we decide which fact-checking methods to use? How can we assess the reliability of verification processes (eg when ordering something online using a credit card or other form of digital payment)?
	Technology
Version	A particular form of something, differing in certain respects from an earlier form, or other forms of the same type of thing; an account of an event from a particular person's viewpoint. For instance, we can tell someone our version of events, or present our EE supervisor with a revised version of our essay following their feedback.
	How do we know whether or not a person's version of events is reliable? How can we tell whether a new version of something is actually better than the version that came before it?
	Human sciences, Language, Technology

Vested interest

An individual's own stake in an investment or project, especially where a financial gain or loss is possible. For instance, companies with a vested interest in a deal may be responsible for leaks about a possible merger. Social networks also have a vested interest in being able to track users, so are bound to be against the idea of people being able to opt out.

How do we know whether or not somebody has a vested interest in something? What are some possible ethical implications of a vested interest? How far should you be obliged to declare your involvement with a person or company?

Human sciences, Politics

Via

Through; by way of; by means of; using. For example, you can send a document via email, arrive via train, or let someone know something via a friend.

How can we assess the reliability of information when it has come to us via someone else (ie second-hand or third-hand)?

Knowledge and the knower

Viability

Ability to work, survive or live successfully. For instance, rising costs may threaten businesses' viability, and successful conception depends on the viability of both the woman's egg and the man's sperm.

How do we know whether something is viable? How do we know whether, or if, one way of looking at the world is more viable from another? How far can we judge the epistemic viability of something?

Human sciences, Natural sciences

Vice

Bad or weak behaviour or quality, especially from a moral standpoint. Epistemic vice is a negative character trait which specifically gets in the way of building, disseminating, or interpreting knowledge. (See also **virtue**.)

Vices can be anything from cigars to hypocrisy. The latter might be counted more specifically as an epistemic vice, as it could get in the way of knowledge. Other examples of epistemic vice might be closed-mindedness, not being sensitive to detail, wishful thinking, or prejudice.

How far can we identify our own epistemic vices? To what extent can epistemic vices, such as gullibility or prejudice, be overcome? How far is it possible to detect epistemic vice in others?

Human sciences, Knowledge and the knower

Virtue

A form of behaviour showing high standards, especially moral ones; a good or useful quality. Epistemic virtue is a positive character trait which actively enables information to be built up, spread around, or interpreted. (See also **vice**.)

For instance, you can extol the virtues of a particular product, such as a car; virtues can also be aspects such as kindness or curiosity. Examples of epistemic virtue might be being honest, being objective, being curious, being attentive to detail, or being creative.

How do we know what virtues we possess? What virtues may help us in the pursuit of knowledge (we might call these epistemic virtues)? How do we know whether a quality such as honesty always enables knowledge to be developed? How can we tell what epistemic virtues (if any) we ourselves possess? How can we ascertain whether or not someone else has a particular epistemic virtue?

Human sciences, Knowledge and the knower

Virtue epistemology

A form of epistemology which focuses on the agent (person doing things) or knower, based on their intellectual or epistemic virtues. (See also **virtue**.)

Virtue epistemology is based on the idea that focusing on individual intellectual strengths is essential in terms of helping us to know what knowledge really involves.

What are the qualities of an excellent thinker? How far are our intellectual virtues (or strengths) stable? How far can these intellectual virtues be acquired if we do not already have them? How do we know what an epistemic virtue is? To what extent are epistemic virtues motivated by a love of truth? How far do epistemic virtues produce knowledge and understanding?

Knowledge and the knower

| Vis-à-vis | In reference or relation to; as compared with. For example, someone may need to speak with you vis-à-vis some upcoming arrangements; foreign companies may also have an edge vis-à-vis a country's national firms. |

How do we know whether there is a relevant relationship, or comparison to be made, between two things?

Knowledge and the knower

| Visible | Able to be seen or noticed easily. For instance, there can be a visible improvement in a student's attitude since they have begun taking private lessons with a particular teacher. Phenomena related to the weather, such as fog or heavy rain, can also decrease how far something is visible. |

If something is not visible, how do we know whether or not it is really there?

Natural sciences

| Vouch | To assert – as a result of your own experience – that something is true or accurately described; confirm that someone is who they say they are, or that they are of good character. For example, you may be able to vouch for your teacher's skills, or vouch for the efficiency of something that you have purchased. |

How do we know whether or not we can vouch for something or someone? If someone vouches for something or someone, how do we know whether or not to trust their endorsement?

Knowledge and the knower

| Watershed | 1. Significant, meaningful; impacting everything that happens afterwards. (Adjective) |
| | 2. A moment in the day after which certain TV programmes cannot be broadcast because they are considered inappropriate for children. (Noun) |

For example, the invention of the printing press might be described as a watershed moment. A TV programme might not be shown until after the watershed (usually 9 pm) if it contains too much swearing or adult imagery for children to see.

Who decides what a watershed moment is? How do we know what counts as a watershed moment? Similarly, who decides what an appropriate time is for a TV watershed to be set at? How do we know what a 'good' watershed time is? How far is the TV watershed still relevant in the 21st century, and how do we know this?

History, Human sciences, Politics, Technology

| Ways of knowing (WOKs) | The methods through which knowledge becomes apparent to us; ways in which we make sense of the world. In our study of TOK, we can talk about eight different ways of knowing: intuition, reasoning, faith, emotion, memory, sense perception, imagination, and language. |

How do we know whether these eight ways are sufficient, or whether there might be more? How far are these ways of knowing actually separate from one another? How far would it be possible to learn about the world through one WOK alone?

Knowledge and the knower

| Weasel words | Words or phrases used to avoid being direct, especially when addressing a difficult issue. |

Weasel words can be used when speakers want to make it appear that they have answered a question clearly, or stated something directly, when they have actually said something vague or inconclusive. Examples of weasel words might include modal verbs such as 'could' or adverbs such as 'possibly'.

How far do weasel words enable their users to abdicate (give up) responsibility? What are some possible ethical implications of using weasel words? What repercussions might the use of weasel words have for knowledge itself?

Language, Politics

Weighting	Emphasis or priority; allowance or adjustment made in order to take account of special circumstances or compensate for a distorting factor.

Weighting

Emphasis or priority; allowance or adjustment made in order to take account of special circumstances or compensate for a distorting factor.

For instance, your teachers may multiply a score from each of your assessments by a particular weighting, depending on the importance of the assignment. Consumers may also decide – at least subconsciously – what weighting to give to quality as well as price when trying to decide what to buy.

How do we know when, why and how to use weighted scores? How far can we ensure that weighted scores are being used fairly? What are the possible advantages and pitfalls of the use of weighting?

Human sciences, Mathematics, Natural sciences

Whataboutism

A way of deflecting from an argument by saying that someone else – who isn't the arguer – is doing something bad as well. (See also tu quoque fallacy.)

Whataboutism accuses tangential parties of wrongdoing so as to undermine an argument's context; this wrongdoing, too, may be tangential, so as to move the topic of an argument away to something that the accuser prefers to discuss instead. For example, in the wake of alt-right violence, an example of whataboutism would be to say 'what about the alt-left?'.

How do we know how to respond to whataboutism? How far can a meaningful discussion be had with someone who uses whataboutism extensively? How do we know whether the use of whataboutism is valid?

Politics

Whimsical

Impulsive, unpredictable or fickle; old-fashioned, sweet, fun, unusual, or twee, in an appealing or amusing way. For instance, somebody can be said to dress in a whimsical style. Even bureaucratic or legal processes can be described as whimsical. For example, if the speaker is wanting to contrast the seriousness of the outcome (eg the citizenship of millions of people) with the triviality of the paperwork involved, or if they wish to imply that those handling the process do not take it seriously.

How do we know whether a judgment or action is whimsical? How far do whimsical actions or events contribute to the development of knowledge?

Knowledge and the knower

Whitewashing

Deliberately attempting to hide unpleasant or incriminating facts about someone or something. In film, whitewashing is a casting practice in which white actors are cast in non-white roles. (See also greenwashing.)

For instance, governments may prefer to ignore or whitewash disturbing aspects of investigations if it makes them look bad. Ethnic minorities in the arts also frequently report that the whitewashing of roles has harmed their careers.

What are some possible ethical implications of whitewashing? How do we know whether whitewashing has taken place? What repercussions might whitewashing have for knowledge as a whole?

The Arts, Language, Politics

Wisdom

Having experience, knowledge, and good judgment. For instance, we might question the wisdom of building a dam close to an active volcano.

How do we know whether we are wise? How far is it possible to achieve or develop wisdom? How far does wisdom have practical applications?

Knowledge and the knower

Wisdom hierarchy

Also known as the DIKW pyramid, the wisdom hierarchy is a model representing the relationships between data (at the base of the pyramid), information, knowledge, and wisdom (at the top).

Some argue that the wisdom hierarchy is problematic because it is presented as a pyramid, whereby knowledge and wisdom is the result of applying finer-grained filters at each level.

How do we know whether the wisdom hierarchy is 'best' presented as a pyramid, or whether it is 'better' presented in some other form (such as a flowchart)? How might this impact the ways in which we perceive knowledge? How do we define each of the four terms used in the wisdom hierarchy? How do we know if one is more important than another, or if/how one leads to another? How do we judge whether raw facts (or data) are usable on their own? How do we differentiate information from data? How far does information make data useful? To what extent can knowledge be defined in reference to information? How far can wisdom be described as 'knowing the right things to do'?

Knowledge and the knower

Wishful thinking	Wishful thinking is the formation of beliefs based on what might be pleasing to imagine, rather than on evidence, rationality, or reality.
	Examples of wishful thinking might be, 'I know in my heart that our home team will win the World Series', going to court to pay a speeding ticket and hoping the case is dismissed or the officer who ticketed you does not show up, or thinking the lesson will end before you have to present in front of the class.
	What effects does wishful thinking have on our decision-making? How far is wishful thinking problematic? To what extent can wishful thinking be described as a conscious mechanism? How far do our beliefs need to match our desires and sense experiences? How do we know whether emotion has a legitimate role in what we choose to believe? What are some possible ethical implications of wishful thinking?
	Human sciences
Wonder	A feeling of amazement or admiration; a surprising event or situation; very good, remarkable or effective; curiosity or a desire to know something.
	"It's a wonder you weren't killed!" "The pyramid is a wonder to behold." "Don't you ever wonder if she's happy?"
	How far is wonder essential to the human condition?
	Knowledge and the knower
Worldview	A particular view of life or the world; a philosophy/set of beliefs developed in relation to this. For instance, religious worldviews could be said to revolve around the battle between good and evil; our worldview can also be shaped by a fundamental event in our lives or aspect of our family background.
	How do we determine what our own personal worldview is? How far can we tell what has shaped our worldview? What implications might this have for how we view knowledge?
	Knowledge and the knower, Religious knowledge
Would	A modal verb indicating the possible consequence of an imagined event or situation; expressing a desire or inclination; expressing hope, opinion, or conjecture; used to give advice; also, when used ironically, can comment on typical behaviour.
	"He would lose his job if he were to be identified." "I wouldn't drink that if I were you." "I would imagine that they'd be home by now." "I would love to work there." "They would say that, wouldn't they?"
	How far does imagining what would happen advance the development of knowledge?
	Knowledge and the knower, Language
Yield	To produce or provide; to give in to an argument, demands, or pressure; also, an amount produced or a financial return. For instance, experiments can yield surprising results, or evidence can yield new clues that are helpful to an investigation. Our applications can also, at times, yield no response, especially when applying for our first jobs after graduation.
	How do we know whether to trust the information yielded? How do we know whether an experiment yields quantitatively precise results for its predictions? How do we judge the extent to which different fields yield knowledge?
	Natural sciences
Zeitgeist	German for 'spirit of the age', meaning the general intellectual, moral, and cultural climate of an era. For instance, someone's songs can capture the zeitgeist of 1960s America. Some artists and writers believe that an era's zeitgeist cannot be known until it is over.
	How far can we determine the zeitgeist of an era while we are still living in/through it? How far do zeitgeists define a particular time period? How do we know what creates a zeitgeist or holds it together? How far does one zeitgeist correspond to one historical period?
	History, Human sciences

External assessment: the TOK essay

Preparing your TOK essay: FAQ

What is the TOK essay, and how do I decide what subject to base it on?

In the TOK essay, you need to show your understanding of how knowledge can work within different areas of knowledge. You do not choose the title – the IB gives you six to choose from. These six titles change every year, but always ask you to refer to at least two areas of knowledge of your choice.

How do I choose my essay title? How do I know if I have chosen well?

As with the exhibition, think about topics and ideas you have studied and discussed in TOK, and see if any of these relate to the topics at hand. You can also consider things which have happened to you in your own life or topics that interest you (inside or outside of school) that could link to the essay titles. Also, make sure you choose your two areas of knowledge carefully, and plan your essay properly (keep reading below for more advice on planning!), to make sure that your essay is balanced all the way through. If you feel like you have lots to say about one area of knowledge in relation to your essay title, but barely anything about the other, you may need to have a rethink. This could mean choosing a different area of knowledge, or even changing your essay title altogether.

> ## Get it right!
>
> Planning out a few different possible essay titles quickly – in relation to various areas of knowledge – can help you to have a better idea of whether you will have enough to say in relation to the essay topic, or whether you will run out of ideas quickly.

When are the titles released?

The IB releases the titles six months before the submission deadline.

Does that mean I have to spend six months working on my essay?

No. This is just to give schools enough time to schedule the essay appropriately around your other assessments. It is also to give teachers enough time to submit your essays to the IB before the deadline. The IB recommends that you spend ten hours of lesson time working on your essay in school. You will spend more time on your essay outside of school.

> ## Examiner tip
>
> Make sure you leave plenty of time to plan and work on your essay. Start **as early as possible**. The first ideas you have are unlikely to be the best ideas you have and will rarely make it into the final version. So allow plenty of time to develop and improve your early thoughts and ideas.

But I'm rubbish at essay-writing! How can I structure it?

Here's one possible essay structure. If you're not feeling confident, you can use this – and the sentence starters provided a bit later in this book – to help you.

Introduction: ◄ **(around 160 words)**

Show the examiner how you will be interpreting the essay question/what you understand by it. Give them a preview (like a movie trailer!) of what you will discuss (don't give away too much… just a little).

Main body: ◄──────────────── **(around 1280 words, split into 4–8 different sections/paragraphs of 160–320 words each)**

Here you explain each of your ideas one by one.

Remember that shorter sentences and paragraphs can be better to help you get your ideas across clearly. You may wish to, for example, devote one paragraph to your claims about the essay title in relation to **one** area of knowledge, followed by one paragraph about possible counterclaims, before then doing the same for your **second** chosen area of knowledge.

Remember to link back to the essay question regularly so that you don't lose focus.

Conclusion: ◄ **(around 160 words)**

Restate your main ideas, using different words. You can start with the main idea from the paragraph right before your conclusion – this will help you to make a good link between your essay's main body and its conclusion. Then work backwards through the rest of the essay, restating your main idea from each section or paragraph, until you end up where you started. (See below for more guidance on drawing up your conclusion.)

Examiner tip

Remember, you should plan your essay out before starting, so that you know how you want to group your ideas together and in what order, so that the whole essay will make sense. (See below for more help with planning.)

Can I amend the essay title I have chosen, or say it in different words?

No. You must use the exact same wording/question that the IB gives – you cannot rephrase it or change any of the words.

How long should my essay be?

Your essay should be **1600 words** long. The IB recommends that most of these words should be in the main body of the essay – no extended **footnotes**! **Quotations** are included in your word count.

I always find drawing up the conclusion difficult. What should I do?

Here are two possible ways to help you draw up your conclusion:

1   Put your essay away so you can't see it, then try to write down your main ideas from memory, to try to work them together into a conclusion.

or

2   Record yourself telling your Mum/Dad/sibling/best friend/anyone who will listen about what you have written in your TOK essay. You can then use this recording as a basis for your conclusion – especially if writing is tricky for you.

Once you have done this, think about the overall importance of these ideas. What brings them together? What do they tell us about knowledge and how we acquire it? Remember, though, that everything you say should follow on logically from what you have said before. No surprises!

Get it right!

To help you create a conclusion for your essay, you can also use the worksheet 'Writing introductions and conclusions'. (See the Elemi website www.elemi-isp.com for this worksheet available as a free download.)

Is the bibliography included in my word count?

No. References, maps, diagrams, charts and so on are not included in the final word count.

What happens if I write more than 1600 words?

Beware! The examiner will stop reading, and will only mark the first 1600 words of your essay.

Yes. And examiners can check how many words you have written – so don't lie.

The IB says your essay should be presented using these features:

- written in size 12 font
- written with double spacing (this means there is an extra blank line between every line that you write).

It also makes sense to:

- use a clear font that is easy to read, like Arial or Times New Roman.
- use normal size margins
- be consistent in how you present your text: are you going to justify the text so that the width of the column is always the same throughout (like many books of fiction) or are you going to keep it arranged so that it only lines up on the left-hand side, as this book is laid out.

This book lines up on the left-hand side of the column, and each line is of a different length.

Also, **don't forget to present your ideas in a formal way**, using appropriate academic language. We've got two tools to help you do that:

- Use the sentence starters/'phrases you can steal' from later in this section (see page 167).
- Use our 'Formal to informal language converter': a worksheet to help you gain a better understanding of what type of language might be expected in your writing. This not only applies to your TOK essay, but also in other subjects, such as History. (See the Elemi website www.elemi-isp.com for free downloadable worksheet.)

Examiner tip

It's just not worth over-writing. Remember your examiner is a human being, not a machine – so you need to make sure you're doing everything you can to make their marking work as easy as possible. They might get frustrated when they see you've overwritten or written your essay in an unusual font that is particularly difficult for them to read on screen. A frustrated examiner might not be as generous as you want them to be! Is it really worth the risk?

Your own ideas should form most of the paper, but it is expected that you use a few outside sources as well. These should be properly **cited/referenced** and **academic honesty** is paramount. You can use an online bibliography generator to help you as well: these automatically generate your citations in the style prescribed by your school (such as MLA, APA, Chicago, or Harvard).

Examiner tip

Online bibliography generators can give you the confidence to know that you have completed your citations (in-text, footnotes, and end-text) correctly. Examples of online bibliography generators include CiteThisForMe.com, MyBib.com, EasyBib.com, BibMe.org, Bibliography.com, Scribbr.co.uk, and ZBib.org.

Your teacher can:

- Explain the requirements of the essay to you and make sure you are familiar with the mark scheme
- Answer any questions you have about the essay
- Check how you are doing/monitor your progress, and check that you have really done the work yourself. This is done through the **Planning and progress form (PPF)**.

During the first meeting:

Your teacher discusses the **prescribed titles** with you and makes sure you are on the way to deciding which essay to do (only you can decide this).

In the second meeting:

You will discuss your initial ideas about your essay with your teacher. They will expect you to show them an **essay plan** or some other evidence of your thoughts (eg notes or bullet points). Your teacher needs to be sure in this meeting that you are exploring and developing your ideas gradually over time and not leaving everything to the last minute.

In the third (and final) meeting:

Your teacher will comment on one draft of your essay. Remember your teacher is only allowed to look through your essay once.

All of these meetings are recorded on the PPF.

You fill out most of it – but there is also a space for a teacher comment at the end. You will also both write your names on the form, with the date on which the form is completed.

Make sure you fill out each section of the PPF right after each meeting – if you leave it too long, you will probably forget what you talked about.

No – your teacher is not allowed to give your draft essay a grade, or to make any changes to the essay. They can give written comments as feedback, but these should be marginal – not in the main body of the essay.

For your first interaction, you will need to discuss the prescribed titles with your teacher, and choose the title for your essay. So, it makes sense to look at the essay titles before the meeting, and perhaps prepare a few possible (very rough) plans. These could take the form of notes or a spider diagram. That way, you will be able to show and explain your thought processes to your teacher much more easily, and seek their guidance on what title(s) may work well for you.

- What does this word in this essay title mean?
- Could I relate this essay title to this area of knowledge?
- Could this essay title link to that time in TOK when we talked about…?

Your second interaction will focus on how your essay-planning has developed so far. If you did not already do the planning activity detailed in the previous step, it's a good idea to have done it by now. If you already did it, you can develop it further, noting possible claims, counterclaims, points and examples that you wish to use.

- What do you think of this possible argument?
- Do you think these two areas of knowledge combine well for this essay title?
- Do you think my plan for this essay title is balanced between the two areas of knowledge I have chosen?

In your final interaction, you should present to your teacher a full draft of your essay. It does not have to be perfect, but should show a reasonably developed introduction, main body, and conclusion.

- Do my ideas link together well?
- Have I developed this point enough?
- Are there any logical holes in my arguments?

Teachers can only give oral feedback at this point – nothing written is allowed.

I submitted my essay already, but I made some extra changes and want to resubmit it. Can I do this?

No – once your essay has been submitted to the IB, it cannot be replaced with a later version. So, make sure what you submit is the very best, final version of your work.

How is the essay marked?

The essay is **externally assessed**: this means that your teacher does not mark it, but that your work is **examined** and **moderated** by IB examiners.

It is worth 10 marks, and has a **weighting** of two thirds (or 67% of your course).

To get 9–10 marks, your essay should be:

✓ Focused

✓ Linked well to different areas of knowledge

✓ Clear and **coherent**

✓ Supported by **specific** examples

✓ Considering the **implications** of these examples

✓ Able to **evaluate** different **points of view**

✓ **Accomplished**.

Putting my essay together

Step 1: Look at my chosen title, and consider key phrases from it that are open to debate.

For example:

> 'Too much of our knowledge revolves around ourselves, as if we are the most important thing in the universe' (adapted from Carlo Rovelli). Why might this be problematic?
>
> (TOK prescribed title, Nov 2020 series)

In this case:

● How much knowledge is 'too much', and why? Who decides?

● The conditional structure 'as if': the author, Carlo Rovelli suggests we are not the most important thing in the universe. Is this correct, in your view? Why or why not?

● Who decides what is important in the universe? What impact might this have on your response?

● Does what is 'important' in this universe matter, if there are in fact multiple universes?

● The question also uses the modal verb 'might' – suggesting that this assertion may be problematic, or it may not.

Step 2: Decide which areas of knowledge I am going to link my question to.

In this case:

- This question focuses on self-awareness, and how we develop and acquire knowledge. One area of knowledge that could be used is the natural sciences – specifically child development and how people develop cognitively and physically from childhood to adulthood. Through this development process is how we acquire a lot of knowledge (from what we are taught in school, and how our brain processes that information, to what will happen if we drop a porcelain cup from a height).

- Another area of knowledge that could be used is religious knowledge. We develop not just self-awareness (eg of our morals and values) but also of the world and our place in it through religious belief (or the lack of it).

Step 3: Plan my essay around the 'pitfalls' of the question noted in Step 1.

To help you plan, you might find it useful to use spider diagrams or bullet points, making links to each area of knowledge.

As part of this process, you could also consider:

- counter-arguments
- the background of the author (if named)
- and how this may impact the view being presented.

(For an example diagram relating to this practice question, see the diagram overleaf.)

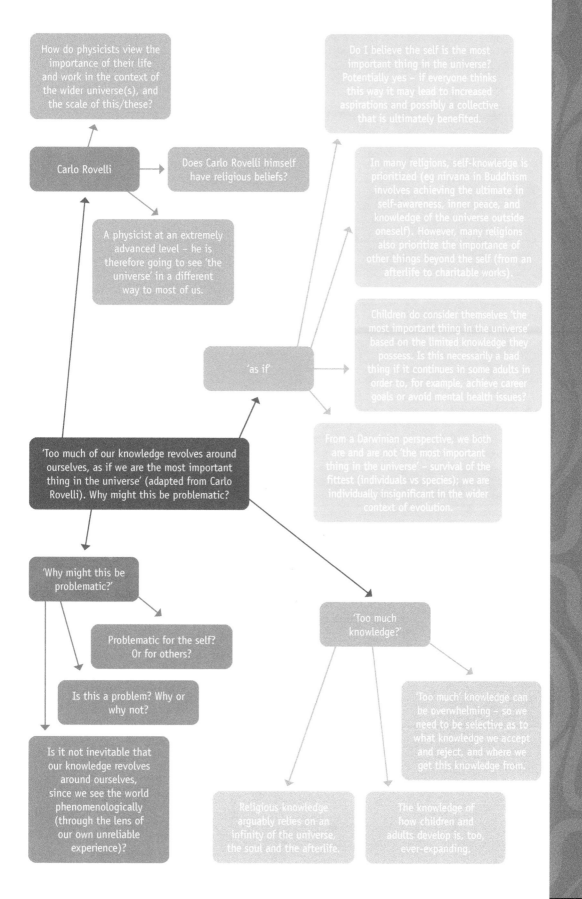

How do physicists view the importance of their life and work in the context of the wider universe(s), and the scale of this/these?

Do I believe the self is the most important thing in the universe? Potentially yes – if everyone thinks this way it may lead to increased aspirations and possibly a collective that is ultimately benefited.

Carlo Rovelli

Does Carlo Rovelli himself have religious beliefs?

In many religions, self-knowledge is prioritized (eg nirvana in Buddhism involves achieving the ultimate in self-awareness, inner peace, and knowledge of the universe outside oneself). However, many religions also prioritize the importance of other things beyond the self (from an afterlife to charitable works).

A physicist at an extremely advanced level – he is therefore going to see 'the universe' in a different way to most of us.

Children do consider themselves 'the most important thing in the universe' based on the limited knowledge they possess. Is this necessarily a bad thing if it continues in some adults in order to, for example, achieve career goals or avoid mental health issues?

'as if'

From a Darwinian perspective, we both are and are not 'the most important thing in the universe' – survival of the fittest (individuals vs species); we are individually insignificant in the wider context of evolution.

'Too much of our knowledge revolves around ourselves, as if we are the most important thing in the universe' (adapted from Carlo Rovelli). Why might this be problematic?

'Why might this be problematic?'

Problematic for the self? Or for others?

'Too much knowledge?'

Is this a problem? Why or why not?

'Too much' knowledge can be overwhelming – so we need to be selective as to what knowledge we accept and reject, and where we get this knowledge from.

Is it not inevitable that our knowledge revolves around ourselves, since we see the world phenomenologically (through the lens of our own unreliable experience)?

Religious knowledge arguably relies on an infinity of the universe, the soul and the afterlife.

The knowledge of how children and adults develop is, too, ever-expanding.

Step 4: Develop each of my bullet points into paragraphs.

As part of this process, you may find it helpful to use some of the key words and phrases (highlighted below in yellow). You will find more examples in the 'Phrases I can steal' section on page 167.

For example:

> Carlo Rovelli states that 'too much of our knowledge revolves around ourselves'. However, this essay will explore why this may not be problematic, in relation to the area of knowledge of the natural sciences, as well as religious knowledge.

Step 5: Link my paragraphs and ideas together using connectives.

As part of this process, take a look at the **connectives** below (highlighted here in pink). Could you make use of these connectives to link your paragraphs?

For example:

> Carlo Rovelli states that 'too much of our knowledge revolves around ourselves'. However, this essay will explore why this may not be problematic, in relation to the area of knowledge of the natural sciences, as well as religious knowledge.
>
> Rovelli also questions our place in the universe, implying derisively, 'as if we are the most important thing in [it]'. As a physicist, Rovelli is perhaps bound to see the world differently from most. Humans individually do indeed seem very small even when compared with just our universe, let alone when considering multiverse theories. One might even question how compatible religious beliefs are with the pursuit of scientific research – especially given that in many religions, self-knowledge is prioritized.
>
> This is particularly true when considering the goal of attaining nirvana in Buddhism.

Step 6: Get my teacher to give me feedback on my first draft.

Here is a TOK teacher's comments on the opening paragraphs above. Read through it carefully – there might be some tips for you in to help you reflect on your own work:

> "Your time may not be best spent on researching the context of the quotation, as it may be more useful to explore your own perspective than Rovelli's. In the same way, the essay is 'only' 1600 words – so re-citing the Prescribed Title's knowledge claim may, again, not be the best use of the limited space you have. The remark about humanity's place in the vast universe/multiverse might be a red herring, unless you develop this theme more in the rest of the essay. Also, by choosing to focus on how compatible religion and science are, you may end up going off topic if you aren't careful. However, the emphasis on the goal of developing self-knowledge in some religious contexts is very promising. Exploring the converse (ie some religious knowledge systems' emphasis on transcendence of the self) would also be helpful, as this will help you to show some counter-arguments to the thesis. You don't need to compare areas of knowledge in the essay, but this can still be a highly fruitful approach, as long as you still link it to the prescribed title's main knowledge claim. Make sure you also take into account the differences between 'production', 'dissemination' and 'acquisition' of knowledge, as well as bias, point of view, and methodological considerations. This will help you to best assess how valid the knowledge claim is.
>
> If this essay carries on in the same way, it will likely receive a 7 or 8 out of 10."

Step 7: Make the necessary changes based on my teacher's feedback.

Consider the comments your teacher has made and make the changes you think are appropriate. You may also find it useful to maybe get a friend or parent to read through your essay as well.

Step 8: Check my work for plagiarism.

Your school/teacher may suggest you use plagiarism checker software or an online checker for this. At the same time, you should also make sure your sources are properly cited.

In the example above, the green highlighting shows where other sources have been quoted.

Step 9: Check the word count, and make the essay shorter if needed.

Whilst it may be difficult (and stressful!) to cut your essay to make it shorter, it is very necessary.

If you need to take out some words, look to ensure that each sentence contributes something valuable to what you want to say. Repetition is an easy mistake to make. Check every sentence contributes something new, rather than saying the same thing using different words. This approach will help you delete entire sentences or entire paragraphs.

If you only need to cut a few words, try:

- taking out conjunctions and rewriting as two sentences
- deleting the word 'that' (it is often used more than necessary)
- using the active voice, rather than the passive voice
- using a verb instead of a noun (eg instead of 'The teacher gave an assessment of the performance', write 'The teacher assessed the performance').

Get it right!

Remember **shorter can mean better**. If you force yourself to cut some words, you may find that your work is more succinct, more concise, and clearer to the reader.

Step 10: Submit my essay!

Phrases I can steal

For each section of your essay, here are some phrases that you might find useful in your own writing.

Introducing

This essay will explore ...

This essay aims to ...

With reference to the areas of knowledge of ...

In relation to the area of knowledge of ...

X can play an important role in addressing the issue of ...

In order to define X, we have to consider ...

This essay will evaluate/examine/analyse ...

This paper contests the claim that ...

This essay explores the ways in which ...

This paper considers the implications of ...

This essay assesses how far ...

Defining terms

Throughout this paper, the term 'X' will refer to ...

It is necessary here to clarify exactly what is meant by ...

The phrase/word 'Y' will be interpreted as follows:

In this essay, the term 'Z' will be used in its broadest sense, to refer to ...

In this paper, the terms 'A' and 'B' are used interchangeably to mean ...

Showing cause and effect

Therefore, ...

Thus, ...

As a result, ...

Due to ...

Owing to ...

Consequently, ...

Because ...

As ...

Since ...

To present others' views

According to ...

As explained by ...

X suggests/states/asserts that ...

Y claims/hypothesises that ...

Z argues that ...

As per the writings of A, ...

Some theorists have posited that ...

Indicating opinion and interpretation

It would seem ...

Perhaps ...

This could ...

It appears ...

This could be justified by ...

Possibly ...

It seems likely ...

One might consider ...

One possible interpretation could be ...

It can be suggested that ...

Acknowledging limitations

There is limited evidence for ...

While establishing X is beyond the scope of this essay, ...

A note of caution is due here, since ...

There is a potential for bias from ...

To add to or further explain ideas

Also, ...

Furthermore, ...

Perhaps more importantly, ...

Moreover, ...

It is also essential to note ...

Additionally, ...

In addition, ...

Subsequently, ...

To give examples

For instance, ...

For example, ...

This can be demonstrated by ...

This is seen when ...

To compare and contrast

Likewise, ...

Similarly, ...

However, ...

In the same way, ...

Meanwhile, ...

Whereas ...

Nevertheless, ...

On the other hand, ...

In contrast, ...

Conversely, ...

Signalling emphasis

Most of all ...

Least of all ...

Most importantly ...

Especially ...

Significantly ...

Notably ...

Specifically, ...

In particular, ...

Expressing significance

This idea/notion is of interest because/due to ...

Most notably, ...

Significantly, ...

It is important to note that ...

It is vital to consider ...

An implication of this is that ...

In conclusion

This (referring to previous paragraph) means/could mean that ...

While it is difficult to assess the importance of X, ...

X nonetheless expands on our understanding of Y

Even though it is not possible to fully assess the impact of Z, ...

Overall, ...

Ultimately, ...

Above all, ...

It can be seen that ...

The principal implication of all of this is that ...

This essay has raised important questions about the nature of ...

Therefore, ...

My checklist

Have I:

- [ ] chosen my essay topic from the six provided by the IB?
- [ ] scheduled my three meetings with my teacher?
- [ ] created my essay plan?
- [ ] filled out the PPF?
- [ ] given examples of my ideas in my essay?

- [ ] submitted a draft of my essay to my teacher for feedback?
- [ ] cited my sources?
- [ ] made sure the essay does not go over the word count?
- [ ] submitted the final version of my essay to the IB?

Internal assessment: the TOK exhibition

Preparing your TOK exhibition: FAQ

What is the exhibition, and how do I decide what subject to base it on?

In the TOK exhibition, you need to show three examples of how TOK exists in the world around us.

This exhibition is like an art exhibition, but with examples of objects which show knowledge processes – how we question and develop knowledge – in the real world. Your exhibition should be based on one of the 35 IA prompts. Your teacher will provide you with these. All three objects therefore need to link to this same prompt.

Get it right!

The IA prompt that you choose must also be used exactly as it is written in the IB guide – the wording cannot be changed in any way.

It is also strongly recommended by the IB that you base your exhibition on *at least one* of the TOK **themes** studied in class. So, for example, don't do your exhibition on an IA prompt relating to indigenous societies if this has not been studied.

Remember all these themes can be reviewed in the glossary in this book.

What is an object? What type of thing can I include?

Objects could consist of any of the following:

- Pieces of art
- Video clips
- News articles
- Photographs
- A text created by you (eg your extended essay!) or someone else (eg a novel)
- Scans (eg of historical documents that you clearly wouldn't be able to bring to class)
- Digital artefacts (eg tweets, memes)
- Items from the real world (eg washing-up gloves, a basketball).

As you can see, these objects can be:

- **real or physically present** in the class (so you can physically bring something with you)

or

- **an image** of the object (for objects where it's clearly not possible for you to bring it in).

If you have other ideas, it is recommended that you discuss these with your teacher.

Remember that the objects, as defined by the IB, must be:

> "pre-existing objects, rather than objects created specifically for the purposes of the exhibition"

This means that it is important that the objects have a real-world context outside the assessment (ie existing in a specific time and place). These contexts should also be specific. So, for example, a sonogram of your baby brother, as opposed to a random sonogram found online.

Get it right!

If you can swap your object for another similar object and find that the commentary still applies then it is probably too general.

As with an art exhibition, the three objects could be placed in a certain sequence that you have chosen, giving viewers of your exhibition a sense of greater meaning and narrative (or story-telling), which you could also explain as part of your commentaries.

Is the exhibition just three objects? Or do I need to do something else?

You need to write a **commentary**, showing each object and identifying its real-world context, explaining why you have included it in the exhibition, and linking each object to the IA prompt. As this should be a maximum of 950 words in total, this comes to around 315 words per object. Citations and references should also be included (note that these do not form part of the word count), as well as a title clearly indicating your chosen IA prompt.

> ### Examiner tip
> You don't have to link each of your objects to each other. You only have to link them to the IA prompt you have chosen. You can link them if you want to – but you don't have to.

How is the exhibition marked?

The exhibition is **internally assessed**: this means that your teacher marks it, but that your work is then **moderated** by IB examiners. If examiners judge that your teacher has marked inaccurately (perhaps too generously, or even not generously enough) then they can change not just your marks but the marks of others in your class.

Your teacher will advise you exactly what to do, but you should put all of the information described above into one file (.doc, .docx or .pdf) so it can be assessed, with photographs of your three objects).

Your TOK exhibition is worth 10 marks, and has a weighting of one third (or 33%) of your course.

To get 9–10 marks, your exhibition should be:

✓ Clearly showing which three objects you have chosen and how they fit in to the real world

✓ Linking well to the chosen IA prompt

✓ Explaining why each object is important to the exhibition

✓ Supported by appropriate evidence

✓ **Convincing, lucid** and **precise**.

If you only provide two objects, you can only achieve a maximum of 6 marks out of 10.

If you do not use one of the IA prompts provided, you will be awarded 0 marks.

Just as with all aspects of your IB Diploma studies and assessment, **academic honesty** is also vital.

Can I work in a group?

No – for the exhibition, you must work by yourself. You may also not use the same objects as anyone else in your class, so make sure you inform your teacher of your choices carefully and do not change any of your objects without telling them.

When will I do my exhibition, and how long will this take?

You must have eight hours of class time to complete the exhibition; during this time, your teacher will:

* explain the exhibition requirements to you
* make sure you understand the **assessment instrument**
* consult with you about what you will include in your exhibition's final version
* give feedback on your first draft of the file that will be sent for moderation to the IB examiners.

It is possible that you will need to spend some time outside of class on the preparation of your exhibition as well. You will do this during the first year of the IB Diploma Programme.

Can I have feedback on my exhibition from my teacher before it is sent to the IB?

Yes – your teacher is allowed to give you feedback on one **draft** of your exhibition file. (As described above, this will be images, commentaries, references and links to the chosen IA prompt). Your teacher can provide oral or written advice on how your work can be improved, but cannot edit your draft directly.

How will the exhibition be held in real life?

Of course, the TOK exhibition is not just a file of work sent to IB examiners – you will do a real-life exhibition in school. Depending on what your school decides is best, this could be:

* within your TOK class
* open to the whole school
* open to parents
* open to other schools in your area (and, by the same token, you could visit theirs)
* accessible online, even.

Preparing my TOK exhibition

A Selecting my prompt

The prompts the IBO publishes are designed so that they are accessible to all students – no matter what you have studied in class. But that doesn't always make it an easy choice.

To help you select the prompt that will work best for you, follow these simple steps:

1 Look through the list of prompts. If you can't think of anything that you studied in class that relates to a particular prompt, then cross that prompt out. This should leave you with a more manageable, shorter list from the 35 prompts given.

2 Think about if the prompts remind you of anything from your own life.

3 Think about objects you have at home that are used frequently perhaps, or objects you have that are meaningful to you. Could these relate to any of the prompts you have left?

> ### Examiner tip
> Sometimes by starting with objects that interest you, they can lead you to an appropriate prompt that fits well with them.

4 You can also consider 'objects' that you don't actually possess, but which still interest you. For example:
   - the Bill of Rights (or a photograph/online picture of it, since you clearly can't bring the actual Bill of Rights to class)
   - a political leader's Twitter feed
   - a YouTube video that you like a lot
   - a still from a video game.

   Could these connect with any of the prompts?

5 Highlight or circle prompts that connect to items you already have, or to objects which interest you.

6 After this process, you should have just a few prompts left. Try to plan them out (say, by making a spider diagram) or discuss them with your friends. If you find that the conversation quickly runs dry, or that you are soon out of ideas when making the spider diagram, then possibly this is not the right prompt for you.

It could be that you like a particular prompt a lot, but just need to find different objects for it. In the same way, you might want to keep the same objects, but choose a different prompt to fit them. Try different combinations and see what works.

Also, remember that your teacher is there to help you. If you have eliminated most of the prompts, but are still trying to decide between two or three of them, consult your teacher with the ideas that you do have. Maybe they will be able to steer you in the best direction for you.

> ### Examiner tip
> Maybe make sure the other person you ask to look over your work is an adult or someone outside your TOK class so as to avoid the risk of **plagiarism**.

B Putting my exhibition together

Below you will see how one student has chosen their IA prompt and put together their selection of three objects to relate to the chosen prompt. This is intended as a model to help explain the process and is not set out as the 'right way' to do it for you.

> ### Examiner tip
> Of course, in the interests of academic honesty, you'd have to select your own prompt and objects. There's no point reproducing what someone else has done in the past, since you'd then find it very difficult to put together a convincing, lucid, and precise exhibition if it's not personal to you alone, so fail to achieve the best marks you can.

Step 1: Choose my IA prompt from the list provided by the IBO.

For example:

30. What role does imagination play in producing knowledge about the world?

Step 2: Choose three objects that could relate to this prompt.

In this case:

1 Your baby cousin's toy car

Chosen because... it links to a small child, and small children have a lot of imagination. This links well to the prompt here, as it raises questions of how can we know if small children are imagining, or just re-enacting scenarios that they have already seen?

2 A copy of your favourite novel

Chosen because... authors require a certain amount of imagination in order to produce novels, again linking to the key word of the chosen prompt.

This raises the relevant question, however, of how far authors are being (auto)biographical, and how far they are truly imagining; in the same way, how do we know whether writers are telling the whole truth, and how far real stories have been embellished with imagination?

Perhaps ultimately, how do we know whether the mixture of truth and fiction (or 'imagination') matters?

Examiner tip

If choosing quite similar objects (eg as here, two pieces of creative writing) then make sure you make clear how their relationship to the prompt is different. This will help you to make sure that your commentary does not become repetitive.

3 A poem you have written about a recurring dream

Chosen because... A poem written by links with the prompt as it, too, is the product of imagination. However, the difference between this and the previous choice – of a novel you have not written yourself – is that you are perhaps 'producing' knowledge in a different way compared to this knowledge having its origins in someone else's (ie the novelist's) experiences, as opposed to your own.

Layout considerations – in this case, the poet makes deliberate choices regarding the syllabic count of each line – also have the capacity to produce meaning and knowledge, in a way that is not so obvious or present in novels.

Step 3: Photograph each of the objects.

In this case:

Image 1: Photograph of my baby cousin's toy car

Image 2: Photograph of my favourite novel

Image 3: Photograph of my poem

Recurring dream

It came out in a pencilled drawing,

making use of shades of blackened grey

and forming frames of rectangles that

trap each other and get smaller.

Smaller they squeezed and tightened their

grip, the pressure struggling to breathe

through the dream. The weight is mighty,

holding my white breath for me

as blackness clamps my body

and my head. I only wake

just as my bones begin

to break. Before that

I felt dead, my white

bright breath letting

me soar above

myself, out-

of-body,

and see

the dream

for what

it was,

and

breathe.

Step 4: Write your commentaries on each of the objects, linking back to your chosen IA prompt.

You might want to construct each paragraph around a particular object that you have chosen. Refer to the 'Phrases I can steal' (on page 175) to help. You can also ask yourself some questions to help you know what to write, such as:

- How does this object connect with the key word/phrase of the prompt (eg imagination)?
- How does this object connect with knowledge, and how we produce and receive it?
- How do we know whether knowledge is attainable in this way or not?
- For questions beginning 'How far', 'What role' and 'To what extent', what are some possible counterclaims, or situations in which this may not be the case? (For example, how do we know whether imagination is really happening in the case of a small child playing, or whether something else is going on?)

The following is one *sample commentary* for the first object above (your baby cousin's toy car).

Transferable phrases that you can use in your own work are highlighted in yellow and **connectives** are highlighted in pink. **Quotations** are highlighted in green. (Refer to the 'Phrases I can steal' section on page 175 for more examples.)

When my baby cousin plays with his toy car, he is to an extent using his imagination to produce and build on his knowledge about the world. Finnish researchers Jenni Vartiainen and Kristiina Kumpulainen asserted in their 2019 research that 'young children can play an active role in co-producing knowledge', which would appear to support this. My baby cousin makes noises that imitate the sound of a car and moves the car around a tabletop in a way that might imitate the movement of real cars (generally in a backwards and forwards direction). He is maybe not creating new knowledge about the world but he is creating his own knowledge about it. He is possibly also using this existing knowledge of the world (imitating cars' sounds and movements based on what he has seen) to then create new knowledge (eg stories about the cars), even if we cannot fully judge this (if it is fully in his own head and not expressed verbally). He also then creates games, such as 'zooming' them off the sofa as fast as possible or pushing them over the top of the sofa (to create a 'hill') for someone to catch. This shows that he is using his imagination in conjunction with the toy car to produce new knowledge, in the form of games he has invented. It could be said that this is innate, not learned, since we (his family members) have not taught him these games – he has made them up himself. However, the knowledge of cars itself does not come from imagination: he is merely reproducing what he has seen in the real world in terms of how cars move and the sounds they make, so imagination's role in producing knowledge might be considered limited in this respect. Ronald Barnett, of London's Institute of Education, also stated that 'through imagination, we could identify ways in which the world […] could be other than it is'. Clearly my cousin's ways of playing with his cars are much more literal than this, and perhaps therefore exhibit less in the way of imagination (as opposed to mere imitation). This links to my other exhibition objects because like with a novel and a poem, the role of imagination is a purely reflective one: it shows existing knowledge about the world rather than creating new knowledge. However, just because imagination is just reflecting the knowledge of the writer, it does not mean that new knowledge is not being created in the mind of the person reading the poem or novel, as it may have made them think about things that they hadn't considered before. This is not the case in the instance of a small child playing with a car: imagination is only reflecting knowledge, not really creating it. At best it is perhaps solidifying burgeoning knowledge.

Step 5: When I have produced all of my photos of my objects, and commentaries to go with them, show them to my teacher for feedback.

Here is a TOK teacher's feedback on the above commentary:

"The exhibition object is well tailored to the prescribed prompt. Focusing on educational theory is an entirely valid approach.

However, a child's cognitive development is something of a 'black box', making this line of inquiry inevitably speculative and indirect. There is also the assumption that play always involves imagination. Furthermore, the contention that the child's use of the toy car demonstrates the role of imagination remains insufficiently substantiated.

The candidate might do better to explore the development of new knowledge. This may be more easily achieved through the use of a scientific prompt or real-world phenomenon, such as a page from CERN's website describing the Higgs Boson. (This was first imagined long before being confirmed experimentally.) This could help the candidate to analyse the prompt more relevantly and directly.

Some connection is made between the car and other objects. This is not obligatory and the candidate may find that they need to cut this out if their commentary overruns. Conversely, it could enhance the exhibition if the candidate is able to make connections between the objects in a consistent and meaningful way throughout their commentary.

If this candidate's exhibition continued in the same way, it may achieve a 5 or 6."

Step 6: Make any changes based on the feedback.

Step 7: Make sure all your images and commentaries are combined in a single file.

Step 8: Submit the final version of the exhibition to the IBO.

Step 9: 'Show' your exhibition in real life, whether online or in person, according to the method decided by your school.

Phrases I can steal

Here are some suggestions for key phases that you could use as part of your exhibition.

Showing possibility or suggestion

This could ...	...is debated...
To an extent	...is debatable...
Might	...may include...
Maybe	Perhaps
To a degree ...	This suggests that ...
Somewhat	This implies ...
Possibly	This would appear to ...
There is limited evidence for ...	It could be said that ...

Showing contradiction, or awareness of other points of view

However, ...	However, ...
Although ...	Whereas...
While it is true that ...	On the contrary, ...
Despite the fact that ...	As opposed to
In spite of ...	At the same time, ...
But	Unlike
Still, ...	Conversely, ...
Nevertheless, ...	Regardless of ...
On the other hand, ...	X notwithstanding, ...
Alternatively, ...	By/in contrast, ...
A counter-argument is ...	That aside, ...
From a different perspective, ...	

Showing restriction

Only if
Except for
Unless
Even if

Introducing evidence or examples

For instance, ...	This shows that ...
As illustrated by ...	Specifically, ...
As revealed by ...	This is demonstrated by ...
In the case of ...	As an example, ...
As shown by ...	This is supported by ...
X asserted that ...	To illustrate, ...

Comparing

… is similar to …	In the same way, …
This complements …	Just as …
Likewise, …	This links to …
Equally, …	Like/As with …

Adding to a point

Moreover, …	Equally, …
Furthermore, …	In addition, …
Additionally, …	Subsequently, …
Again, …	Consequently, …
Also, …	To elaborate, …
As…	As well as …
More importantly, …	Another …

To present widely known ideas

Commonly …	Almost all …
Numerous …	… is usual …
Several …	More than …
Most …	The majority …
… is prevalent …	Usually, …
Many …	

To present unusual or less commonly seen ideas

Seldom …	Few …
A few …	… is uncommon …
Less than …	… is rare …
Fewer than …	Not many …
Rarely …	… is scarce …
Unusually, …	… is unusual …

Concluding

So, …	Ultimately, …
Overall, …	Therefore, …
Clearly, …	Thus, …

My checklist

Have I…

- ☐ chosen my exhibition prompt from the list provided by the IB?
- ☐ chosen my three objects?
- ☐ told my teacher what my three objects are?
- ☐ made sure my objects link to my prompt?
- ☐ written my commentaries for each object?
- ☐ checked that all the commentaries together do not add up to more than 950 words?
- ☐ taken photos of my three objects?
- ☐ put my photos and commentaries into a single file?
- ☐ asked my teacher for feedback on my commentaries?
- ☐ fine-tuned my commentaries based on the feedback given by my teacher (eg getting another person to look over it to make sure it is clear and that there are no logical 'holes' in the argument)?
- ☐ submitted the final version of my exhibition file to the IB?

CPSIA information can be obtained
at www.ICGtesting.com
Printed in the USA
LVHW070021120522
718422LV00016B/558